Ritual and Rhetoric in Leviticus

Ritual and Rhetoric in Leviticus: From Sacrifice to Scripture uses rhetorical analysis to expose the motives behind the writing of the central book of the Torah/Pentateuch and its persuasive function in ancient Judaism. The answer to the question "Who was trying to persuade whom of what by writing these texts?" proves to be quite consistent throughout Leviticus 1–16: Aaronide high priests and their supporters used this book to legitimize their monopoly over the ritual offerings of Jews and Samaritans. With this priestly rhetoric at its center, the Torah supported the rise to power of two priestly dynasties in Second Temple Judaism. Their ascendancy in turn elevated the prestige and rhetorical power of the Torah, making it the first real scripture in Near Eastern and Western religious traditions. Rhetorical analysis of Leviticus therefore has implications not only for the form and contents of that book, but also for understanding the later history of the rhetoric of priesthood, of sacrifice, and, especially, of scripture.

James W. Watts is Professor and Director of Graduate Studies in the Department of Religion at Syracuse University. He is the author of *Psalm and Story: Inset Hymns in Hebrew Narratives* (1992) and *Reading Law: The Rhetorical Shaping of the Pentateuch* (1999) and editor of *Persia and Torah: The Theory of the Imperial Authorization of the Pentateuch* (2001).

Ritual and Rhetoric in Leviticus

From Sacrifice to Scripture

James W. Watts

Syracuse University

CAMBRIDGE
UNIVERSITY PRESS

CAMBRIDGE UNIVERSITY PRESS
Cambridge, New York, Melbourne, Madrid, Cape Town, Singapore, São Paulo

Cambridge University Press
32 Avenue of the Americas, New York, NY 10013-2473, USA

www.cambridge.org
Information on this title: www.cambridge.org/9780521871938

First published 2007

Printed in the United States of America

A catalog record for this publication is available from the British Library.

Library of Congress Cataloging in Publication data

Watts, James W. (James Washington), 1960–
Ritual and rhetoric in Leviticus : from sacrifice to scripture /
James W. Watts.
p. cm.
Includes bibliographical references and index.
ISBN 978-0-521-87193-8 (hardback)
1. Bible. O. T. Leviticus – Criticism, interpretation, etc. 2. Bible. O. T. Leviticus –
Language, style. 3. Cohanim. 4. Ritual. 5. Purity, Ritual – Judaism. I. Title.
BS1255.52.W38 2007
222'.1306–dc22 2006034240

ISBN 978-0-521-87193-8 hardback

To my father,
John D. W. Watts,
in loving gratitude for exemplifying
such a strong model of creative biblical scholarship
and allowing me the freedom to follow it

Contents

Contents

9. The Rhetoric of Scripture

Abbreviations

4QMMT	E. Qimron and J. Strugnell, *Qumran Cave 4. V. Miqsat Ma'ase ha-Torah* (Discoveries in the Judean Desert 10) Oxford: Clarendon, 1994.
ANET	*Ancient Near Eastern Texts Relating to the Old Testament.* Ed. James B. Pritchard. 3rd ed. Princeton: Princeton University Press, 1969.
Ant.	Flavius Josephus, *The Antiquities of the Jews*
AOAT	Alter Orient und Altes Testament
ARM	*Archives royals de Mari*
BETL	Bibliotheca ephemeridum theologicarum lovaniensium
BHS	*Biblia Hebraica Stuttgartensia.* Ed. K. Elliger and W. Rudolph. Stuttgart: Deutsche Bibelstiftung, 1983.
Bib	*Biblica*
BZABR	Beihefte zur Zeitschrift für Altorientalische und Biblische Rechtsgeschichte
BZAW	Beihefte zur Zeitschrift für die alttestamentliche Wissenschaft
CB:OT	Coniectanae Biblica: Old Testament Series
COS	*The Context of Scripture: Canonical Compositions, Monumental Inscriptions, and Archival Documents from*

	the Biblical World. Ed. William W. Hallo. 3 vols. Leiden: Brill, 1997, 2000, 2002.
CTH	Emmanuel Laroche. *Catalogue des texts Hittites.* Paris: Klincksieck, 1971.
DCH	*Dictionary of Classical Hebrew.* Ed. David J. A. Clines. Sheffield: Sheffield Academic Press/London: Continuum, 1983–.
DJD	Discoveries in the Judaean Desert
FRLANT	Forschungen zur Religion und Literatur des Alten und Neuen Testaments
HAL	Koehler, L., W. Baumgartner, and J. J. Stamm. *Hebraisches und aramäisches Lexikon zum Alten Testament.* Leiden: Brill, 1967–1995.
HKL	R. Borger. *Handbuch der Keilschriftliteratur.* 3 vols. Berlin: de Gruyter, 1967–1975.
HUCA	*Hebrew Union College Annual*
JANES	*Journal of Ancient Near Eastern Studies*
JAOS	*Journal of the American Oriental Society*
JBL	*Journal of Biblical Literature*
JCS	*Journal of Cuneiform Studies*
JQR	*Jewish Quarterly Review*
JSOT	*Journal for the Study of the Old Testament*
JSOTSup	Supplements to *JSOT*
JTS	*Journal of Theological Studies*
KAI	*Kanaanäische und aramäische Inschriften.* Ed. H. Donner and W. Röllig. 2nd ed. Wiesbaden: Harrassowitz, 1966–1969.
KHAT	Kurzer Hand-Commentar zum Alten Testament
KTU	*Die keilalphabetischen Texte aus Ugarit.* Ed. M. Dietrich, O. Loretz, and J. Sanmartin. AOAT 24/1. Neukirchen-Vluyn: Neukirchener Verlag, 1976.
LXX	Septuagint Greek translation and verse numbers
MT	Masoretic Text
NAB	New American Bible version

NICOT   New International Commentary on the Old Testament
NJPS   New Jewish Publication Society version
NRSV   New Revised Standard Version
NSKAT   Neuer Stuttgarter Kommentar Altes Testament
OBO   Orbis biblicus et orientalis
OTL   Old Testament Library
P   Priestly source
RB   *Revue Biblique*
SAA   State Archives of Assyria
SBL   Society of Biblical Literature
TDOT   *Theological Dictionary of the Old Testament.* Ed. G. J.
          Botterweck and H. Ringgren. Trans. J. T. Willis, G.
          W. Bromiley, and D. E. Green. 8 vols. Grand Rapids:
          Eerdmans, 1974–.
VT   *Vetus Testamentum*
VTSup   Supplements to *Vetus Testamentum*
WAW   Writings from the Ancient World
WBC   Word Biblical Commentary
WMANT   Wissenschaftliche Monographien zum Alten und Neuen
          Testament
ZAW   *Zeitschrift für die alttestamentliche Wissenschaft*

Preface

This book has its origins in three strands of research that have become more intertwined the longer I have pursued them. The first is rhetorical analysis of biblical and other ancient texts. I became interested in rhetoric when I noticed that the Hebrew Bible instructs its readers in how to use the Torah (Pentateuch) by memorizing it and reading it aloud (Deuteronomy 4: 6–9, 31: 9–13) and then models this usage in stories about prominent characters (Moses in Exodus 24, Joshua in Joshua 8, King Josiah in 2 Kings 22–23, and Ezra in Nehemiah 8), reading it aloud to the assembled people of Israel and Judah. The fact that the text presents itself as suited for public reading suggested to me that it may have been intentionally shaped with rhetorical considerations in mind. Exploring the consequences of this insight for the structure and contents of the Pentateuch led to my book *Reading Law: The Rhetorical Shaping of the Pentateuch* (1999). That book did not, however, present detailed rhetorical analyses of specific pentateuchal texts. This book begins to make up for that lack by subjecting the early chapters of Leviticus to close scrutiny from a rhetorical perspective (Chapters 2 through 6). Using Aristotle's definition of rhetoric as the art of persuasion, these studies ask the question "Who was trying to persuade whom of what by writing these texts?" The answer proves to be quite consistent throughout Leviticus 1–16 and casts these chapters in a rather different light from that in which they appear in most contemporary scholarship. Since biblical texts play rhetorical roles long after their original authors and their intended audiences have died, however, rhetorical analysis must also inquire into their subsequent use for purposes of persuasion. Chapters 7 through 9 present thematic studies of the rhetorical influence of the early chapters of Leviticus on later religion and culture.

Some readers may wonder why I chose Leviticus as the place to demonstrate the usefulness of rhetorical analysis for detailed exegesis of the Pentateuch. Others of its books – most obviously Deuteronomy and perhaps Exodus – might seem more likely subjects for rhetorical analysis. The systematic and didactic tendencies of the first half of Leviticus have not led many interpreters to explain its form and contents in terms of persuasion. These characteristics of the book, however, make it the perfect place to test the thesis that the Torah, as a whole, was shaped for purposes of mass persuasion. If I can demonstrate the power of rhetorical analysis on Leviticus, its importance for much of the rest of the Pentateuch will follow more naturally.

There are other reasons behind my focus on Leviticus 1–16. Another strand of my research involves the use and interpretation of ritual texts. The Torah's ritual instructions have been an object of scholarly fascination since ancient times, generating a great deal of historical and theological speculation. The division between Judaism and Christianity has also made them a traditional site of interreligious polemic. Victorian-era cross-cultural comparisons and the later, more rigorous observations of field anthropologists stimulated interest in comparing ancient Israel's practices with those of other traditional cultures. As a result, ritual studies has become a burgeoning field of inquiry within religious studies, and applying its insights to Leviticus has seemed natural to an increasing number of biblical scholars. Israel's ritual practices can no longer be observed directly, however, and are known to us only through ancient texts, a situation presenting methodological problems that have been insufficiently analyzed. Chapter 1 lays out the case for needing to reconsider how to interpret the meaning and significance of rituals that are available to us only through the mediation of ancient texts written with diverse rhetorical interests in mind. That methodological critique then provides the justification for using rhetorical analysis in the subsequent chapters to establish interpretation of these ritual texts on firmer ground.

My third strand of research has to do with the function of iconic books. It is plain from the religious practices of many modern groups that books of scripture frequently function as material symbols in addition to (or even in place of) serving as texts to be read. Several chapters in this book indicate the ways in which the rhetoric of Leviticus serves, among other things, to elevate its own authority in ritual matters. Chapters 7 and 9 point out that in the Second Temple period, this rhetoric elevated the Torah to iconic status alongside the Jerusalem temple itself. Thus textual rhetoric and ritual practice combined to create ancient Judaism's most religiously potent icon.

Despite these common interests, the chapters of this book were written as independent essays. Readers may wish to start with whichever chapter piques their interest the most. As my earlier comments indicate, however, the chapters build a cumulative case for using rhetorical analysis to interpret the significance not just of biblical ritual texts but also of the whole Torah and, by implication, the entire Jewish and Christian collections of scriptures and their function in ancient and contemporary religious communities.

Three of these chapters are expanded versions of articles previously published in other venues. Chapter 2 appeared as "The Rhetoric of Ritual Instruction in Leviticus 1–7," in *The Book of Leviticus: Composition and Reception* (ed. R. Rendtorff and R. A. Kugler; VTSup 93; Leiden: Brill, 2003), 79–100. Chapter 3 was published as " '*Olah*: The Rhetoric of Burnt Offerings," in *Vetus Testamentum* 66/1 (2006): 125–137. Chapter 9 presents a slightly expanded version of "Ritual Legitimacy and Scriptural Authority" that appeared in the *Journal of Biblical Literature* 124/3 (2005): 401–417. I am grateful to E. J. Brill and the Society of Biblical Literature for permission to reproduce them here.

Many people have read and commented on various parts of this book, which is stronger as a result. I owe a debt of gratitude to Carol Babiracki, Dixie Evatt, Frank Gorman, George Heyman, Tazim Kassam, Jason Larson, Heather McKay, David L. Miller, Edward Mooney, Dorina Miller Parmenter, Gay Washburn, and John D. W. Watts as well as interlocutors at various conferences in which I have presented versions of these essays. Responsibility for all remaining defects is, of course, purely my own.

Ritual and Rhetoric in Leviticus

Introduction: Ritual Text and Ritual Interpretation

In a book about medieval rituals, Philippe Buc argued: "Texts were forces in the practice of power. They should not be decrypted for (elusive) facts about rituals and then set aside."[1] He arrived at this conclusion by observing that ritual meaning was a gamble and was always contested in medieval societies and in medieval texts. As a result, Buc reached a negative conclusion about how far medieval texts can be used in the study of ritual:

> Ultimately there can be no anthropological readings of rituals depicted in medieval texts. There can only be anthropological readings of (1) medieval textual practices or perhaps (2) medieval practices that the historian has reconstructed using texts, with full and constant sensitivity to their status as texts. The latter is nonetheless much more difficult (especially for data-poor eras), less reliable, and allows only a circumscribed realm of appropriate questions and possible results.[2]

What Buc calls "data-poor eras" must surely include the times in which the ritual texts of the Bible were written. We know so little

[1] Philippe Buc, *The Dangers of Ritual: Between Early Medieval Texts and Social Scientific Theory* (Princeton: Princeton University Press, 2001), 259.
[2] Buc, *Dangers of Ritual*, 4.

about them that dates for the composition of the priestly strand (P) in the Torah/Pentateuch range over five centuries. Yet anthropological readings of ritual instructions and stories in the books of Leviticus and Numbers have multiplied in recent decades. They have been motivated by a wish to use twentieth-century parallels to understand Israel's ancient ritual practices, but they have also been used by interpreters to reconstruct the theological rationales behind the rituals. The search for the "meaning" of sacrifice, for example, remains an abiding preoccupation of biblical scholars as well as other students of religion.[3]

Buc's methodological warnings serve as a useful starting point for reconsidering how to interpret ancient ritual texts and, through them, ancient rituals. To set the stage for the following investigations of biblical ritual texts, this chapter evaluates the search for the "meaning" of the rituals in Leviticus in light of current theoretical debates about ritual. Those debates include disagreements over the definition and contents of the category "ritual" itself. For my purposes in studying ancient texts, I have found the description of ritual proposed by Jonathan Z. Smith most useful. He drew on earlier observations by Sigmund Freud and Claude Levi-Strauss to maintain that ritual draws attention to and makes intentional the ordinary practices of everyday life.[4] "Ritual relies for its power on the fact that it is concerned with quite ordinary activities placed within an extraordinary setting, that what it describes and displays is, in principle, possible for every occurrence of these acts."[5] Thus ritual turns everyday routines such as washing oneself, entering and leaving a room, and eating meals into

---

[3] As illustrated by the titles of three recent books: Christian Eberhart, *Studien zur Bedeutung der Opfer im Alten Testament. Die Signifikanz von Blut- und Verbrennungsriten im kultischen Rahmen* (WMANT 94; Neukirchen-Vluyn: Neukirchener Verlag, 2002); William K. Gilders, *Blood Ritual in the Hebrew Bible: Meaning and Power* (Baltimore: Johns Hopkins University Press, 2004); David Janzen, *The Social Meanings of Sacrifice in the Hebrew Bible: A Study of Four Writings* (BZAW 344; Berlin: De Gruyter, 2004).

[4] Jonathan Z. Smith, "The Domestication of Sacrifice," in *Violent Origins* (ed. R. G. Hamerton-Kelly; Stanford: Stanford University Press, 1987), 191–235 [193–95].

[5] Jonathan Z. Smith, *To Take Place: Toward Theory in Ritual* (Chicago: University of Chicago Press, 1987), 109.

deeply meaningful practices by focusing attention on them, formalizing them and, often, by prescribing precisely how they get done.[6] Ritual texts, then, are texts that describe or mandate the performance of such rituals.

I start this methodological review with the work of one scholar, Jacob Milgrom, whose dominant influence over contemporary scholarship on biblical ritual texts is irrefutable. Placing his approach in the context of ritual theories that developed out of studies in anthropology and comparative religions will lay the basis for a new approach to interpreting biblical and other ancient ritual texts.

Jacob Milgrom as Interpreter of Ritual

Jacob Milgrom dedicated his career to explaining the details of ancient Israel's ritual and legal practices. His writings are characterized by close attention to philological details and exhaustive examinations of every ancient parallel that may shed light on the biblical text, as well as constant interaction with the interpretive traditions – ancient, medieval, and modern. These features of his work make it invaluable and essential reading for the study of ritual and law in the Bible. Milgrom's conclusions arose from and depended on his methodological commitments, however, which remained consistent from his earliest writings to his most recent ones. It is these presuppositions that I want to contextualize and evaluate within the modern discussion of ritual generally.

Milgrom has been quite specific about the presuppositions that he used to study ritual texts. In *Cult and Conscience* (1976), he introduced his approach with these words:

> I assume the Priestly Code makes sense. . . . it is a self-contained system – logical, coherent and whole. A system is built on postulates, but, in our

---

[6] For a broad survey of "ritual-like" activities under the categories of formalism, traditionalism, invariance, rule-governance, sacral symbolism, and performance, see Catherine Bell, *Ritual: Perspectives and Dimensions* (New York: Oxford University Press, 1997), 138–69.

case, they are nowhere stated. Instead, they are ensconced in the laws and rituals, especially in their technical vocabulary.[7]

His aim then was to demonstrate the *rationality* of P's regulations within the context of ancient Israelite society.

Milgrom also emphasized the *realistic* character of Israel's cultic rules, that is, that they describe real features of ancient Israel's religion and society. He repeatedly denied that the rules and laws of Leviticus and Numbers are utopian: they do not simply dream of a pure cult and society but describe actual practices, or at least what the writers hope will become actual practices. As a result, Milgrom claimed to be describing the rational system that underlay, not just ritual texts, but also ancient Israel's cult and society, at least in so far as they conformed to the prescriptions of Leviticus and Numbers. And he suggested that in large measure they did: in his Numbers commentary, Milgrom said that the laws "provide a window to the life of ancient Israel."[8]

In taking this approach, Milgrom consciously assumed a particular position on the spectrum of interpretive approaches to the Bible's ritual rules, one in which he has a lot of company. He also took a position on the spectrum of theoretical approaches to the study of ritual. It is his position in the latter context that I want to describe more fully here.

The view that the rituals of an ancient or indigenous people are rational and realistic can readily be recognized as the distinctive thesis of a particular school of anthropologists influential in the middle of the twentieth century. On the basis of Emile Durkheim's arguments that societies generate their own symbolic representations, a series of researchers interpreted rituals and beliefs in such "functionalist" terms to show that they are rational within the culture in which they are

---

[7] Jacob Milgrom, *Cult and Conscience: The Asham and the Priestly Doctrine of Repentence* (Leiden: Brill, 1976), 2.

[8] Jacob Milgrom, *Numbers Bmdbr*, JPS Torah Commentary (Philadelphia: Jewish Publication Society, 1990), xxxvi.

found.[9] Thus E. E. Evans-Pritchard, to choose a famous example, demonstrated the internal consistency of the beliefs of the Sudanese Nuer people and their effectiveness within Nuer society. He thereby undermined older views that characterized ancient and primitive peoples as superstitious, that is, irrational.[10] Mary Douglas's famous studies of purity rules applied such functionalist anthropological approaches to ancient Israel's practices, among other cultures.[11] A subsequent phase of anthropological research has argued for the independence of some symbolic and ritual systems from social structures, emphasizing the self-contained rationality of such systems even more.[12]

Milgrom was well aware of this anthropological research, and he referred approvingly to the methods of anthropologists such as Evans-Pritchard, Victor Turner, and Douglas.[13] Therefore, though he did not represent himself as an anthropologist, placing him in this company does no injustice to his work. Milgrom's insistence on the rationality of Israel's rituals corresponds with the same claim made by these anthropologists for various indigenous practices and beliefs. His claim that the biblical legislation is realistic corresponds with the functionalist view that religious beliefs mirror society and serve to support social structures. He made the connection himself by using, as an epigram for his article "Rationale for Cultic Law," the following quotation from Turner: "Anthropologists . . . hold that at their 'deepest level' ritual reveals values, which are sociocultural facts."[14]

---

[9] Emile Durkheim, *Elementary Forms of Religious Life* (tr. J. W. Swain; New York: Free Press, 1965 [French original, 1912]).

[10] E. E. Evans-Pritchard, *Nuer Religion* (New York: Oxford University Press, 1974 [1956]); see also Victor Turner, *The Forest of Symbols: Aspects of Ndembu Ritual* (Ithaca: Cornell University Press, 1967).

[11] Mary Douglas, *Purity and Danger: An Analysis of Concepts of Pollution and Taboo* (New York: Praeger, 1966).

[12] E.g., Clifford Geertz, *The Interpretation of Culture* (New York: Basic, 1973).

[13] Even if he differed with details of the latter's views on Leviticus; see Milgrom, *Leviticus 1–16, Leviticus 17–22, Leviticus 23–27* (Anchor Bible 3; 3 vols.; New York: Doubleday, 1991, 2000, 2001), 1:442–3, 726, 728.

[14] Milgrom, "Rationale for Cultic Law: The Case of Impurity," *Semeia* 45 (1989): 103–10 [103].

Placing Milgrom in this company provides a useful context within which to evaluate his contribution. Like the anthropologists discussed above, Milgrom has been very concerned about defending biblical ritual practices against charges of superstition or empty ritualism. His demonstration of the systematic relationship between purity regulations and sacrificial practices and his search for how such practices reinforce ethical norms have been major factors in moving biblical studies away from the derogatory assumptions of previous generations of scholars, just as these anthropological studies have placed a brake on generalizations about "primitive" beliefs and practices.

These anthropological approaches have been criticized, however, and it is fair to ask to what extent Milgrom's work is vulnerable to the same criticisms. One criticism has noted that a focus on the meaning of symbolic systems, either in terms of their social function or in terms of their internal consistency, has difficulty dealing with change over time.[15] These approaches have trouble taking into account phenomena such as anachronistic meanings and symbols that no longer apply directly to the culture in which they are found or, on the other hand, symbols and rituals that are intended to promote change rather than serving to preserve the status quo. As a result, some theorists of ritual have moved to more performative approaches that emphasize the conscious volition of the individual or group engaged in these practices.[16]

On the face of it, Milgrom's description of the rituals of Leviticus does not appear vulnerable to the same criticism. He certainly recognized and looked for historical changes in ritual practices.[17] He went

[15] For this criticism, see, e.g., Jonathan Z. Smith, "The Domestication of Sacrifice," 207–8.

[16] See, e.g., Victor Turner's theories of "dramatism" (*The Ritual Process: Structure and Anti-Structure* [Ithaca: Cornell University Press, 1969]) and Catherine Bell's survey of performative approaches (*Ritual: Perspectives and Dimensions*, 72–83).

[17] Jonathan Klawans has criticized Milgrom for using theories of historical evolution on the grounds that they prevented Milgrom from describing a consistent symbolic interpretation of the sacrifices in Leviticus. Taking Douglas's theory of purity as a model, Klawans called for a consistently symbolic interpretation of all of Leviticus

to great pains to trace the historical relationship between different ritual and legal texts, and argued at length for re-ordering the Penta-teuchal sources to place the composition of P prior to Deuteronomy in Israel's monarchic period. He even occasionally noted "vestiges" of older beliefs in P's legislation, though he dismissed their significance for the overall system.[18] Thus historical concerns have been very much at the forefront of his work.

At another level, though, this criticism finds some foothold in Milgrom's approach. He dealt with change *between* different texts but presupposed a unified and static symbolic system within the texts themselves and the rituals they describe. For example, in "The Chang-ing Concept of Holiness," Milgrom argued that H ("holiness" texts that dominate the latter part of Leviticus) expanded P's strict appli-cation of the idea of "holiness" in reaction to the criticisms of Isaiah of Jerusalem.[19] So one text (H) revises the views of an earlier text (P) in reaction to the criticism found in a third (Isaiah). As a descrip-tion of the ways texts and their writers interact, there is nothing inher-ently implausible here. It is not clear, however, from his discussion how such arguments were translated into ritual and legal practice, if at all. What Milgrom calls the *realism* of the texts, that is, their equivalence to Israel's ancient practices, becomes less and less evident the more the interaction of the texts is emphasized, just as the "functionalism" of

("Ritual Purity, Moral Purity, and Sacrifice in Jacob Milgrom's *Leviticus*," *Religious Studies Review* 29/1 [2003]: 19–28). Milgrom has responded to Klawans by insisting that only P texts represent rituals in a consistent symbolic system; H texts as well as the Hebrew prophets employed looser, metaphorical formulations ("Systemic Differences in the Priestly Corpus: A Response to Jonathan Klawans," *RB* 112 [2005]: 321–9). In contrast to Klawans, my critique (below) makes virtually the opposite criticism of Milgrom's work and the work of many other scholars, especially Douglas: by interpreting Leviticus in terms of symbols and metaphors that are not explicit in the text, they impose a theology on it that the book does not express.

[18] E.g., Milgrom, *Leviticus*, 1:44; idem., "The Changing Concept of Holiness in the Pen-tateuchal Codes with Emphasis on Leviticus 19," in *Reading Leviticus: A Conversation with Mary Douglas* (ed. J. F. A. Sawyer; JSOTSup 227; Sheffield: Sheffield Academic Press, 1996), 65–75 [65].

[19] Milgrom, "Changing Concept," 74–5.

symbolic systems becomes less evident to anthropologists in the face of historical social change. Given the ancient debates in Israel over how rituals should be practiced, the *actualization* of a particular view in Israel's ritual practices needs separate demonstration.

A second criticism has been leveled at functionalist and symbolic approaches to ritual that questions whether rituals can be explained effectively by reducing them to systems of meanings at all. Are rituals only means for communicating symbols? Maybe not. This criticism points out that ritual practices, such as animal offerings, are usually far older than their interpretation by ancient texts, not to mention by modern ethnographers and interpreters. It is difficult to show that any one symbolic interpretation of them is widely shared by those who participate in the rituals themselves. In other words, the power of a ritual for its participants may not necessarily depend on its symbolic interpretation, or at least on the participants' agreement on any one symbolic interpretation.

This point is likely to surprise many readers, so a brief review of some of the arguments for it may be helpful. John North noted among the ancient Romans, for example, a general lack of expositions of the meaning of their own ritual offerings. Despite a pervasive preoccupation with correct ritual practice, "a striking feature of this tradition is the degree of variation to be found in the interpretation and even the reporting of the rituals of annual festivals." North concluded that "an important characteristic of Roman ritual is its capacity to take on new levels of meaning as new situations arise.... It is precisely because of the shortage of fixed theology or doctrines that ritual programs can adjust themselves – through omitting, adding, misunderstanding, and reinterpreting – to new conditions of life."[20] Making the same observation from a more theoretical perspective, Jonathan Z. Smith argued

[20] John A. North, "Sacrifice and Ritual: Rome," in *Civilizations of the Ancient Mediterranean: Greece and Rome* (ed. M. Grant and R. Kitzinger; New York: Scribner's, 1988), 983, 984.

that rituals serve to call attention to the details of regular life rather than focusing on deep issues of meaning. He concluded therefore that the purification and sacrificial rituals of Jerusalem's temple, for example, served primarily to draw distinctions: "There is no possibility of decoding the meaning of the causes of impurity – they signify sheer difference. Nor is there any relationship of equivalence between the modes of purification and the forms of impurity – they signify sheer change in status, sheer difference. . . . For it is not the term but the relations that mattered."[21] Walter Burkert criticized all theories of the original meaning of this or that ritual behavior. He pointed out ritualistic animal behaviors and argued that "ideas do not produce ritual; rather, ritual itself produces and shapes ideas, or even experience and emotions."[22] Fritz Staal went so far as to conclude that "ritual is pure activity, without meaning or goal."[23]

Again, the fact that Milgrom is interpreting texts shields his work from the brunt of this criticism, because texts convey verbal meanings in much more obvious ways than do rituals (even if a precise description of how texts convey meaning confounds philosophers – a problem I will not delve into here). As Milgrom readily pointed out, however, biblical texts describe and prescribe rituals, but do not bother to explain them. Biblical interpreters, unlike ethnographers, cannot interview Israelite priests and ask them to interpret the rituals themselves. (Even if they could, one might wonder to what extent the explanations would have been made up simply to answer the ethnographer's questions.) So interpreters of ritual texts must seek explanations on the basis of the ritual acts themselves. When the texts do not provide symbolic explanations of the rituals they describe, interpreters find themselves open to the charge of imposing symbolic systems not intrinsic or necessary

[21] Smith, *To Take Place*, 108.
[22] Walter Burkert, *Homo Necans: An Anthropology of Ancient Greek Sacrificial Ritual and Myth* (trans. P. Bing; Berkeley: University of California Press, 1983; German original, 1972), 28.
[23] Fritz Staal, "The Meaninglessness of Ritual," *Numen* 26/1 (1979): 2–22 [9].

to the rituals.[24] To put this point in Milgrom's terms, the *rationality* of the rituals and their textual descriptions may be questioned, not as in previous generations as a way of denigrating the thought of ancient or indigenous peoples but rather as pointing to the possibility that the rituals of any society cannot be reduced to and explained as symbolic systems alone.

None of this is to deny the contribution that Milgrom has made to understanding ancient Israel's religion by showing that the Bible's ritual legislation *can* be understood as a rational symbolic system that *could* have regulated actual ritual practice. In fact, I personally do not doubt that some people did in fact understand the rituals in systematic ways similar to those that Milgrom has described and that such considerations did shape ritual practices at some times. But who did so, and when?[25] The relationship between symbolic interpretation, ritual, and text still needs to be explored for all the periods of Israel's ancient history, insofar as we have any evidence for it.

Milgrom has accomplished a necessary task for biblical studies by demonstrating that biblical ritual can be interpreted rationally and realistically. The comparisons I have made here do not undercut this accomplishment but rather point out that they prepare the way for the next step. The theoretical problem of ritual and its relationship to society and interpretation needs to be worked out in the triangular relationship between Israel's ancient rituals, texts, and society as that relationship changed over time.

[24] Bryan D. Bibb made a similar point, noting that both performances of rituals and the ritual texts that describe them contain ambiguities that leave worshippers and readers room for personal interpretation. Eliminating the ambiguities by elaborate logical constructions or detailed source critical divisions undermines this function ("This Is the Thing that the Lord Commanded You to Do: Ritual Words and Narrative Worlds in the Book of Leviticus" [Ph.D. Dissertation, Princeton Theological Seminary, 2005], 99–100).

[25] Milgrom was aware of the multivalence of sacrifice, at least cross-culturally (*Leviticus* 1:443; "Systemic Differences," 322), but he did not grapple with the methodological problem that such multiple meanings, much less an absence of any symbolic interpretation at all, pose to any description of a symbolic system behind ritual practices.

Recent Ritual Interpretations of Leviticus

These criticisms do not apply only to Milgrom's work. Other interpreters joined him in the effort to reconstruct the theological under-
pinnings of P's ritual system. Baruch Levine and William Hallo, for
example, found descriptive ritual texts from Mesopotamia more realistic than rituals in the Bible, because "they are dispassionate administrative accounts which record actual events, rather than projecting
pious performance."[26] Levine argued that the more idealized ritual
narratives and prescriptions in the Bible nevertheless developed out
of more archival genres and so reflected actual temple practice. He
noted P's fondness for the language of legal reasoning and the role of
persuasion in shaping prescriptive texts: "The transformation of temple records into ritual codes of law illustrates how form responds to
ideology, and how customary practices assume the authority of law
and commandment."[27] Adrian Schenker emphasized the rationality
of P's ritual texts: "Their liturgical-theological thought is rational and
reasonable."[28]

Frank Gorman employed more recent anthropological theories (by
Geertz, Douglas, Turner, and Rappaport among others) than did
Milgrom to describe rituals as P's means for "actualizing and 'bodying
forth' the story" of creation.[29] He drew on studies of ritual space and
ritual time as keys to understanding cultural cosmologies in order
to derive the priests' cultural worldview from their rituals. Gorman
therefore described P's ritual system as "the meaningful enactment of

---

[26] Baruch A. Levine and William W. Hallo, "Offerings to the Temple Gates at Ur,"
HUCA 38 (1967): 17–58 [18].

[27] Baruch A. Levine, *Numbers 1–20*, Anchor Bible 4 (Garden City: Doubleday, 1993), 82;
idem, "The Descriptive Tabernacle Texts of the Pentateuch," *JAOS* 85 (1965): 307–18
[314].

[28] Adrian Schenker, "Die Anlässe zum Schuldopfer Ascham," in *Studien zu Opfer und
Kult im Alten Testament* (ed. A. Schenker; Tübingen: Mohr Siebeck, 1992), 45–66 [45]
"Ihre liturgische-theologischen Denken ist rational und einsichtig."

[29] Frank H. Gorman, Jr., *Leviticus: Divine Presence and Community*, International Theological Commentary (Grand Rapids: Eerdmans / Edinburgh: Handsel, 1997), 5.

world in the context of Priestly creation theology."[30] His discussion treated ritual texts, their authors' beliefs, and their culture's world-view as interchangeable. In a similar way, David Janzen emphasized the social meaning of ritual as demonstrated by ethnographic field studies. He argued that the meaning of a ritual depends on its social context and cannot be determined apart from it. Janzen therefore described the "rhetorics of ritual," by which he meant the persua-sive effects of ritual performances.[31] His interpretation of P's rituals depended therefore not only on understanding P's theology but also on the worshipper understanding P's theology: "Sacrifice *is* obedience. It is an act that makes sense only if the holiness worldview makes sense, and so whenever Israelites perform it in P they acknowledge that it is a necessary act, necessary because P's worldview of holiness makes it so."[32]

Roy Gane has developed a systematic interpretive approach to ancient rituals. He combined elements of ritual theory with systems theory and applied them to ancient Near Eastern texts, including Leviticus 16.[33] Gane followed Fritz Staal in emphasizing that rituals have syntactic structures, that is, they function in terms of pure rela-tions ("intrinsic activity"), not in terms of intrinsic symbolic meanings that attach to individual activities, objects, or people. But he also insisted that rituals perform a "cognitive task" by establishing commu-nication and interaction with otherwise inaccessible divine or demonic beings. Gane presupposed, with his teacher Milgrom, that ancient rit-ual texts provide modern interpreters direct access to the rituals whose dynamic structure and cognitive tasks he can interpret. His method found an internal logic in rituals rather than exposing their social func-tion, but he did not address the problem that texts may reflect interests and meanings different from the rituals they describe.

---

[30] Idem, *The Ideology of Ritual: Space, Time and Status in the Priestly Theology* (JSOTSup 91; Sheffield: JSOT Press, 1990), 9.
[31] Janzen, *The Social Meanings of Sacrifice*, 4–5, 9–35.
[32] Janzen, *The Social Meanings of Sacrifice*, 110–11.
[33] Roy E. Gane, *Ritual Dynamic Structure* (Piscataway, NJ: Gorgias, 2004).

Among other interpreters, the dependence on anthropological theories of ritual may be less apparent, but the tendency to equate P's ideas with the social function of ritual in ancient Israel remains strong. For example, after quoting Turner that "rituals reveal values which are sociological facts," John Hayes stated, "The rituals of Leviticus embody and reveal a systematic theological thought-world."[34] Alfred Marx reconstituted "P's theology of sacrifice" by moving from detailed descriptions of the structure and form of P's document to a discussion of P's vocabulary of offerings to, finally, a description of the structure and meaning of the offerings. He described this meaning in terms of its "function" – presumably in Israel's religion and society – and his conclusion that "atonement is not the principal aim of the sacrificial cult" was not limited to a characterization of P's intent alone.[35] In the discussions of Hayes and Marx, the line between text and ritual has disappeared.

That is typical of the way P's ritual legislation has been interpreted in much of the scholarship, even more so in the past than the present. To take only the most prominent example, Julius Wellhausen established the relative chronology of pentateuchal sources on the basis of the stages of religious and social development that they reflect. At the same time, he argued that D and P were created as revisionist, and in the latter case, restorationist documents that reflect the "artificial systematizing of given materials."[36] His confidence in being able to distinguish inductively between rules that reflected ancient practice and those that legislated changes to those practices has been shared by much of the field.

---

[34] John H. Hayes, "Atonement in the Book of Leviticus," *Interpretation* 52 (1998): 5–15 [6].

[35] Alfred Marx, "The Theology of Sacrifice According to Leviticus 1–7," in Rolf Rendtorff and Robert A. Kugler (eds.), *The Book of Leviticus: Composition and Reception* (VTSup 93; Leiden: Brill, 2003), 103–20 [117, 119]. He has argued that the Hebrew Bible provides unusual access to understanding the function of sacrifice in ancient society (Marx, *Les systèmes sacrificiels de l'Ancien Testament: Formes et functions du culte sacrificial à Yhwh* [VTSup 105; Leiden: Brill, 2005], 3; but cf. 144–45).

[36] Julius Wellhausen, *Prolegomena to the History of Israel* (Gloucester, MA: Peter Smith, 1973; German 1st ed., 1878), 405.

There are a few exceptions to this interpretive tendency. Erhard Gerstenberger emphasized P's rhetoric and therefore was able to distinguish between the writers' intentions for their intended audience (which for Gerstenberger were diaspora Jews in the Second Temple period) and the meaning of the offerings for ritual participants. For example, he distinguished between P's emphasis on the *ʿōlāh* as an atonement offering and the fact that Israel, like most traditional cultures, invoked the more universal notion of a food gift to understand religious offerings generally.[37] Both conceptions therefore show up in Leviticus. Saul Olyan has also been careful to distinguish "biblical representations of ritual action" from actual historical practice. "Prescriptive texts may reflect a utopian or revisionist program more than actual practice at any particular time or place . . . , though I do not doubt that some prescriptive texts reflect some community's practice at some point in time. The problem is identifying who, where, and when."[38]

Critiques of the tendency to equate the meaning of ritual texts with the meanings of rituals have been voiced more explicitly by William Gilders and Wesley Bergen. Both noted the paucity of symbolic interpretations of ritual in biblical texts and criticized the tendency of biblical scholars to regard rituals as having only one meaning, which proper textual exegesis can expose. They argued instead that interpreters must take seriously the fact that rituals are usually multivocal and ambiguous, that is, they mean different things to different people and often convey no clearly articulated symbolism to those who participate in them.[39] They also pointed out the methodological stumbling block that ancient texts present to ritual interpretation: Gilders noted, "Interpreting a textually represented ritual requires attention to the text

---

[37] Erhard Gerstenberger, *Leviticus: A Commentary*, OTL (tr. D. W. Stott; Louisville: Westminster John Knox, 1996), 34–7.

[38] Saul M. Olyan, *Rites and Rank: Hierarchy in Biblical Representations of Cult* (Princeton: Princeton University Press, 2000), 13.

[39] Gilders, *Blood Ritual*, 3–6; Wesley J. Bergen, *Reading Ritual: Leviticus in Postmodern Culture* (JSOTSup 417; London: T&T Clark, 2005), 1–3.

as well as to the ritual. Both must be interpreted. . . . For this reason, we must distinguish carefully between the 'world of the text' and a living, historical context in which ritual activity takes place."⁴⁰ As a result of these methodological cautions, Gilders focused on the indexical meaning of ancient Israel's blood rituals, which is their significance for indicating the status and changes in status of ritual participants, especially the priests. Bergen used performance theories of rituals to make a similar point, that the meaning of the ritual can be found only by participating in it. He argued, however, that the textualization of ritual in Leviticus resulted in ritualized reading taking the place of ritual offerings: "Thus, the textualization of the ritual is balanced by the ritualization of the text. . . . So there is no loss of ritual, only its transformation."⁴¹

Despite these exceptions, most contemporary interpretations of Leviticus continue to make facile connections between its ritual instructions and narratives, its theology, and Israel's ritual practices. One recent book exemplifies this tendency and has received a very positive reception. I will therefore subject it to a more sustained analysis and critique to illustrate fully the difficulties that this interpretive tendency can lead to.

Reading Mary Douglas Rereading Leviticus

Mary Douglas is a well-known anthropologist who in the 1960s wrote a very influential book (*Purity and Danger*, 1966) on beliefs about purity and pollution in a variety of cultures, including ancient Israel. She

---

⁴⁰ Gilders, *Blood Ritual*, 9, 11.
⁴¹ Bergen, *Reading Ritual*, 8. The rest of his book elaborated on these insights: "Two tensions propel this book. The first is the tension between the question 'What do rituals do?' and the question 'What do texts do?' These questions are not separable in a study of Leviticus, since Leviticus is a text prescribing and influencing action. The questions are not separable in a text which continues to have an effect on the world, even though the actions that result from an encounter with the text are not those prescribed by the text" (p. 10).

later became disenchanted with the application of her own theory to the Bible, because purity rules in this case do not seem to distinguish between levels of Israelite society. At most, they distinguish priests from the rest of Israel, and Israel from the rest of the nations.[42] In her recent treatment of the issue (*Leviticus as Literature*, 1999), she maintained that her theories of purity still apply cross-culturally, but the Bible is an exception to them.[43] According to her new line of thinking, Leviticus concerns itself with theology rather than society, and its purity laws exhibit theological rather than social distinctions. P intends to present "a theory of God, his attributes, and his actions" by means of ritual analogies.[44] She therefore embarked on a more comprehensive analysis of all of Leviticus (and, elsewhere, of Numbers)[45] in which purity laws became only one element of her exploration of its structure, logic, ritual concerns, and theology. Unlike Milgrom and Marx, she did not see the rituals as reflecting Israel's religion and society but rather, like Gorman, as creating a particular worldview: "Leviticus presents its philosophical doctrines in the form of rules of behaviour. Its paradigm lesson about God and existence is enacted on the body of a sacrificial animal, or on the altar, or on the body of a human person."[46] Nevertheless, despite her skepticism that the text reflects society, the meaning of the ritual as described by P and the meaning of P's text is still the same.

This new interpretation depends on far more than observations drawn from comparative anthropology. In fact, in her recent work Douglas drew on her anthropological background relatively little except for occasional ad hoc observations about particular practices. The bulk of her argument applied theories of comparative logic, schemes of formal and structural literary analyses, and theological

---

[42] Mary Douglas, *Leviticus as Literature* (Oxford: Oxford University Press, 1999), vii.
[43] Douglas, *Leviticus as Literature*, viii.
[44] Douglas, *Leviticus as Literature*, 12.
[45] Mary Douglas, *In the Wilderness: The Doctrine of Defilement in the Book of Numbers* (JSOTSup 158; Sheffield: Sheffield Academic Press, 1993).
[46] Douglas, *Leviticus as Literature*, 39.

meditations to the contents of Leviticus. She seemed quite unconcerned with, if not unaware of, methodological conflicts between these
different approaches. She wove them together to create an exposition
of Leviticus' "studied elegance and powerfully contrived structure. A
literary composition that is so impressive could suggest that writing a
theological treatise was the full achievement."[47]

Douglas's book on Leviticus has been met with enthusiasm from
many reviewers,[48] and it is easy to see why. She presents Leviticus
as much more compatible with modern ethics and theology than one
might think from a casual reading of the book. She therefore continues
the efforts of Milgrom and others to present Leviticus as rational and
realistic, and she extends the thesis into a far more systematic depiction
of Leviticus' literary structure and theological message.

I find Douglas's major theses, however, to be quite implausible.
Her analysis of Leviticus provides a rather extreme example of mixing
textual meaning and ritual significance and folding both into a theological superstructure provided by the interpreter.[49] Given the welcome
reception her book has received, it seems worthwhile to subject it to
sustained critique as a paradigmatic example of the problems of a kind
of interpretation that is widespread in biblical scholarship. In what
follows, I distinguish four major theses that Douglas wove together in
her analysis of Leviticus in order to discuss them separately.

---

[47] Douglas, *Leviticus as Literature*, 7.
[48] E.g., the five reviews by Suzette Heald, Lester L. Grabbe, Don Handelman, Alan F.
Segal, and Ronald S. Hendel, "Book Review Forum on Mary Douglas's *Leviticus as
Literature*," *Journal of Ritual Studies* 18/2 (2004): 152–91.
[49] This critique is, of course, not new, though it needs repeating. Almost 40 years ago,
Ernest Gellner sarcastically characterized the aim of the social-function theory of
religion as "to enable us to attribute meaning to assertions which might otherwise
be found to lack it" ("Concepts and Society," in *Sociological Theory and Philosophical
Analysis* [ed. Dorothy Emmet and Alasdair MacIntyre; New York: Macmillan 1970],
115–49). Jonathan Z. Smith quoted Gellner and went on to suggest that "scholars of
religion in the future will shift from the present Romantic hermeneutic of symbol and
poetic speech to that of legal-exegetical discourse" (*Map Is Not Territory: Studies in
the History of Religion* [Leiden: Brill, 1978], 298). Mary Douglas's influence on biblical
studies seems to be taking this discipline in the opposite direction.

One of her theses has to do with the mode of thought that Leviticus employs. Douglas argued that Leviticus does not employ discursive thinking, that is, reasoning that argues rationally from cause to effect. It rather works by deploying multiple layers of analogies, explaining one thing by presenting another that is analogous to it. Douglas cited many studies that document the dominance of such analogous or "correlative" thinking in traditional societies, including classical China and archaic Greece, as well as among lower-class people in modern Britain.[50] She argued that in ancient Jewish culture, such analogical reasoning lost ground to discursive thinking due to the dominating influence of Deuteronomy. As a result, the interpretive tradition lost any knowledge of the analogies that give Leviticus its meaning and has ever since struggled unsuccessfully to translate the book into discursive thought.[51]

Douglas's use of the distinction between analogic and discursive reasoning suffers from three difficulties. They range from her description of the modes of thinking, through her historical reconstruction of the relationship between the writers of Leviticus and the writers of Deuteronomy, to the application of the distinction to the text of Leviticus. Her own examples suggest that analogic and discursive thought are not necessarily incomprehensible to each other (though children from disadvantaged lower classes may find them so).[52] She described cultures in which they have and do interact.[53] Douglas also noted that

---

[50] Douglas, *Leviticus as Literature*, 15–16, 26–7, 36–7.

[51] Douglas, *Leviticus as Literature*, 28–9.

[52] Douglas, *Leviticus as Literature*, 36, 42.

[53] For example, she noted that the analogical thought she finds in Leviticus bears many similarities in form and content with Jewish mysticism (Kabbalah) from the late medieval and early modern periods (*Leviticus as Literature*, 28). But in the Judaism of these periods, rational philosophy competed with Kabbalah for religious prestige and influence. (This debate led to competing methods of Jewish biblical interpretation as well: for a summary, see Barry D. Walfish, "An Introduction to Medieval Jewish Biblical Interpretation," in *With Reverence for the Word: Medieval Scriptural Exegesis in Judaism, Christianity, and Islam* [ed. J. D. McAuliffe, B. D. Walfish, and J. W. Goering; Oxford: Oxford University Press, 2003], 3–12.) Analogic and discursive modes of thought were in conflict, but were hardly incomprehensible to each other,

modern science uses models, which are analogies, from one sphere of experience to describe another. She did so to argue that analogical reasoning is no less rational than it is discursive.[54] Scientists, however, clearly have no problem using both analogies and discursive reasoning. These examples undermine her argument that Leviticus' analogies were inevitably misunderstood by Deuteronomists and later discursive (especially modern) interpreters.[55]

The notion that the writers of Deuteronomy fundamentally misunderstood Leviticus is also historically implausible. The Jewish scribes and priests that made up the Deuteronomistic and Priestly schools did not hail from different times and cultures, but rather shared the culture and traditions of mid-first millennium B.C.E. Judaism.[56] Mutual incomprehension at the level of fundamental misunderstanding between such groups is unlikely, though a rivalry that could lead to the intentional embrace of different modes of discourse is not. The fact, however, that ideological differences can and do lead to mutual incomprehension between groups is not the same thing as claiming that their modes of reasoning make misunderstanding inevitable. Conscious ideological commitments rather than unconscious modes of logic separate such groups.

Finally, Douglas cannot explain why Leviticus never makes its analogies explicit, except to argue that in traditional cultures this was unnecessary.[57] Traditional cultures, however, often make their cosmological analogies explicit. To take just two examples of analogies involving bodies (such as Douglas found throughout Leviticus for both human and animal bodies): the Babylonian creation epic, *Enuma*

and it should be noted that, in the short run at least, kabbalistic analogies won the contest for a popular following, and the competition between them still goes on today.

54 Douglas, *Leviticus as Literature*, 19–21, 25, 28.

55 Douglas, *Leviticus as Literature*, 14, 20, 29. Her insistence on the necessary conflict between analogical and discursive reasoning also contradicted her description of the religion of Leviticus as essentially "modern" in its theological conception (1–2, 15).

56 Douglas, *Leviticus as Literature*, 28.

57 Douglas, *Leviticus as Literature*, 46, 177, 180, 188.

Elish, unequivocally describes the cosmos as created from the slaughtered body of the mother goddess,[58] and a variety of Indo-European traditions extend the body/cosmology analogy to society as well, to justify distinctions between social classes.[59] Leviticus itself is capable of making analogies explicit: it mandates performance of one ritual on the analogy of the instructions already given for another (7:7) and legislates against mistreatment of aliens by drawing an analogy with Israel's experience in Egypt (19:34). The writers of Leviticus could also have made microcosmic analogies explicit if they had wished, but these are nowhere to be found. Their complete absence from the book suggests a possibility that Douglas refused to consider, namely, that the writers were not thinking in such analogies to begin with, or at least had no intention of conveying any such analogies to the readers of this book.

That brings me to the second major thesis of Douglas's *Leviticus as Literature*. She argued that the book deploys a master analogy between Mount Sinai and the Tabernacle, and between both and the bodies of animal sacrifices as well as of human Israelites. Furthermore, she outlined the literary structure of Leviticus in a form that mirrors the architectural structure of the Tabernacle, so that reading the book becomes analogous to touring that sanctuary. The initial problem with this proposal has already been mentioned: nowhere does Leviticus make any of these analogies explicit, as Douglas admitted.[60]

Now it is possible that certain analogies could become so commonplace that writers expect readers to recognize their implicit evocation. That argument, however, becomes less plausible the further this particular set of analogies is extended. The association between mountains and sanctuaries was a commonplace of ancient Near Eastern religious thought and certainly played a big role in reflections about

---

[58] *COS* I.III, lines iv:125–40, v:55–65.

[59] See the examples cited by Bruce Lincoln, "Sacrificial Ideology and Indo-European Society," in *Death, War and Sacrifice: Studies in Ideology and Practice* (Chicago: University of Chicago Press, 1991), 167–75.

[60] Douglas, *Leviticus as Literature*, 75.

the Jerusalem temple, such as are found in the Psalms. Therefore, an implicit analogy between Mount Sinai and the Tabernacle pitched at its base is not unlikely. The analogy between human and animal bodies on the one hand and the mountain and Tabernacle on the other is, however, not attested in other biblical texts. Douglas could only cite explicit parallels from a variety of unrelated cultures.[61] Since another of her theses involves a radical disjunction between the religion of the biblical writers and other ancient cultures (discussed below), such parallels alone cannot present convincing evidence for the existence of this implicit analogy in Leviticus.

Douglas's use of the parallel seems very arbitrary as well. She makes the mountain's top analogous to the animal's entrails because the mountaintop, like the innermost part of the sanctuary, is off-limits to anyone but Moses or Aaron. By extending the Tabernacle analogy to animal and human bodies, however, the "head" ($r\bar{o}\check{s}$) of the mountain ends up at the opposite end of the continuum from the head of the animal. While Douglas was quick to seize on obscure linguistic connections or puns elsewhere to buttress her analogies, here she ignored a very obvious linguistic association because it contradicted her argument. It is more likely that Leviticus never intended any analogy between mountain or Tabernacle and animal or human bodies at all.

There are even stronger reasons to reject Douglas's contention that the literary structure of Leviticus has been shaped by this analogy with the Tabernacle (and with Mt. Sinai and with bodies). It is not because biblical texts do not celebrate sanctuaries; many obviously do (Pss 48, 84, 87, 122; Exod 25–31, 35–40), and some may even be shaped to provide a literary equivalent of a pilgrimage to a shrine.[62] The problem is rather that Douglas's structure highlighted otherwise

---

[61] Douglas, *Leviticus as Literature*, 68, 78–9.
[62] Mark S. Smith has plausibly argued that Exodus is structured as a pilgrimage; see *The Pilgrimage Pattern in Exodus* (JSOTSup 239; Sheffield: Sheffield Academic Press, 1997).

obscure elements as key to the book's structure. Thus the short story of the half-alien blasphemer (Lev 24:10–23) becomes a key transition (the Tabernacle's second "screen") simply because it is a narrative in contrast to its instructional context. The whole scheme depends on the selection of a few elements, often linguistic puns in passing references,[63] while ignoring many other features that have usually been read as of greater structural significance. As a result, Douglas's division of the book into three sections, consisting of Leviticus 1–17, 18–24, and 25–27, is highly idiosyncratic and corresponds to that of no other commentator on the book.

The third major thesis of *Leviticus as Literature* revised Douglas's earlier explanation of the list of clean and unclean animals in Leviticus 11. In *Purity and Danger*, Douglas had argued that the priestly writers considered clean all animals that conformed to the conventional mode of motion (walk, fly, swim) of the habitats (land, air, or water) that they inhabit.[64] They judged unclean those animals that use inappropriate locomotion for their contexts, such as shellfish that walk on the sea bottom. In the newer work, however, Douglas found such a mechanical explanation inappropriate to Leviticus' theology of divine compassion and argued instead for an ethical motive behind the list of animals. Now she considered the designation of "abominable" a means for protecting weak animals that might be easy prey.[65] She found a close analogy between food laws against eating blood and homicide laws against shedding blood.[66]

Her argument rested in part on the distinction in Leviticus 11 between what is *ṭāmēʾ*, "unclean" (certain land animals; vv 4–8, 24–47), and what is *šeqeṣ*, "abominable," and *šiqqēṣ*, "regarded as abominable" (certain creatures of the air and sea; vv 10–23). Interpreters have usually regarded the latter term as intensifying the effect of the former,[67] but

---

[63] Douglas, *Leviticus as Literature*, 194–7, 218–30, 237–45.
[64] Douglas, *Purity and Danger*, 69–71.
[65] Douglas, *Leviticus as Literature*, 1–2, 135–6, 141, 151, 171–4.
[66] Douglas, *Leviticus as Literature*, 232.
[67] E.g., John E. Hartley, *Leviticus* (WBC 4; Dallas: Word, 1992), 157.

Milgrom argued that the different terms distinguish between inedible animals that convey corpse pollution (*ṭāmēʾ*, "unclean,") and those that do not (*šeqeṣ*). The latter may not be eaten, but their corpses do not convey pollution, an especially important qualification because water containing the latter would not be declared unclean due to contact with them.[68]

Douglas adopted Milgrom's observation but argued that the book's underlying concern is not with the status of water containing shell-fish and insect corpses but rather with protecting these animals from indiscriminate slaughter. She rooted this view in the divine assertion in Genesis 1 that all of creation is "good" and wondered "why the good kind God would create abominable animals?" From this starting point, her approach was entirely theological: "God is not capricious and inconsistent. . . . Of course he would not let his human clients abuse his other creatures. . . . Ritual purity is a kind of two-way protection, a holy thing is protected from profanation, the profane thing is protected from holiness."[69] In Leviticus 11, this worked out to mean that because the corpses of land animals pollute on contact, "the rule against touching a dead animal protects it in its lifetime. Since its carcass cannot be skinned or dismembered, most of the ways in which it could be exploited are ruled out, so it is not worth breeding, hunting, or trapping."[70] Douglas thought the P writers regarded water creatures without fins or scales as lacking ability to escape (fins) or defenses (scales), and so should not be preyed upon. "It means that, though contact with these creatures is not against purity, harming them is against holiness."[71]

There are more difficulties with this position than just the oddity of the idea that highly armored shellfish might seem defenseless. The more serious problem involves P's motivation for making the distinction

---

[68] Milgrom, *Leviticus,* 1:656–9.
[69] Douglas, *Leviticus as Literature,* 11.
[70] Douglas, *Leviticus as Literature,* 141.
[71] Douglas, *Leviticus as Literature,* 168.

that, as usual in Leviticus, is not stated explicitly. Milgrom found the motive in the need to justify the purity of water sources, which at least invokes the book's explicit concern with pollution. Douglas replaced that motive with a concern to protect weaker creatures, an idea that is not even explicit in the Genesis texts she cited.[72] Modern readers, of course, find a biblical call to defend threatened wildlife quite attractive, and Douglas catered to our biases. But the argument finds no explicit basis in Leviticus or the Pentateuch.

Douglas's fourth major thesis placed Leviticus within a history of Israelite religion. She argued that the book presents a revisionist religion that systematically eradicates and replaces the role of demonology in divination and sacrifice.[73] Douglas noted that in many cultures, including those of the ancient Near East, sacrifice served as a means of divination, of determining the will of the gods and the reasons that events, especially bad events, were occurring. Once divination identified the supernatural source of a problem, sacrifice also provided a means for propitiating the relevant gods or driving away the afflicting demons. Most ancient and traditional societies explained ritual purification as a means for expiating demonic influences. Biblical writers, however, rejected sacrificial divination and beliefs in demons out of hand, leaving the ritual systems of sacrifice and purification largely without a theoretical justification.

This is the most plausible of Douglas's major theses. Unlike the others, it is supported by passages in Leviticus that explicitly condemn ritual divination of various sorts (Lev 19:26, 31; 20:6, 27). It also explains something that has puzzled interpreters for millennia, namely, the book's failure to interpret the meaning of sacrifices and other rituals. Douglas suggested that the absence of ritual explanations is part and parcel of the polemic against other religious systems: the theory of

---

[72] She seems to have forgotten that the same deity who declared all the animals good also destroyed many of them *en masse* with flood in Genesis 6–9 – predation on the weak indeed!

[73] Douglas, *Leviticus as Literature*, 2–5, 9–10, 11, 107, 113, 122–3, 132, 189.

demonic influences has been deliberately stripped from Israel's ritual system, leaving little theoretical explanation for the practices.[74] This argument is interesting and worth exploring further.

It does not, however, support Douglas's contention that the priestly writers replaced beliefs in demons with theological analogies.[75] Leviticus describes a theological cosmology and microcosmic analogies no more than it does a demonology. One might insist, as Douglas does, that the priestly writers must have filled this explanatory gap in some way or another. Perhaps they did, but they did not write those explanations down in Leviticus. If the expulsion of demon beliefs from Israel's religion created a deficit of theoretical explanations for temple rituals, Leviticus does nothing to supply them. Douglas used her imagination to fill the gaps theologically, which is perhaps the only reasonable way that moderns can do it. The ancient writers of Leviticus do not seem to have felt the same need. Neither did the writers of many ritual texts from other ancient cultures, as I have already noted.

[74] One might question whether divination practices and beliefs about demons were as universal in other cultures, especially other ancient cultures, as Douglas suggested, or that the priestly writers' repudiation of demonology is as thorough as she thought. Her evidence for demon beliefs in other ancient cultures (*Leviticus as Literature*, 189) is not very deep and deserves a more thorough examination in relation to ancient practices of divination and purification. The idea that the priestly writers repudiated demonology has been defended at length by Yehezkel Kaufmann (*Toledot ha'Emunah ha Yisre'elit*, 4 vols. [2nd ed.; Jerusalem: Mosad Bialik, 1952], 1:525–33, 539–45; 2:*passim*), but was challenged by Levine (*In the Presence of the Lord: A Study of Cult and Some Cultic Terms in Ancient Israel* [Leiden: Brill, 1974], 79–91; *Leviticus*, 250–3) who found apotropaic and prophylactic magic aimed at warding off demonic forces throughout the priestly ritual texts, and especially in the scapegoat ritual of Leviticus 16. Milgrom, on the other hand, denied that demons have any vitality in priestly thought (*Leviticus*, 1:1079).

[75] Douglas, *Leviticus as Literature*, 12. In a critique of Douglas's work, Antony Cothey noted this problem and proposed that Leviticus presents its ritual procedures as practical, rather than symbolic, responses: "We may find it helpful from our perspective to describe its role as symbolic; and this is true as far as it goes; but we should recognize that the problems to which the ritual actions provided a solution and also the effectiveness of the God-given remedy were both held by the priestly writers to be fully real" ("Ethics and Holiness in the Theology of Leviticus," *JSOT* 30 [2005]: 131–51 [150]).

Aside from these four large theses, Douglas provided many interesting observations about specific passages in Leviticus. These were often drawn from comparisons with other cultures revealed by anthropological study and are, to my mind, the most interesting parts of her book. For example, she drew on studies of the role of oath taking and divination in the judicial practices of various societies to elucidate the issue of so-called inadvertent sins and their ritual resolution in Leviticus 4–5.[76] Douglas also called on interpreters to consider whether rituals such as circumcision and purification may have played a prophylactic function that affected the purity of new mothers and lepers.[77]

Douglas rethought her original theories about purity in Leviticus because she could not find any social function for the book's purity laws. That is because she dismissed the book's explicit interest in distinguishing the roles and privileges of priests as "obvious" and, since it received no further discussion, apparently trivial.[78] In her earlier book on Numbers, Douglas devoted a chapter to considerations of hierarchy after having elaborated on the Bible's depiction of ancient Israel as an individualistic "enclave" culture. She concluded by noting the irony of having "a hierarchical hereditary priesthood editing the ancient texts of an individualist culture," but continued that "there is no sign that they are imagining that they could introduce a hierarchical community" and that the book of Numbers "is utterly republican in tone," by which she meant that it makes no room for royalty.[79]

Like so many other interpreters, Douglas failed to draw any connection between the priestly rhetoric in the Torah and the priestly hierocracy that gradually accumulated temporal as well as religious authority in Jerusalem in the Persian and Hellenistic periods (see Chapter 7).

---

[76] Douglas, *Leviticus as Literature*, 127, 131–2.

[77] Douglas, *Leviticus as Literature*, 181–2.

[78] Douglas, *Leviticus as Literature*, vii.

[79] Douglas, *In the Wilderness*, 82. Contrast this with Olyan's nuanced appraisal of the deep implications for social hierarchy of the dichotomies between holy/common and clean/unclean that are elaborated in P (*Rites and Rank*, 27–35, 54–61).

Instead, she reconstructed theological analogies unsupported by the text. Interpretation should rather start with the obvious priestly interests of the book and try to meet the ancient authors on their own ground by taking those interests seriously as well. All the evidence suggests that the priesthood was by far the most important component of human society in the worldview of the writers of Leviticus.

That does not mean that I am advocating a return to an exclusive emphasis on social function, as in Douglas's earlier work. It is quite possible that cosmology and even microcosmic analogies may play a role in P's ideas.[80] Interpretation of these texts, however, must be guided by their explicit statements if it is to be defensible either on discursive or analogical grounds.

The Difference Between Texts and Rituals

The point of these critiques has been to argue that interpreters need to distinguish more carefully between a ritual text's explicit assertions, the ritual practices reflected in it, and the "meaning" of either the text or the ritual. The tendency of interpreters, with a few exceptions, to slide easily from discussing P's intentions to describing the religious meaning and social effects of various rituals obscures distinct interpretive questions that should be distinguished, but rarely are. Let me distinguish five such questions:

1. *Why did P write about these rituals?* The usual list of answers – instruction manual for priests or for laity, or a theology of sacred space and practice – fails to plumb the rhetorical possibilities of the P document. Gerstenberger's commentary provides a first step toward exploring these issues, though I do not think that P primarily addresses diaspora congregations. The priestly writers make overt and sustained attempts to convince

---

[80] See Yohan Yoo, "A Theory of Purity from the Perspective of Comparative Religions" (Ph.D. Dissertation, Syracuse University, 2005).

hearers and readers to perform the offerings, to perform them in this particular way, to accept the authority of this document over ritual performances, and to accept the monopoly of the Aaronide priests over all ritual offerings. Such overt persuasion should be given much greater attention in descriptions of the purpose of Leviticus than it has to date.

2. *What did P think the rituals meant?* This question has received the lion's share of attention, but it is usually assumed that this was also P's purpose (= question 1). That assumption receives little if any explicit warrant from the text. While the efforts to rehabilitate P's image against the charge of empty ritualism are most commendable, we should remembered that P's theology must always be "reconstituted" because P does very little to make it explicit. The texts do not necessarily reflect the meaning of the rituals.

3. *Do P's descriptions reflect actual practice?* This has been roundly debated as a conflict between utopian and realist interpretations of P. But many of the scholars who insist on P's realism have also pointed out P's innovations in ritual practices. If P was promulgated to *change* existing practices, then the degree to which it reflected actual practices at the time of its composition requires careful evaluation. Furthermore, the setting of these ritual instructions in the Tent of Meeting, which no longer existed when P was written, gives the entire composition a utopian and even nostalgic cast.[81] Given P's eventual canonical status as part of the Torah, P's innovations probably succeeded in becoming at least part of Israel's ritual practices, though perhaps not always in the way its authors intended since it was canonized together with Deuteronomy's rules, with which priests had to harmonize it.

4. *What did these rituals mean in ancient Israel?* Just because P's texts became authoritative does not mean P's implied interpretations did. I think Douglas overstates the problem by insisting that Deuteronomy necessarily led to P's being misunderstood, but we must nevertheless take into account the possibility that the priestly writers' notion of ritual meaning did not

---

[81] So Bergen argued that Leviticus "deliberately creates readers who recognize that their participation in the act of reading the text involves imaginary participation in a dead ritual" (*Reading Ritual*, 31).

necessarily become the interpretation and teaching of Second-Temple-era priests, much less of the general population, even when they were trying to follow P's instructions. Gilders's warning hits the mark: "Even for 'native' cultic specialists, as well as for 'lay' participants in ritual performances, ritual acts are characteristically multivalent, and there is diversity of interpretation even within unified cultic communities."[82]

5. *How did these rituals function in ancient Israel?* This question poses the problem of the "latent" function of ritual, to use Gilders's vocabulary (borrowed from R. K. Merton) and Bergen's distinction between a ritual's purpose and its effects.[83] Many interpreters collapse the rituals' meaning with their religious and social function.[84] Prominent theorists of sacrifice, however, from Robertson-Smith through Freud to Girard, have claimed that sacrificers did not understand the true function of sacrifice in their own societies. (For a survey and analysis of these theories of sacrifice, see Chapter 8.) Therefore an answer to the question of what a ritual meant to ancient people is not necessarily an answer to the question of how and why the ritual functioned within ancient society.

These questions distinguish textual interpretation from ritual interpretation. Interpreting a text about a ritual does not interpret the meaning of the ritual (except sometimes – but not always – its meaning for the author of the text), and conversely the meaning or function of the ritual is not the same thing as the meaning of the text describing the ritual. In other words, *texts are not rituals and rituals are not texts.* Let me elaborate briefly on each of these propositions in turn.

Texts are not rituals: Commentators frequently note the gaps in P's accounts of rituals, which make it impossible to reconstruct the whole ritual from what the text records. Rather than complaining about what

---

[82] Gilders, *Blood Ritual*, 141.

[83] He took seriously Lev 1:4's assertion that the purpose of the ʿōlāh offering is to atone, but noted that the ritual could nevertheless have many other effects (Bergen, *Reading Ritual*, 4).

[84] E.g., Eberhart: "Eine konkrete, kultische Bedeutung bzw. Funktion wurde mit den verschiedenen Opferarten ohne Zweifel assoziiert" (*Studien zur Bedeutung der Opfer*, 6).

is missing, we should ask why the text includes what it does. What did the writer wish to accomplish by communicating precisely these points?

Ritual texts may be (in fact, usually are) motivated by concerns other than the interpretation of ritual meaning. Not just in the Bible, but across many traditions and cultures, traditional practitioners offer few explanations for their rituals.[85] That is not for lack of discussions about rituals in traditional sources. But rhetoric that instructs, commemorates, or encourages practices (didactic ritual texts, sermons, votive inscriptions, etc.) is more likely to describe and commend a ritual than to explain it.[86] So rather than explaining a ritual's meaning, P's rhetorical goals may include the validation of the ritual and its form on the basis of ostensibly ancient textual authority, and/or persuasion to motivate performance of the rituals, and/or persuasion to accept the whole text's authority (torah) because of its authoritative instruction on ritual performance. (See Chapter 2.) So texts are not rituals: the text's meaning may or may not have anything to do with the ritual's meaning in the mind of the author, much less its meaning and function within ancient culture.

Furthermore, narrow investigations of the "meaning" of a text's words may miss its broader rhetorical function as an instrument for persuasion. Such persuasion may use ambiguity and mystery as much as meaning and clarity to try to influence its audience. A rhetorical analysis of ritual texts should therefore be alert to the possibility that some passages were intentionally written to be hard to understand and consider what persuasive purposes such deliberate obfuscation might

---

[85] On the lack of ancient explanations for Greek rites, see Marcel Detienne, "Culinary Practices and the Spirit of Sacrifice," in *The Cuisine of Sacrifice among the Greeks* (ed. M. Detienne and J.-P. Vernant, tr. P. Wissig; Chicago: University of Chicago Press, 1989; French 1979), 1–20 [5]; for Roman rites, see North, "Sacrifice and Ritual: Rome," 981–6.

[86] There are still communities that read the Pentateuch's instructions for offerings as mandating ritual practices: in addition to the well-known example of the Samaritans, some Christian traditions in Africa practice ritual slaughter with conscious reference to Leviticus (see the summary and literature cited by Bergen, *Reading Ritual*, 53–7).

have served. Rituals, of course, may also serve persuasive purposes, so some interpreters have investigated the "rhetorics of ritual."[87] Even if that was the case for Israelite offerings, however, there is no *a priori* reason to think that a ritual's persuasive purpose would match the rhetorical intentions of authors who write about that ritual. Ritual texts are not rituals and cannot be presumed to match the rituals they describe in either meaning or rhetoric.

Rituals are not texts: Rituals do not always require symbolic reduction to the extent that those trained in Talmudic debates or allegorical theology or Eucharistic disputes or formalist and symbolist anthropology usually assume. Unlike texts that are unavoidably linguistic and necessarily involve signs and symbols, rituals are not necessarily heavily invested in systems of symbolic interpretation. Though many do in fact carry with them a tradition of symbolic interpretation and controversy (e.g., the Christian Eucharist), others are remarkably free of symbolic commentary, even in modern Western society. Consider, for example, the university ceremonies of commencement and convocation, which, despite their pageantry, give little attention to interpretive commentary. Like their ancient priestly counterparts, the ritual texts of college and university administrators focus primarily on encouraging participation and mandating proper practice, not on elaborating the symbolism of the rites. At most, written programs will include a few paragraphs about academic hoods and gowns and university arms and other symbols, but the ceremony itself usually receives no commentary. Its meaning is presented as self-evident.

Rituals have no clear author by whose authorial intent we can try to explain them. Their meanings are as multifarious as all the people who participate in them, observe them, or write or read about them. Though some ritual texts do claim divine or semi-divine authorship of key rituals and this claim is sometimes used by authors and speakers to try to define their meaning (biblical examples include quotations of Moses about Passover in Exod 12:24–27 and of Jesus about the Eucharist in

---

[87] Janzen, *Social Meaning of Sacrifice,* 9–35.

1 Cor 11:23–26), they more often simply authorize the practice itself (Moses about the Day of Atonement in Lev 16, Jesus about baptism in Matt 28:19). Claims to divine authorship of rituals are patent attempts to persuade readers to perform the rites and, perhaps, to interpret them in a particular way. As such, they are themselves indications that the ritual's performance and/or meaning was contested. To grant precedence to one author (ancient or modern) or authority or tradition of interpretation is to accede to one party's claims in a many-sided contest of interpretations (see Buc).

As a result, some theorists and historians have questioned whether rituals can be effectively explained by reducing them to a system of meanings at all (e.g., Fritz Staal, J. Z. Smith). Stanley Stowers put the issue bluntly: "Practices cannot be reduced to ideas."[88] We should take seriously the possibility that rituals are not primarily or necessarily means for communicating symbols, unlike texts.

Rhetoric and Ritual Interpretation

How then should rituals be interpreted? Nancy Jay helpfully distinguished action from interpretation in her comparative analysis of sacrifice:

> The meaning of any action not only varies with the way in which it is interpreted, it *is* the way in which it is interpreted. . . . For meaning is not a simple and direct product of action itself, but of reflection upon it. And the act of reflection is always another act, socially situated in its own way.[89]

This point can be verified from the study of any ritual, whose interpretations often vary dramatically among both participants and

---

[88] Stanley K. Stowers, "On the Comparison of Blood in Greek and Israelite Ritual," in *Hesed ve-Emet: Studies in Honor of Ernest S. Frerichs* (ed. Jodi Magness and Seymour Gitin; BJS 320; Atlanta: Scholars, 1998), 179–94 [189].

[89] Nancy Jay, *Throughout Your Generations Forever: Sacrifice, Religion and Paternity* (Chicago: University of Chicago Press, 1992), 8.

theorists. Thus an analysis of ritual meaning should always be not only an interpretation of interpretations, but one which is also sensitive to *uninterpreted rituals* as well. Everyone both performs and interprets rituals, but often not the same ones.[90] (For further discussion of this point, see Chapter 8.) Though Buc's thorough review of the uses of ritual in Western thought shows the decisive role of interpretation in textual descriptions of rituals; in the end he preserved the common distinction between interpretive and noninterpretive cultures.[91] It is, I think, more accurate to say that every culture emphasizes symbolic interpretation of some rituals and experiences, and not others. The differences in their choice of what to interpret produce surprise and incomprehension from foreigners. It is a mistake to assume the existence of native ritual interpretations in the absence of any evidence for them.

If texts, such as P, do not provide symbolic explanations of the rituals they describe, interpreters find themselves open to the charge of imposing symbolic systems not intrinsic or necessary to the rituals. A given text may have been realistic at one time and utopian at another; a given ritual may have been given symbolic interpretation at one time and not at another; a given society may have had conflicting rituals, texts, and interpretations interacting at the same time. In fact, all of these possibilities are inherently probable for any culture and period.

Two commendable impulses – namely to defend P against charges of "empty ritualism" and to defend the "realism" of most of P's descriptions of ancient rituals – have led interpreters to collapse the distinction between ritual and interpretation. I do not mean to denigrate these concerns. As to the first, Buc chronicled how deeply the prejudice against "ritualism" permeates Western history and culture. As to the second issue, reconstructions of Israel's religious history depend almost entirely on the descriptions of ritual provided by texts. When we

---

[90] Contra Jay, *Throughout Your Generations Forever*, 13.
[91] Buc, *Dangers of Ritual*, 247.

deal with these issues, however, we must keep the distinctions between texts, rituals, and interpretations clearly in mind.

It is also worth remembering that in antiquity rituals do not seem to have required interpretation unless and until they were contested. Within Greek culture, discussions of the meaning of sacrifice were stimulated by groups, such as the Orphics and Pythagoreans, that were critical of the socially dominant institutions.[92] And the dominant traditions maintained their position more by the force of custom and tradition than by intellectual apologetics. That remains true even in modernity, despite the emphasis in rabbinic/scholastic/academic traditions on the rationales behind the rituals: within congregations, custom and tradition often trump intellectual rationales in determining normative practice.

It may be that once the Torah's ritual legislation became the normative temple law of Jerusalem, its status was secured by the prestige of the Temple and its traditions. It required no theological interpretation at all, but only interpretation as to how to apply it in practice. If anything, it may be that the normative ritual legislation lent its prestige and authority to the narratives and civil laws of the Pentateuch because of their presence together in the same Torah, rather than the other way around. Thus the stories and moral rules that we are more accustomed to considering the sources of "theology" may historically have gained their scriptural status by their association with ritual legislation (see Chapter 9).

When a text describes rituals, the first question interpreters should ask is "why?" The answer is often given explicitly in the text: rituals are usually described to persuade people to perform them, or to perform them in this particular way, or to accept the text and/or its author's authority to mandate the ritual and, perhaps, to officiate over it. Attention to the purposes served by ritual texts should therefore lead to analyzing their means of persuasion, that is, their rhetoric.

---

[92] Marcel Detienne, "Culinary Practices," 5–8.

Persuasion has been a traditional subject of rhetoric, its theories, and its modes of analysis.[93] Theories of rhetoric first developed in ancient Greek culture from which later Western forms of rhetorical analysis and instruction derive. No comparable theories of persuasion seem to have developed in ancient Israel or other pre-Hellenistic Near Eastern cultures. All human cultures, however, develop conventional modes of persuasion that shape the words of their speakers and writers.[94] Though rhetorical criticism has come to be associated in biblical studies with purely literary analysis of structure and style, ancient and modern rhetorical analysis has usually addressed such issues from the larger perspective of argumentation, asking how speakers and writers influence their listeners and readers. Literary study then becomes more than an analysis of the text itself; it aims to understand texts as transactions between authors and audiences.[95] An emphasis on rhetoric calls attention to both the literary features of a text and the real writers and readers whose ideas motivated its formation and later use. When biblical texts give overt indications of being formulated for persuasive purposes, and most do, rhetorical analysis provides a means for bringing together critical observations from both historical and literary studies to explain their form and function. Rhetorical analysis calls attention to the text's function in transactions between people, both at the time of its composition and in later social situations.

In what follows, I examine the ritual instructions and stories in Leviticus from a rhetorical perspective in order to place interpretation of both texts and rituals on methodologically firmer ground. Five chapters examine various aspects of the book's ritual texts to describe

---

[93] For a survey and discussion of the history of rhetoric in terms of persuasion, see Kenneth Burke, A *Rhetoric of Motives* (Berkeley: University of California, 1950) 49–55, 61–2.

[94] For studies of the rhetorical practices of non-Greco-Roman cultures, see the essays in Roberta Binkley and Carol Lipson (eds.), *Rhetoric Before and Beyond the Greeks* (Albany: SUNY Press, 2004).

[95] See Dale Patrick and Allen Scult, *Rhetoric and Biblical Interpretation* (JSOTSup 82; Sheffield: Almond, 1990), esp. 12.

their original purpose and the means they use to try to persuade their intended audiences to accept them. Then the following three chapters turn to the actual effects of Leviticus' ritual rhetoric on the power of ancient Jewish priests (Chapter 7), the cultural idea of sacrifice (Chapter 8), and the authority of scripture (Chapter 9). Throughout, I try to take seriously Jay's admonition that interpretations of rituals are always "interpretations of interpretations." Readers may feel that contact with the "real" meaning of the rituals has been lost along the way, but that is only because any impression of such ritual immediacy was an illusion to begin with. We can never go back and observe, much less participate in, ancient Israel's temple ceremonies. All we can do is read the texts that describe, legislate, and polemicize about them to try to understand how their authors used ritual for rhetorical purposes.

2

The Rhetoric of Ritual Instruction

Formal and structural features of Leviticus 1–7 distinguish these chapters as some of the most systematic texts in the Hebrew Bible. In a collection of literature otherwise noted for its sweeping narratives and urgent sermons, these methodical instructions for the performance of five kinds of offerings, presented twice in different arrangements, have suggested to many interpreters that they preserve examples of an ancient genre of ritual instruction. However, the identification of a ritual genre in these chapters (and elsewhere in the Pentateuch) has failed to account for all of the features of this material. The present form of Leviticus 1–7 can be better understood as a product of the same process of generic mixture and allusion apparent in many other biblical texts.

I have argued elsewhere that the large-scale structure of the Pentateuch and several of its constituent parts has been shaped by a rhetorical strategy that combines diverse materials for persuasive effect. Thus the narratives of Genesis and Exodus ground the authority of the divine lawgiver on the basis of past acts of creation, blessing, and salvation; the laws and instructions of Exodus, Leviticus, and Numbers stipulate behavior in the present; while the blessings and curses that conclude Leviticus and Deuteronomy, and that in the larger context characterize Deuteronomy as a whole, depict the possible futures deter-mined by Israel's response to the laws. This story-list-sanction pattern can be recognized in some other ancient Near Eastern texts of vari-ous types and reflects a strategy employed in various literary genres to increase their persuasive impact. Thus the macro-structure of the Pen-tateuch seems designed to maximize its persuasive impact on ancient Jews who read it or, more likely, heard it read.[1]

Leviticus 1–7 furthers the Pentateuch's persuasive agenda and was designed for that purpose. Of course, these chapters also instruct, but instruction frequently involves persuasion as well.[2] Leviticus 1–7 has been shaped not only to instruct worshippers and priests how to perform various offerings, but also to persuade them to do exactly as these texts stipulate and to accept these texts as the ultimate authority for such ritual performances.[3] To demonstrate these claims regarding the form and function of Leviticus 1–7, I will first argue that previous efforts to describe their form and function on the basis of genre have not accounted for the text as it appears in the Hebrew Bible. I will then

---

[1] James W. Watts, *Reading Law: The Rhetorical Shaping of the Pentateuch*, Biblical Seminar 59 (Sheffield: Sheffield Academic Press, 1999).

[2] In an exhaustive analysis, David M. Carr has recently shown how literary texts were used in ancient Near Eastern and Mediterranean scribal cultures, including Israel's, not only to educate but also to "enculturate" students into an elite professional class of bureaucrats and/or into the ruling social class (*Writing on the Tablet of the Heart: Origins of Scripture and Literature* [Oxford: Oxford University Press, 2005]). He doc-umented that persuasion, ranging from physical discipline to intellectual stimulation, was used to get students to memorize classical texts that then molded their thinking and motivations to the cultural prescribed norm.

[3] Baruch J. Schwartz argued similarly for the persuasive formulation of biblical law: "The 'laws' in the Torah form part of a story, according to which they were spoken in order to be proclaimed, they were to be proclaimed in order to convince, they were to convince in order to be observed, and they were to be observed in fulfillment of the Sinai covenant.... [T]he laws, as well as the story in which they are contained, were composed in order to be read publicly and understood, to have a lasting, pedagogical, persuasive influence on later generations of listeners" ("Prohibitions Concerning the 'Eating' of Blood in Leviticus 17," in *Priesthood and Cult in Ancient Israel* [ed. G. A. Anderson and S. M. Olyan [JSOTSup 125; Sheffield: JSOT, 1991], 34–66 [35]; idem, *Selected Chapters of the Holiness Code – A Literary Study of Leviticus 1–9* (Hebrew) [Ph.D. Dissertation, Hebrew University of Jerusalem, 1987], 1–24).

compare the rhetorical features of these chapters with other ancient Near Eastern texts dealing with rituals, to lay the basis for describing their rhetorical function in the context of Leviticus and the Pentateuch as a whole.

The Search for Ritual Genres

In twentieth-century criticism, the genre of ritual instructions has been analyzed from two different directions: form-critical reconstruction of its oral form, and comparative analysis of its ancient parallels. Each approach, however, produced a reconstructed genre quite different from the texts of Leviticus 1–7. The latter was then presumed to have been modified in distinctive ways to fit later social or literary contexts. Reviewing these theories will illustrate the difficulties that genre analysis encounters in Leviticus 1–7.

Interpreters in the mid-twentieth century mounted a major effort to isolate and analyze the forms of oral priestly teaching and to categorize them by genre.[4] This movement found its fullest and most direct application to Leviticus 1–7 in Rolf Rendtorff's monograph *Die Gesetze in der Priesterschrift* (1954).[5] Rendtorff isolated in Leviticus 1 and 3 a genre of short instructions for the performance of offerings that he labeled "ritual." It is characterized by stereotypical short verbal sentences formulated in impersonal perfect verbs except for an introductory imperfect, and by concluding formulas.[6] Leviticus 2, 4, and 5 reflect this form to a lesser extent, so Rendtorff concluded that this material originally took other forms that were secondarily adapted to

---

[4] E.g., J. Begrich, "Die priesterliche Tora," in *Wesen und Werden des Alten Testaments* (ed. P. Volz; BZAW 66; Berlin: A. Töpelmann, 1936), 63–88; Gerhard von Rad, *Deuterononium-Studien* (rev. ed.; Göttingen: Vandenhoeck & Ruprecht, 1948), translated by D. Stalker as *Studies in Deuteronomy* (SBT 9; London: SCM, 1953).

[5] Rolf Rendtorff, *Die Gesetze in der Priesterschrift: eine gattungsgeschichtliche Untersuchung* (FRLANT 44; Göttingen: Vandenhoeck & Ruprecht, 1954).

[6] Rendtorff, *Gesetze* 12.

the "ritual" pattern. Leviticus 6–7 do not reflect this form or any other and probably had a scribal origin.[7] Klaus Koch built on Rendtorff's analysis but defined the ritual genre on the basis of sequences of converted perfect verbs alone, which allowed him to find it in more texts in Leviticus 1–7 and in Exodus 25–40.[8] Rendtorff admitted that it is difficult to reconstruct the original setting of the "ritual" genre because its social context is not reflected in Leviticus 1–7 or almost anywhere else in the Hebrew Bible. He suggested, however, that the strict stylization and stereotypical repetition notable in Leviticus 1 and 3 show that they were intended for oral recitation, perhaps as sentences spoken to accompany offerings.[9]

Two difficulties hindered this form-critical attempt to establish the genre of these ritual texts. First, it was not able to discover convincing evidence for the original settings in which ritual genres of instruction developed.[10] Rendtorff himself has since backed away from any attempt to identify these original settings, preferring to speak of a "ritual style" rather than an oral genre.[11] Second, the observation that much of this material stemmed from editorial modifications of the hypothetical original genres raised the question of whether there ever was an oral tradition behind these edited texts. Rolf Knierim dismissed the case for a ritual genre because it did not account for the form of the present text. He argued that the casuistic ("if . . . then . . . ") formulation of Leviticus 1:2b–9 must be taken seriously for genre analysis, in which case the material can only be classified as case law.[12] Casuistic law is a scribal

---

[7] Rendtorff, *Gesetze* 14, 19, 20, 33–4.
[8] Klaus Koch, *Die Priesterschrift von Exodus 25 bis Leviticus 16: eine überlieferungsgeschichtliche und literarkritische Untersuchung* (FRLANT 53; Göttingen: Vandenhoeck & Ruprecht, 1959), 46–76.
[9] Rendtorff, *Gesetze,* 22–3.
[10] See the critique by Karl Elliger, *Leviticus* (Handbuch zum Alten Testament 4; Tübingen: Mohr [Siebeck], 1966), 30–1.
[11] See his *Leviticus* (Biblischer Kommentar: Altes Testament 3/1; Neukirchen-Vluyn: Neukirchener Verlag, 1985), 18–19.
[12] Rolf P. Knierim, *Text and Concept in Leviticus 1:1–9: A Case in Exegetical Method* (Forschungen zum Alten Testament 2; Tübingen: Mohr [Siebeck], 1992), 10, 65, 95.

genre, so there was never an oral form of this material.[13] Yet Knierim, like Rendtorff and Koch, abstracted the material's genre out of the context in God's instructions through Moses (vv 1–2a). He justified doing so by arguing that, though case law can be used for didactic purposes, that use does not explain why the material was formulated this way.[14] However, his grounds for this conclusion, that the material's impersonal style does not fit instruction, remained purely impressionistic. Thus Knierim's modification of the form-critical project by focusing on the extant text and on scribal genres still abstracted the text's genre from its role in its literary context. As such, it did not contribute much toward explaining why the text was chosen or written to function within the book of Leviticus as it stands.

The second approach to ritual genre has emphasized scribal practices from the start. Comparative studies of ancient ritual texts have sought to explain the material's form and arrangement through a scenario of textual development. In a series of articles, Baruch Levine has argued that ancient ritual texts began as archival records of offerings. Out of these records the genre of "descriptive ritual" developed, composed of texts that record in indicative verbs the performance of liturgies and rites. Such descriptive rituals appear in Akkadian, Hittite, and Ugaritic sources and probably served as instructions for priests and other liturgical actors. Only much later, however, did such texts get recast in a more hortatory form as prescriptive rituals to reflect their didactic role.[15] In the Hebrew Bible, Levine focused his attention on texts such as Exodus 35–39, Leviticus 8–9, and Numbers 7:10–88 that

---

[13] Knierim, *Text and Concept*, 103.

[14] Knierim, *Text and Concept*, 7, 98–100, 106.

[15] Baruch A. Levine, "Ugaritic Descriptive Rituals," *JCS* 17 (1963): 105–11; idem, "The Descriptive Tabernacle Texts of the Pentateuch," *JAOS* 85 (1965): 307–18; idem, "The Descriptive Ritual Texts from Ugarit: Some Formal and Functional Features of the Genre," in *The Word of the Lord Shall Go Forth: Essay in Honor of David Noel Freedman* (ed. C. L. Meyers and M. O'Conner; Winona Lake: Eisenbrauns, 1983), 467–75; idem, *Numbers 1–20*, 81–2; idem, with Hallo, "Offerings to the Temple Gates at Ur," 17–58; idem, with J.-M. de Terragon, "The King Proclaims the Day: Ugaritic Rites for the Vintage (*KTU* 1.41–1.87)," *RB* 100 (1993): 76–115.

describe past ritual events rather than prescribing future ritual actions. His analysis suggested that passages such as Leviticus 1–7 stand at the end of a long process of textual development from temple archive through descriptive rituals to prescriptive rituals.

Levine's isolation of the descriptive ritual genre depended on a survey of texts from a wide variety of cultures, which is both his theory's strength and its weakness. The number of texts strengthens the argument that this form reflects a genre, that is, a recognizable group of literary conventions governing the text's form and contents. The label "descriptive," however, depends on interpreting verbal forms as indicatives that can and have been read otherwise. Some of Levine's Ugaritic examples in particular have been interpreted as prescriptive rituals, despite his arguments to the contrary.[16] The comparative evidence allowed Levine to point to specific examples of each stage of development, which otherwise would be lacking in the biblical material. The Bible does not preserve any examples of the original archival form, which must be hypothesized on the basis of texts from other ancient cultures.[17] Comparative analysis of ritual texts, however, has been able to find parallels for only some of the features of biblical prescriptive texts. It has so far been unable to present good parallels to the divine voicing and hortatory address of these ritual instructions and has been forced to depend on hypothetical developments in the genre to account for them.[18]

---

[16] Johannes C. de Moor argued that "the ritual texts of Ugarit are usually of the prescriptive type, listing in a very terse style instructions for knowledgeable people, apparently priests" and translated them accordingly (*An Anthology of Religious Texts from Ugarit* [Nisaba 16; Leiden: Brill, 1987], 157).

[17] "Except for brief descriptions of ritual acts in poetic passages, ritual content in the Bible is always treated either as a divine command presented prescriptively, or as an event presented in narrative form" (Levine, "Descriptive Tabernacle Texts," 314).

[18] I must note that Levine's goal in describing "descriptive rituals" was to establish a better basis for describing ancient cult practices. He argued that descriptive rituals are more reliable depictions of actual performances than are prescriptive texts that are frequently idealistic (Levine and Hallo, "Offerings to the Temple Gates," 17–18). Thus he isolated the genre for purposes of reconstructing the history of religion, not originally to explain the present form of biblical texts.

Rendtorff, Koch, Knierim, and Levine worked by identifying a genre that then became the basis for analyzing the text. Whether using inductive form-critical analysis or comparisons of ancient ritual texts, they attempted to explain the present text as derived from hypothetical oral or written antecedents described on the basis of genre. Both the form-critical and comparative methods end up, however, as analyses of ideal types rather than of actual biblical texts, because some features of the extant text do not conform to the proposed genres. Invariably they describe the present form of the biblical text as having undergone further textual development that differentiates it from the ritual genres they have described.

These approaches to biblical ritual texts use an overly strict understanding of genre. Even Knierim, who aimed to analyze genre within the present text rather than applying an *a priori* genre to the text, ended up doing so anyway because his conception of the case law genre was too inflexible.[19] The Hebrew Bible demonstrates a flair for juxtaposing and mixing various genres (narrative, law, instruction, oracle, etc.) and modes (prose, poetry) of expression in the same compositions. Psalms and other poems appear in contexts of narrative prose (Genesis 49, Exodus 15, 1 Samuel 2, etc.) and prophetic poetry (Habakkuk 3).[20] Narrative always surrounds collections of laws in the Pentateuch. These are only some of the most obvious examples of juxtaposed genres in the Hebrew Bible, and they reflect practices also attested in other ancient Near Eastern literatures. Though some inset genres, such as

---

[19] Similarly, Gerstenberger, who despite emphasizing the hortatory features of Leviticus, nevertheless regarded them as secondary, because "where in the world are legal books composed in direct, admonitory address?" (*Leviticus,* 25). See, however, the examples of second person address that I cite in what follows.

[20] For analysis of these combinations, see Watts, *Psalm and Story: Inset Hymns in Hebrew Narrative* (JSOTSup 139; Sheffield: JSOT Press, 1992); idem, "Psalmody in Prophecy: Habakkuk 3 in Context," in *Forming Prophetic Literature: Essays on Isaiah and the Twelve in Honor of John D. W. Watts* (ed. J. W. Watts and P. R. House; JSOTSup 235; Sheffield: Sheffield Academic Press, 1996), 209–23; idem, "Biblical Psalms Outside the Psalter," in *The Book of Psalms: Composition and Reception* (ed. Peter W. Flint and Patrick D. Miller; VTSup 99; Leiden: Brill, 2004), 288–309.

psalmody, are well attested in independent compositions, others seem to appear conventionally as insets in other frameworks, ancient law collections being a notable example. Therefore the large-scale features of Hebrew and other ancient literatures should warn interpreters to expect the juxtaposition of genres and their literary conventions in many texts.

Genres are not immutable forms but rather repertoires of literary conventions available to speakers and writers that allow them to play on the expectations of their audiences.[21] Descriptions of genres are useful for describing the cultural expectations that readers and hearers have of texts. Such expectations come into play in the reading of any text and the hearing of any speech, regardless of how far that text or speech may deviate from conventional forms. Deviations from genre use these conventions no less than do rigid reproductions of a traditional form; they just aim for a different effect on their audience, as David Damrosch noted:

> Genre is the narrative covenant between author and reader, the framework of norms and expectations shaping both the composition and the reception of the text. Genre is always a shaping force, though never a determining one in the case of truly creative work, and it can be studied in its uses, its adaptations, its transformations, and even its repressions, over the history of the composition and rewriting of biblical narrative.[22]

---

[21] For a convenient survey of genre theory and its application to ancient texts, see Tremper Longman, III, *Fictional Akkadian Autobiography: A Generic and Comparative Study* (Winona Lake, IN: Eisenbrauns, 1991), 3–21. An ambitious attempt to write a genre history linking Mesopotamian and Hebrew literatures can be found in David Damrosch, *The Narrative Covenant: Transformations of Genre in the Growth of Biblical Literature* (San Francisco: Harper & Row, 1987). I find Damrosch's understanding of genre and his comparative method very congenial, but I am not convinced that Hebrew narrative developed out of epic (see my *Psalm and Story,* 194–6).

[22] Damrosch, *Narrative Covenant,* 2.

Genre identification depends on the comparison of large numbers of texts from the same literary culture. The lack of extant extra-biblical Hebrew literature from the centuries in which the biblical texts were composed greatly hampers the identification of genres because of the small number of examples available. It is no accident, then, that the description of psalm genres rests on much firmer grounds, because of the larger number of examples, than does genre analysis of almost any other kind of Hebrew literature, and it is relatively easy to isolate a psalm within a larger work.[23] Detailed descriptions of rituals do not appear nearly as frequently in biblical literature, so describing their various genres and distinguishing them from their frameworks cannot proceed with the same confidence. Even without knowing, however, which forms were recognized as genres by ancient audiences and which represent creative modifications and amalgamations of diverse genre elements, one can still describe some of the effects that certain literary conventions were intended to have on their audiences by observing their use in other literatures. Such texts often state overtly some of the motives for their composition. Comparisons with other ancient literatures can therefore show how particular devices tended to be used, even if we cannot be sure whether they conventionally appeared together as part of a recognizable genre or not.[24] Description of the

---

[23] For the latter, see Watts, "'This Song': Conspicuous Poetry in Hebrew Prose," in *Verse in Ancient Near Eastern Prose* (ed. J. C. de Moor and W. G. E. Watson; AOAT 42; Neukirchen-Vluyn: Neukirchener Verlag, 1993), 345–58; idem, "Psalmody in Prophecy," 209–23.

[24] Koch reevaluated his earlier form-critical efforts on the basis of such comparisons ("Alttestamentliche und altorientalische Rituale," in *Die Hebräische Bibel und ihre zweifache Nachgeschichte: Festschrif für Rolf Rendtorff* [ed. E. Blum et al.; Neukirchen-Vluyn: Neukirchener Verlag, 1990], 75–85). On the basis of Akkadian parallels, he produced a much more flexible definition of ritual genre to include casuistic structures and second person address, rather than just a sequence of perfect verbs. He considered these parallels to be confirmation of the existence of such an originally oral ritual genre. On the basis of this handful of texts, however, one cannot tell whether the ancients would have recognized this as a distinct genre or simply as a combination of conventions used to describe rituals in various genres.

rhetorical effects produced by conventional features of the text will lead to a better understanding of the extant text than will reconstructing some original genre within it.

Rhetorical Features of Leviticus 1–7

Both form-critical and comparative methods have found support from features of Leviticus 1–7 (and other collections of ritual instructions in the Pentateuch): while various of its formal features suggest oral composition and delivery, its structure and contents remind one of ritual texts from ancient Near Eastern archives. The narrative framework, however, that casts Leviticus 1–7 as divine prescriptions delivered through Israel's paradigmatic lawgiver, Moses, highlights the persuasive intent behind this text's formulation as it stands.

The narrative frame depicts this material as oral instruction. Like all the other instructions and laws in the Pentateuch, these chapters portray themselves as speeches. God is the speaker, as in most of Exodus 20 through Numbers. The immediate audience is Moses, but he is told to repeat these instructions to the people of Israel (Lev 1:1–2; 4:2; 7:23, 29) or to the priests, Aaron and his sons (6:2, 18 [LXX vv 9, 25]), who are all then the intended recipients within the story. Interpreters are no doubt correct in finding behind the rhetoric of this story the historical conditions and political hierarchies of early Second Temple Judaism or late monarchic Judea at the earliest: God's voice delivers the prescriptions of priestly and provincial (or royal) powers to Jews whom the Pentateuch repeatedly urges to identify themselves with Israel of the exodus and wilderness period (e.g., Exod 12:14–27; 13:3–16; 23:9; Lev 19:34; Deut 5:15; 29:14–16; etc.). Casting this material as oral instruction fits such later historical contexts just as well as the period of wilderness wandering depicted in the story, for the Hebrew Bible depicts *torah* even in these later periods being read aloud from written texts to large assemblies of people (2 Kings 22–23;

Nehemiah 8).[25] Thus the frequent mention of "you/your" in these chapters seems intended to reinforce in the intended audience the sense of authoritative instructions directed at them.[26]

That does not mean they originated as oral compositions. Biblical narratives describe law *readings,* that is, secondary orality based on written texts (Exod 24:3–8; Deut 31:9–13; Josh 8:30–35; 2 Kings 22–23//2 Chronicles 34; Nehemiah 8). The Sinai traditions themselves vacillate between depicting the original revelation of divine law as written on tablets (Exod 24:12; 31:18; 32:16; 34:1; Deut 5:22; 9:10) or as delivered orally to Moses, who then wrote it down (Exod 24:4; Deut 31:9, 24–26). This reminder that the interaction between oral and written compositions ran in both directions should warn interpreters against too sharp a distinction between the modes of presentation. And of course, despite the formal features and explicit evocation of oral rhetoric, comparative analysis of oral origins is ultimately forced to depend on written texts, since that is all that survives, and is therefore limited to whatever oral forms the texts happen to preserve.

Increasing numbers of Ugaritic, Hittite, and Akkadian ritual texts (most recently, those from Emar) have been published and anthologized, providing an opportunity to place Leviticus' ritual instructions within a wider cultural context. Yet the prescriptive and hortatory cast of Leviticus 1–7, as well as most other biblical texts containing ritual instructions, does not allow one to simply include them within the same textual genre. Rather than limiting the comparison to texts of a predetermined genre, a comparison of Leviticus 1–7 with *any* ancient texts exhibiting similar features and contents will be more helpful for assessing its rhetorical effect. By not restricting comparisons in advance on the basis of genre, the whole range of literary conventions at work

---

[25] On public readings of law and their rhetorical significance, see Watts, *Reading Law,* 15–60.

[26] So rightly, Gerstenberger (*Leviticus,* 26), though his arguments for placing this audience exclusively in the Persian-period diaspora are not convincing.

in these chapters can be assessed and their effects analyzed. I will discuss the major literary features of Leviticus 1–7, focusing first on the narrative framework (God tells Moses to tell Israel or the priests), and then turning to the form and style of the contents.

Framework

Leviticus 1:1–2 depicts the material that follows as quoted direct speech by God through Moses to people and priests. Similar introductions that appear with increasing frequency in these chapters (4:1; 5:14, 20; 6:1, 12, 17 [LXX 6:1, 8, 19, 24], 7:22, 28) keep drawing this scenario to readers' and hearers' attention. Comparative analysis suggests that they do so to increase the text's persuasiveness.

Divine voicing of laws and instructions is the norm in the Hebrew Bible, but rare in other ancient Near Eastern texts. There divine prescriptions appear most often in narratives, where deities are likely to issue orders to each other and to humans. As one would expect, such commands tend to be occasional, limited to the situation depicted in the story, such as when Ea or YHWH orders Utnapishtim or Noah to build a boat (Gilgamesh xi; Gen 6:11–9:17). Sometimes deities prescribe cultic acts in such stories, such as when El commands offerings to start a military campaign in the Ugaritic legend of Kirta. More commonly, humans present offerings and prayers on their own initiative, such as Utnapishtim/Noah do at the end of the flood stories. The deities' role is to respond appropriately. This pattern of human initiative and divine response appears in many other stories involving ritual worship. Even in Kirta, where a deity commands offerings, the plot turns not on El's command of offerings but on Kirta's initiative in vowing gifts to the goddess Athirat that he later forgets to provide, and so suffers that deity's anger as a consequence.[27]

---

[27] *KTU* 1.14–1.16; translated by N. Wyatt, *Religious Texts from Ugarit: The Words of Ilimilku and His Colleagues* (Biblical Seminar 53; Sheffield: Sheffield Academic Press, 1998), 176–243; and by Dennis Pardee in *COS* 1.102.

Instructional, legal, and didactic literatures are more likely to be presented in human, rather than divine, voices. Kings such as Hammurabi voice the Mesopotamian law codes, though they claim divine support for doing so. Some Hittite ritual texts begin, "Thus says X: if/when . . . then I do as follows. . . ."[28] The Punic tariffs begin by citing a committee of prominent citizens that established them: "Tariff of priestly revenues set up by the thirty men who are in charge of the revenues, in the time when Hillesba'l the mayor, was head."[29] More often, the authorities behind ritual instructions remain anonymous.

Ritual instructions, however, also appear within royal dedicatory inscriptions from various ancient Near Eastern cultures. Here kings regularly claim credit for instituting one or more cults and sometimes for ordaining the rites to be performed there, especially the kinds and amounts of offerings. Thus in a second millennium B.C.E. Akkadian inscription, the Kassite king Kurigalzu reported that, to accompany his land grant to an Ishtar temple, "3 kor of bread, 3 kor of fine wine, 2 (large measures) of date cakes, 30 quarts of imported dates, 30 quarts of fine(?) oil, 3 sheep per day did I establish as the regular offering for all time."[30] Similar cultic mandates are found in New Kingdom Egyptian inscriptions, such as, "I assigned to [Amun] thousands of oxen, so as to present their choice cuts,"[31] and in the eighth century Luwian/Phoenician bilingual inscription of Azatiwada: "a yearly sacrifice: an ox; and at the time (season) of plowing: a sheep; and at the time (season) of reaping/harvesting: a sheep."[32] The fourth-century Naucratis stela depicts Pharaoh Nectanebo I ordering on behalf of the

---

[28] CTH 407, 410, 757; translation by Billie Jean Collins in COS 1.62, 1.63, 1.64.

[29] KAI 69; translation by Dennis Pardee in COS 1.98.

[30] HKL 1.136; translation in Benjamin Foster, Before the Muses: An Anthology of Akkadian Literature (3rd ed.; Bethesda, MD: CDL, 2005), 365–6.

[31] A stela of Amenhotep III from his mortuary temple in Thebes; translation by Miriam Lichtheim, Ancient Egyptian Literature (3 vols.; Berkeley: University of California, 1973–80), 2:46.

[32] H. Çambel, Corpus of Hieroglyphic Luwian Inscriptions (Berlin: De Gruyter, 1999), vol. 2; translations by J. D. Hawkins and K. Lawson Younger, Jr., in COS 2.21, 2.31.

temple of Neith that "one shall make one portion of an ox, one fat goose, and five measures of wine . . . as a perpetual daily offering. . . . My majesty has commanded to preserve and protect the divine offering of my mother Neith."[33] These texts testify to royal interests in cultic matters, especially the quantities of offerings to various temples. Priests, on the other hand, rarely claim to be the authorities behind cultic teachings, though the Hittite texts mentioned above are a notable exception.[34]

Oracular texts are the most likely ancient genre to portray a deity mandating offerings and other rites, as YHWH does in the Pentateuch. Thus an occasional ritual command appears among the oral oracles reported to the king in the eighteenth-century B.C.E. Mari letters: "The god has sent me, saying 'Hurry up and deliver a message to the king that a *kispum* offering be performed for the spirit of Yahdun-Lim" and "Send to your lord the following message: The new month has now begun, and on the fourteenth day, the *pagrā'um* offerings should be executed. Not a single offering may be neglected."[35] The goddess Ishtar addresses the Assyrian king Esarhaddon in a similar fashion in one of the seventh-century oracles of her priestesses: "You could rely on the previous word I spoke to you, couldn't you? Now you can rely upon the later word, too! Praise me! When the daylight declines, let torches flare! Praise me before them!"[36]

It must be noted, however, that oracles more often portray deities ordering military and building campaigns than issuing cultic instructions, an observation that applies to the narrative and prophetic texts of the Hebrew Bible as well. In this respect, oracular texts mirror the

---

[33] Translation by Lichtheim, *Ancient Egyptian Literature*, 3:88–9.

[34] At Ugarit, while colophons to the major epics credit priests – Ilimilku "the sacrificer" wrote or copied both the Baal cycle (*KTU* 1.6 vi) and Keret (*KTU* 1.16 vi) – no such colophons appear in the ritual texts.

[35] *ARM* 3.40, 2.90; translations by Marti Nissinen, *Prophets and Prophecy in the Ancient Near East* (WAW 12; Atlanta: SBL, 2003), 55–6; cf. *ANET* 624.

[36] SAA 9 1.10 vi 1–32, translated by Nissinen, *Prophets and Prophecy,* 110. R. D. Biggs translated the first lines in a more confrontational tone: "Why did you not act on the earlier oracle which I gave you? Now you shall act on this one" (*ANET* 605).

concerns of royal inscriptions, which probably reflect the interests at work in the preservation of these texts more than the inherent tendencies of oracles. The oracles were recorded in the Mari letters and were preserved in Esarhaddon's archive because they dealt with royal concerns. Private oracular pronouncements, which were no doubt very common, were less likely to be written down and preserved. The degree to which they may have dealt with ritual matters can therefore not be ascertained. There is one text, however, that suggests that the royal and oracular genres may have influenced each other and that the speeches of kings and of gods could be interchangeable. The ambiguous "Marduk Prophecy," probably from the twelfth century B.C.E., ends with the god Marduk mandating a schedule of offerings, apparently for King Nebuchadnezzar, that reads:

> 40 quarts [], of 40 quarts [], of 10 quarts of flour, 1 quart of [], 1 quart of honey, 1 quart of butterfat, 1 quart of figs(?), 1 quart of raisins, 1 quart of alabstron [oil], 1 quart of finest [] without alkali(?), 1 regular sheep, a fatted calf will be burned for this spirit. Month, day, and year I will bless him![37]

If this interpretation of the last column is correct, then king and deity here reverse places, with the deity mandating (funerary) offerings on behalf of the king in exactly the same manner that kings mandate divine offerings in royal commemorative inscriptions. Since gods were traditionally thought of as royalty, and some kings were portrayed as gods, the merging of divine and royal voices should come as no surprise.[38]

The framework of Leviticus 1–7, which periodically introduces God issuing instructions through Moses, resembles not so much the form of

---

[37] R. Borger, "Gott Marduk und Gott-König Šulgi als Propheten," *Bibliotheca Orientalis* 28 (1971): 3–24; translation by Foster, *Before the Muses*, 388–91; cf. Longman, *Fictional Akkadian Autobiography*, 132–42.

[38] Borger compared the Marduk Prophecy with the Prophecy of Shulgi as similar texts: the first has a royal deity speak and the second a deified king ("Gott Marduk," 3–24).

ancient ritual texts narrowly defined as it does the forms of expression used in royal and oracular texts dealing with cultic matters among other things. Therefore considerations of the chapters' literary genre need to include this wider range of texts. Furthermore, the royal and oracular genres make explicit rhetorical claims that ritual texts, especially Levine's "descriptive" rituals, may not: they clearly aim to *persuade* their audience to undertake a particular course of action, usually to preserve the temple or the king's other accomplishments, especially the inscription itself. The framework's evocation of royal and oracular genres should not be viewed as applying the conventions of some other genre to a basically "ritual" text, for ritual prescriptions are at home in these genres as well. Rather, the writers of Leviticus 1–7 used various literary conventions traditionally associated with ritual concerns to shape a text to serve their purposes. Their use of royal and oracular rhetoric in the framework emphasizes by literary convention the royal authority of the divine speaker and demonstrates the persuasive intent behind these chapters.

Contents and Style

Royal and oracular texts, however, contain nothing to compare with Leviticus 1–7's detailed stipulation of ritual performance. For such descriptions, we must turn to those texts usually classified by the term "ritual." Yet even among ritual texts from other ancient cultures, nothing has so far been found that matches the form and content of these chapters. That is less surprising when one notes the diversity of form and content among ancient ritual texts. There is no single ritual genre into which all these texts fit. They share only an emphasis on the details of cultic ritual, and it is therefore for reasons of contents rather than form that they tend to be classified together.

The prescriptive formulation of most rituals in the Bible contrasts with the predominance of descriptive rituals in other ancient cultures, as Levine has demonstrated. Nevertheless, prescriptive rituals are not unknown in Ugaritic, Akkadian, and Punic sources. These sources also parallel specific features of Leviticus 1–7. The systematic repetition that characterizes especially Leviticus 1–3 can also be found in Punic tariffs that consist principally of repeated introductory phrases: "In (the case of) a X, (whether it be) a whole offering, or a presentation offering, or a whole wellbeing offering, the priests receive Y. . . ."[39] An atonement ritual from Ugarit repeats six times an almost identical liturgy applied to three types of offerings (ox?, sheep, donkey) and two kinds of worshippers (men, women).[40]

The casuistic ("if/when . . . , then . . .") formulation that is characteristic of priestly style throughout P's legal and instructional corpus also appears as a prominent structural feature of some Hittite and Ugaritic descriptive rituals. Several Hittite texts begin: "If the troops are defeated by the enemy, then they prepare the 'behind the river' ritual as follows" or "When [they] cleanse a house . . . , its treatment is as follows. . . ."[41] Among the Ugaritic corpus, a prescriptive list of required offerings and actions begins, "When Athtart-of-the-Window enters the pit in the royal palace, pour a libation . . ." and another list of offerings ends with a liturgy introduced casuistically: "Here begins (the liturgy): If a strong one attacks your gates, a warrior your walls, raise your eyes to Baal (saying)."[42]

Even the second person address, "you shall . . . ," that appears frequently in Leviticus 1–7 as well as other ritual instructions in the Hebrew Bible, appears also in ritual materials from other ancient cultures, such as the Ugaritic list of offerings (*KTU* 1.119), otherwise in third person, that ends with the second-person liturgy quoted above. The Ugaritic atonement rite (*KTU* 1.40) mixes first- and second-person exhortations in its casuistic introductions ("whenever you sin . . . this is the sacrifice we make. . . .") and continues to alternate between them throughout. Several Akkadian texts from the Seleucid

[39] *KAI* 69; translation by Pardee in *COS* 1.98.
[40] *KTU* 1.40; translation by Wyatt, *Religious Texts*, 342–7.
[41] *CTH* 426, 446; translation by Collins in *COS* 1.61, 1.68.
[42] *KTU* 1.43, 1.119; translations by Wyatt, *Religious Texts*, 357–9, 416–22.

era describing rituals for repairing temples are consistently structured in second-person casuistic form.[43]

Though many ancient ritual texts focus on just one aspect of a ritual, others reflect the same range of interests as Leviticus 1–7: types of offering, nature of the animals, worshipper's duties, priestly duties, priestly prebends, and so on. Thus some of the rituals from Emar list the types and amounts of offerings due every deity on particular days but also describe the course and timing of processions, various ritual actions, and the distribution of offered meats and other commodities, including priestly prebends.[44]

These comparisons show that the literary features of Leviticus 1–7 also appear in ancient texts dealing with rituals in other Near Eastern cultures, but they are dispersed throughout various texts in such a way as to undermine efforts to identify specific genres by constellations of features. There is no evidence, therefore, that the priestly writers started with some pure genre, whether oral or written, and then modified it through successive scribal additions taken from other literary contexts. That does not mean that no genre conventions influenced the writing of these chapters, but simply that every writer and editor who left a mark on these chapters worked, as we should expect, with various literary conventions traditionally used to portray rituals. Every stage of the text's development was influenced by such genre conventions. Though this conclusion might seem like an obvious observation about the constraints on virtually any writer or editor of any culture, it has a negative consequence for critical study of biblical texts: genre distinctions cannot be used as evidence for editorial modifications of texts. If writers and editors could use and mix genre conventions at will, and evidence from many parts of the Hebrew Bible suggest that they could and did, then hypothetical reconstructions of the original text or

---

[43] F. Thureau-Dangin, *Rituels accadiens* (Paris: E. Leroux, 1921), 34ff, translated by A. Sachs, *ANET* 339–42. For other Akkadian rituals in the second person, see ibid., 334–8, 343–5.

[44] *Emar* 373, 385, 387, 446; translated by Daniel Fleming in *COS* 1.123, 1.124, 1.126.

tradition that exemplified the "pure" genre are creative fantasies. I do not mean by this to deny that editorial modifications of biblical texts occurred. Other evidence suggests that they are pervasive throughout the biblical books, but genre analysis provides no basis for recognizing them.[45] Comparative analysis of literary conventions does, however, provide a powerful tool for exposing the intentions that shaped the extant text.

The Rhetorical Purpose of Leviticus 1–7

Interpreters have offered many suggestions for what purpose the instructions in Leviticus 1–7 may have originally served. Some of the more recent comments show the range and nature of the opinions. For example, Anson F. Rainey described Chapters 1–5 as a "Handbook for Priests."[46] Similarly, Meir Paran suggested that this material was designed to facilitate rote memorization by priests.[47] Martin Noth ventured the opinion that the original audience for these instructions in oral or written form were lay people needing instruction on how to make their offerings.[48] David W. Baker concluded that, like the Punic tariffs, this material was inscribed on a monument at the sanctuary to inform both laity (Leviticus 1–5) and priests (Leviticus 6–7).[49] Rendtorff suggested tentatively that the material's strict stylization and stereotypical repetition suggest that it was intended for liturgical recitation, perhaps as sentences to accompany the offerings.[50]

---

[45] Contra Koch, "Alttestamentliche und altorientalische Rituale," 78.
[46] "The Order of Sacrifices in Old Testament Ritual Texts," *Bib* 51 (1970): 487.
[47] *Forms of the Priestly Style in the Pentateuch: Patterns, Linguistic Usages, Syntactic Structures* (Hebrew), (Jerusalem: Magnes, 1989), xiii.
[48] *Leviticus: A Commentary* (OTL; Philadelphia: Westminster, 1965; German, 1962), 20.
[49] David W. Baker, "Leviticus 1–7 and the Punic Tariffs: A Form Critical Comparison," *ZAW* 99 (1987): 188–98; see also idem, "Division Markers and the Structure of Leviticus 1–7," in *Studia Biblica* 1978 (ed. E. A. Livingstone; JSOTSup 11; Sheffield: JSOT, 1979), 9–15.
[50] *Gesetze*, 22–3.

Knierim argued that ritual case law was written to systematize ritual performance.[51]

What these suggestions all share in common is an attempt to find the *original* purpose for this material, that is, before it was excerpted into Leviticus and the Pentateuch and therefore before it was refashioned to fit this context. Evaluations of its purpose in its present context tend to be mechanical and topical, noting that the instructions for offerings must logically precede the stories about those offerings in Leviticus 8–10. Though this explanation for the position of these chapters is no doubt correct, it offers no insight into how their present shape and contents were intended to affect their audiences. All the efforts to imagine the purpose served by these texts have focused on their presumed original rather than their actual shape, under the influence of the idea that only from the pure genre can the text's setting and purpose be discerned. If, however, all features of the present text were written under the influence of genre conventions, as I have argued earlier, then the shape of the present text should also be intended to evoke certain kinds of responses and should theoretically offer clues as to what motivated its construction in this form. Furthermore, reconstruction of the form and function of earlier strata in the text can only proceed confidently if the form and function of the extant text has been fully analyzed first, for only then (if at all) can editorial seams be distinguished from intentional literary features.

Because of their focus on hypothetical original genres, the suggestions listed earlier miss the persuasive orientation of Leviticus 1–7. Comparisons with other biblical texts also obscure this persuasive element, because within the Hebrew Bible Leviticus 1–7 looks less hortatory than, for example, Deuteronomy, the Wisdom literature, the prophets, or the priestly Holiness Code (Leviticus 17–27). As a result, readers of the Bible are struck by these chapters' systematic, impersonal, and repetitive style. Knierim, for example, argued that "Deuteronomy's

---

[51] Knierim, *Text and Concept*, 103–6.

appeals to joy are based on the parenetic and therefore inevitably psychological language and intentionality of Deuteronomy. The priestly legal corpus is composed in 'legislative' language. It is not parenetic."[52] Mary Douglas took this distinction further, arguing that Leviticus contains only analogic reasoning of a mytho-poetic form, in contrast to Deuteronomy's discursive and abstract logic. Only in the latter is speech "used for persuasion, challenge, and argument."[53] If, however, one shifts the basis of comparison to other ancient Near Eastern ritual texts, the picture changes. Many ancient descriptive rituals and temple records outdo Leviticus 1–7 for mechanical repetition of detail and the absence of all hortatory devices.[54] On the other hand, those texts that parallel these chapters' use of an authoritative royal/divine speaker also make explicit their persuasive agenda: royal and oracular texts clearly express their goal of persuading readers and hearers to engage in certain behaviors and not others.

Once we have noted the persuasive shaping of Leviticus 1–7, the systematic and repetitive style appears in a different light. Repetition that may well seem redundant to a silent reader can sound very motivating to a skilled speaker's audience. The repetition of structural elements and of refrains has a long history in oral rhetoric because it helps an audience anticipate a speaker's direction and respond appropriately to the speaker's cues. Within such repetition, slight variation can convey considerable emphasis.[55] Therefore the systematic and repetitive character of these chapters can be understood as bearing out, rather than conflicting with, the framework's presentation of them as oral

[52] Knierim, *Text and Concept*, 81.
[53] Douglas, *Leviticus as Literature*, 40; see also 20, 29, 36–8, 41–65.
[54] See Levine's discussion of Ugaritic administrative records of rituals, such as *KTU* 1.91 and 1.104 ("Ugaritic Ritual Texts," 468), and of descriptive rituals in all his publications listed in note 15.
[55] The Roman theorist, Quintilian, emphasized the need for repetition in legal argumentation: "We shall frequently repeat anything which we think the judge has failed to take in as he should" (*Inst. Orat* 8.2.2–4). For a discussion of the rhetorical function of repetition and variation throughout the Pentateuch, see Watts, *Reading Law*, 68–74.

speeches.[56] God is represented as a speaker who, through Moses, urges people and priests to engage in specific behaviors. If these speeches seem much less vivid than other biblical texts, that is only because the hortatory emphasis is even more pronounced elsewhere.

Leviticus 1–7 has been composed of repetitive structures bounded by refrains (e.g., *'iššēh rēaḥ nîḥôaḥ lYHWH*, "a fire-offering of soothing scent for YHWH," 1:9, 13, 17; 2:2, 9, 11, 16; 3:5, 16; *wĕkipper 'ălēhem hakkōhēn wĕnislaḥ lāhem*, "the priest will make atonement for them and they will be forgiven," 4:20, 26, 31, 35; 5:6, 10, 13, 16, 18, 26 [LXX 6:7]), with minor variations in the structure and refrains marking changing emphases and subjects (e.g., the pronouns in the refrain of forgiveness punctuating Lev 4–5). Major shifts in structure draw special attention and mark climaxes, such as the prohibition on consuming fat and blood (3:16b–17) that breaks out of and concludes the description of routine offerings in Leviticus 1–3. Damrosch rightly noted that the three-fold structure of Leviticus 1–3 "gives these chapters a certain lyrical aspect" and that the presentation of the offerings is staged dramatically.[57] Despite the long-standing tradition of reading such repetitive structures as dull and uninspiring, their effect in oral readings would instead be exciting and motivating. Indeed, since repetition and refrains often mark the climax of speeches, their appearance here provides further evidence that the Pentateuch reaches its climax in Leviticus.[58]

To whom was Leviticus 1–7's persuasive rhetoric addressed, and to what end? Is the intended audience composed of religious professionals like the priests, diviners, and exorcists for whom many of the Ugaritic,

---

[56] Contra Knierim, *Text and Concept*, 7, 99–100.

[57] David Damrosch, "Leviticus," in *The Literary Guide to the Bible* (ed. R. Alter and F. Kermode; Cambridge, MA: Belknap/Harvard, 1987), 67–8.

[58] For other arguments for this conclusion, see Joseph Blenkinsopp, *The Pentateuch: An Introduction to the First Five Books of the Bible* (New York: Doubleday, 1992), 47; Knierim, *The Task of Old Testament Theology: Method and Cases* (Grand Rapids: Eerdmans, 1995), 367; Watts, *Reading Law*, 59. On the rhetorical function of repetition and refrains, see *Reading Law*, 68–73, 97–102.

Hittite, and Emar ritual texts seem to have been intended? Or are they lay people, such as those to whom the Punic tariffs, most royal inscriptions,[59] and perhaps even a few of the Ugaritic rituals were aimed? Clearly, ancient texts with ritual contents could address either group or both, so neither of the audiences mentioned in Leviticus is inherently improbable. If it were not for the fact that Leviticus explicitly distinguishes between these two audiences (Moses is directed to the people in 1:2; 4:1; 7:22, 28; to the priests in 6:2, 18 [LXX 6:9, 25]), one might think the sharp distinction between them to be anachronistic.

One effect of presenting the major offerings twice, once explicitly addressed to the people of Israel as a whole (chapters 1–5) and once explicitly addressed to the priests (6:1–7:21), is to subject both groups to the words that God spoke to Moses, that is, to *this* law. That may explain why the phrase *zō't tôrat*, "this is the law for...," appears exclusively in the materials directed at priests (6:2, 7, 18 [LXX vv 9, 14, 25]; 7:1, 11).[60] Perhaps *torah* here does not name a genre, as many interpreters have thought, but rather serves to emphasize the authority of these instructions over the priests, precisely those who are mandated to teach divine law (Lev 10:10–11). The point then would be to insist that *this,* and not anything else, is the authoritative regulation governing each particular offering. The prominence of negative stipulations – what should *not* be done (6:5, 6, 10, 16, 23 [LXX 6:12, 13, 17, 23, 30]; 7:15, 19, 23, 24, 26) – in these latter chapters and their rarity in Leviticus 1–5 (only 3:17) confirms that these rules were written to supplant competing practices: "this is torah (not that)."

The text asserts its authority over those who teach it. No one in Israel can claim to be exempt from its provisions or to have other

---

[59] Royal inscriptions that employ the story-list-sanction strategy usually address other kings and royal officials, and a less defined lay audience beyond them; see Watts, "Story-List-Sanction: A Cross-Cultural Strategy of Ancient Persuasion" in *Rhetoric Before and Beyond the Greeks* (ed. Roberta Binkley and Carol Lipson; Albany: SUNY Press, 2004), 197–212 [206–7].

[60] Though 7:11–21 seems to be aimed at the worshipper despite the superscription in 6:18.

instructions that supersede it. That is not to say that these instructions cannot be supplemented; their incomplete character in fact requires supplementation in many ways. Among other things, nowhere in these chapters or elsewhere in the Bible is it specified exactly how the animals are to be killed or what prayers or liturgies (if any) are to be spoken or sung to accompany the offerings. But by addressing explicitly both religious professionals and laity, Leviticus 1–7 enhances its own authority over all who participate in the cult and so reinforces its status as authoritative cultic legislation. Despite the technical nature of many of these instructions, they address all Israel to persuade the people not only to perform the offerings as instructed, but even more to recognize and accept this text's authority to dictate religious obligations. The address to the priests, framed as it is within the divine speeches directed to the people, simply reinforces this claim by making clear that even the cultic professionals in the performance of their office are not exempt from this text's authority. For example, by saying *zōʾt tôrat hāʿōlāh*, "this is the law of the *ʿōlāh*," Lev 6:2 [LXX v 9] requires what 1 Chr 16:40 reports, that the priests *lĕhaʿălôt ʿōlôt . . . ûlĕkol hakkātûb bĕtôrat YHWH ʾăšer tsiwwāh ʿal yiśrāʾēl* "offer the *ʿōlāh . . .* in accordance with everything written in the law of YHWH which he commanded Israel."

No doubt these chapters, like the royal and oracular texts that their framework evokes, intend to persuade the people of Israel and their priests to perform their religious offerings and to do so correctly, as specified here. Within the wider context of the priestly writings and the Pentateuch as a whole, however, these chapters aim also to reinforce the authority of Torah, specifically its authority over religious performance in the Temple. By publicly stipulating the forms of Israel's offerings, they position priests and laity to monitor each other's performance with the text as arbiter of correct practice. Thus an ironic consequence of Leviticus 1–7's role in the Pentateuch was to shift cultic authority from the priesthood to the book. Of course, the priests continued to wield enormous influence because they not only controlled the Temple rites but also were authoritative interpreters of the book. But the presence of ritual legislation in the Pentateuch made the basis for their performances available to the public and therefore open to public scrutiny. The record of fierce debates over cultic practice between temple priests, Pharisees, and Qumran covenanters in later Second Temple times shows that this rhetorical potential in the Pentateuch's ritual texts did not go unrecognized.[61]

Conclusion

Like any other composition, Leviticus 1–7 weaves together various literary conventions to affect its audience. The framework that repeatedly and with increasing frequency designates the speaker as YHWH claims not only divine but also royal authority for these instructions. Its designation of the intended audience as all Israel, with the priests explicitly included, specifies these laws' jurisdiction over all proper ritual performance. The contents' repetitive formulation in prescriptive casuistic style lends a heightened intensity to its provisions that is reminiscent of oral rhetoric. The frequent second-person forms of address make clear the direct application to its intended audience.

All of these features of Leviticus 1–7 fit comfortably in the range of literary conventions typical of ancient ritual texts. None are likely to have been considered unusual or exceptional by Leviticus' intended audience. Though there is insufficient comparative evidence to determine if their combination produced a recognizable genre in Hebrew literature, neither is there any evidence that they were written through some dramatic modification of prevailing genres, whether oral or written.

These chapters were shaped to be read aloud to Jews as part of the larger Pentateuch. They contribute to the Pentateuch's rhetoric by

---

[61] See, e.g., the halakhic letter from Qumran, *4QMMT* (E. Qimron and J. Strugnell, *Qumran Cave 4. V. Miqsat Ma'ase ha-Torah* [DJD 10; Oxford: Clarendon, 1994]), and Josephus, *Ant.* 12.297, 18.15.

emphasizing the supreme authority and jurisdiction of this Torah in Israel, especially over Israel's worship in the Temple. They therefore do more than instruct readers and hearers in proper religious performance. They aim to persuade them that these instructions must be normative, along with the rest of Pentateuchal law.

3

The Rhetoric of Burnt Offerings

The *ʿōlāh*, "burnt offering," is the paradigmatic offering in the Hebrew
Bible. Of all the many technical terms from Israel's cultic worship,
the *ʿōlāh* is most frequently mentioned, and, when multiple offerings
are listed, it is almost always listed first. The *ʿōlāh*'s prominence cannot be credited to its actual dominance in ritual: the *šělāmîm*, "peace
or communion offerings," that were eaten by worshippers and priests
must have outnumbered the offerings burnt whole on the altar. The
offerings would otherwise have impoverished both priests and lay people. That expectation is confirmed by passages that list the numbers
of both kinds of offerings: *ʿōlôt* account for only one out of six animals
offered by the elders of Israel according to Numbers 7, and slightly
more than one out of ten at Hezekiah's temple rededication according
to 2 Chronicles 29. Nevertheless, except when reveling in the sheer
number of offerings,[1] the stories and ritual instructions of the Bible
grant the *ʿōlāh* pride of place.

The *ʿōlāh*'s priority in biblical rhetoric requires examination if we
are to understand the motives of the writers and the effects these texts

[1] E.g., by claiming that Solomon offered 142,000 animals to dedicate the new temple
   (1 Kings 18:63).

had upon early readers and hearers. That is especially true of the most systematic description of Israel's offerings in the Bible, the instructions of Leviticus 1–7. I have argued in Chapter 2 that this material contains various indications that it was shaped to persuade readers/hearers not only to follow its prescriptions but also to accept its authority as *torah*. In the context of this persuasive effort, we may well wonder what advantage was gained by beginning both sets of instructions (Lev 1– 5 [LXX 1:1–6:8]; 6–7 [LXX 6:8–7:38]) with the *ʿōlāh*. But the same question can be asked of biblical rhetoric generally: what does the *ʿōlāh*'s rhetorical preeminence tell us about biblical rhetoric and its influence on later religious traditions?

Explanations for the ʿŌlāh's *Priority*

1. Convention: The question of why the *ʿōlāh* is mentioned so frequently and almost always first has received some, but not very much, attention from interpreters. The very conventionality of the *ʿōlāh*'s priority in offering lists has led most readers to accept it without question. There can be no question that this convention was widely shared by the Hebrew Bible's many authors: not only the priestly authors of Leviticus (including H), but also Deuteronomy[2] and other non-P strands of the Pentateuch,[3] the Deuteronomists[4] and the prophets,[5] the Psalmists[6] and the Chronicler[7] place the *ʿōlāh* first in lists of offerings and even in the paired clichés, *ʿōlāh/zebaḥ*, "burnt offering/animal offering" and *ʿōlāh/šĕlāmîm*, "burnt offering/peace offering."[8] The handful of

---

[2] Leviticus 12, which usually places it first in a string of offering terms but once uses it as an umbrella term for all offerings: vv 13–14.

[3] Exod 18:12; 24:5.

[4] Joshua 22 (4x); 1 Sam 6:15, 15:22; 2 Kings 5:17; etc.

[5] Isa 43:23; Jer 6:20; 7:21, 22; 17:26; 33:18; Ezek 40:42; 44:11.

[6] Pss 40:70; 51:21; 66:13–15.

[7] 1 Chron 16:1–2; 21:26; 2 Chron 7:1; 29:23–32; etc.

[8] Levine described the merismic (cliché) quality of these pairs: "A descriptive analysis of the frequent pairs *ʿōlāh-zebaḥ* and *ʿōlāh-šĕlāmîm* can tell us relatively little about

exceptional cases where ʿōlāh follows zebaḥ (paired: Exod 10:25; Hos 6:6; Ps 50:8; 1 Chr 29:21; in a longer sequence: Ps 40:6–7) or, in one case, minḥāh (Ps 20:4), probably reverse the conventional order to emphasize the end of the line or colon by placing ʿōlāh there.[9] The use of a convention, however, is not self-explanatory. Authors can choose to be conventional or not, and that choice affects how the text will be received by hearers and readers who recognize a convention or a departure from it. Following convention is usually a method for gaining acceptance and sometimes for escaping notice. Flaunting convention, on the other hand, intentionally draws attention, but at the risk of rejection. So what rhetorical goals did placing the instructions for the ʿōlāh at the beginning of Leviticus try to achieve? The systematic detail of Leviticus 1 and the following chapters would seem to draw attention rather than avoid it. However, the conventional sequence of offerings in Leviticus 1–3, ʿōlāh, minḥāh, zebaḥ šĕlāmîm,[10] underscores the presentation of these chapters as standard, indeed, definitive instructions for Israel's most important cultic practices. The first pericope (Lev 1:3–9) contains an unusual number of interpretive

---

the šĕlāmîm, in particular, because most occurrences are clichés, or merisms," e.g., Exod 10:25. "The same reservation may be applied to most attestations of the pair ʿōlāh-zebaḥ in biblical sources, some of which actually refer to non-monotheistic rites [Footnote: Exod 18:12; Josh 22:28; I Sam 15:22; II Kings 5:17, 10:24; Isa 56:7; Jer 7:20–2; Ps 50:18, 51:8]. Even in codified passages, where one would expect a more technical usage to obtain, the pair ʿōlāh-zebaḥ seems to retain a merismic quality" (e.g., Lev 17:18). The references in 1 Sam 6:15 and 2 Kings 16:15 are "largely proverbial. . . . The situation with the pair ʿōlāh-šĕlāmîm is somewhat different, though there, too, the element of cliché is noticeable" (In the Presence of the Lord, 21–2).

9 Even more consistent than the ʿōlāh's conventional priority is the fact that the šĕlāmîm always come last, both in pairings and in longer lists of offerings (except in Leviticus 1–5; see Chapter 2). So one may also ask why, rhetorically, the šĕlāmîm are always last? I suggest that this is related to the question of the ʿōlāh's priority. The questions are two sides of the same coin. Cf., however, the argument of Martin Modéus that the word šĕlāmîm is a gloss that was added throughout the Hebrew Bible to specify that a zebaḥ was performed at the legitimate altar (Sacrifice and Symbol: Biblical šĕlāmîm in a Ritual Perspective [CB:OT 52; Stockholm: Almqvist & Wiksell, 2005], 201–370).

10 For this exact sequence of terms, see Josh 22:23, but cf. the variety of formulations in vv 27–29.

terms that distinguish this initial portrayal of the *ōlāh* as exemplary.[11] So the beginning of Leviticus seems to follow convention: because the *ōlāh* always comes first, writers who wish to have their prescriptions accepted as normative will of course treat it first.

Writers, however, rarely aim only to reproduce convention, because that provides little motivation for writing in the first place. We may expect, therefore, to find that texts use conventional figures and structures to hide their innovations. What innovations does the conventional language of the early chapters of Leviticus try to hide? That is difficult to say, but various indicators hint that the prescriptions for the *ḥaṭṭā't* and *'āšām* in Leviticus 4–5 aimed to change existing practices. Milgrom suggested a hypothetical history of the offerings to account for these rhetorical features:

> The burnt offering...may originally have been the only sacrifice offered except for the *šĕlāmîm*, which provided meat for the table. This would account for the widespread attestation in the early sources of the *ōlâ* and the tandem *ōlâ wāzebaḥ/ûšĕlāmîm*.... With the advent of a tabernacle/temple, however, it became imperative to devise specific sacrifices to purge the sacred house and its sancta of their contamination and desecration. Thus the purification and reparation offerings, respectively, were devised. These two sacrifices, once introduced into the sacrificial system, became the expiatory sacrifices par excellence and ultimately usurped the expiatory function of the burnt offering for the individual. That these two sacrifices are later than the burnt, cereal, and well-being offerings is shown by the fact that the latter offerings are provided with no cases. The motivations for bringing them are taken for granted. Not so for the purification and reparation offerings: their cases are spelled out in detail precisely because knowledge of them is not widespread.[12]

---

[11] So Eberhart, *Studien zur Bedeutung der Opfer*, 69, who pointed to *qorbān*, "offering" (v 3), *kappēr*, "atone" (v 4), *'iššēh*, "fire offering" (v 9), and *rêaḥ nîḥôaḥ*, "soothing scent" (v 9).

[12] Milgrom, *Leviticus*, 1:176.

Though Milgrom's assumptions about the historical setting for these changes are debatable, he astutely described the distinctive rhetorical treatment that the ḥaṭṭāʾt and ʾāšām receive (see Chapter 4). His last sentence could be stronger, however: P's regulations for the ḥaṭṭāʾt and ʾāšām were written not only to spread knowledge of them but also to assert the authority of their innovations and deflect criticism, since ritual changes are almost never uncontroversial. The instructions directed specifically to priests in Leviticus 6–7 repeatedly emphasize their own status as *torah* and include numerous prohibitions of various practices, all of which indicate that they, too, were written with the expectation of meeting resistance.[13] Therefore, the systematic elucidation of ritual conventions in the early chapters, inaugurated by the instructions for the ʿōlāh, seems to lay the basis for persuading hearers and readers to accept the rest of P's ritual legislation as authoritative *torah* also.

2. *Logical Priority:* A second explanation for the ʿōlāh's prominence in biblical texts asserts that its position reflects its logical priority. Anson Rainey put forward this argument when he explained the different sequences of biblical offerings on the basis of their chief interests. He distinguished an administrative order of offerings (ʿōlāh, minḥāh ḥaṭṭāʾt, ʾāšām, šělāmîm) that is concerned chiefly with the quantity of offerings and priestly prebends, from a procedural order ([ʾāšām] ḥaṭṭāʾt, ʿōlāh with minḥāh, šělāmîm) that depicts the actual ritual sequence.[14] According to Rainey, the administrative order lists first the "most holy" offerings, that is, those of which the lay worshipper could not eat, and arranges them in order of number or frequency, from the most frequent, the ʿōlāh which was always to be accompanied by the minḥāh (Num 15:1–21; 28:1–29:40), to the least common, the ʾāšām. This reasoning does not apply to the šělāmîm, which were the most numerous of all but relegated to last in the administrative order because they were not restricted from the laity. Rainey's description of the administrative

---

[13] See Chapter 2 of this book. The prohibitions are in 6:5, 6, 10, 16, 23 [LXX 6:12, 13, 17, 23, 30]; 7:15, 18, 19, 23, 24, 26.
[14] Rainey, "The Order of Sacrifices," 485–98.

order is cogent but gives insufficient attention to the *šĕlāmîm*. More thought should be given to why a focus on the quantity of offerings would wish to leave this category for last, even though it accounted for the vast majority of all offerings. The influence of a broader cultural convention seems to have come into play here.

Leviticus 1–5, however, presents the offerings in yet another order: *'ōlāh, minḥāh, šĕlāmîm, ḥaṭṭā't, 'āšām*. Rainey described this as a "didactic" order, a "pedagogical classification for the training of sacerdotal specialists" in which the offerings are "grouped according to *logical* or *conceptual* association."[15] The logical categories governing this arrangement are, according to Rainey, the offerings of *rêaḥ nîḥôaḥ*, "soothing scent," in Leviticus 1–3 as distinct from the expiation offerings of Leviticus 4–5. His argument pointed to a real difference in the thematic emphases of this material, though it is not maintained with total consistency: according to 1:4, the *'ōlāh*'s role is specified as atonement, and in 4:31, the *ḥaṭṭā't* of a common person is described as *rêaḥ nîḥôaḥ lYHWH*. But more troubling than such quibbles over consistency is Rainey's failure to explain what is pedagogically advantageous about this "didactic" order. He adduced no evidence outside Leviticus 1–5 that the distinction between expiation offerings and offerings of pleasing odor was formative for Israel's cultic practice, nor did he explain why the categorization here uses the *rêaḥ nîḥôaḥ*/expiation distinction rather than the "most holy" distinction used in the administrative order. Is one more "logical" than the other? Why would a sequence that accords neither with the quantity of offerings nor with the procedural order help "the officient . . . learn the job"? "Logic" is not a self-evident criterion of organization; it must be grounded in some relevant frame of reference if it is to be cogent to the hearers and readers.

Furthermore, various literary features of Leviticus 1–7 indicate that it was shaped for persuasive as much as for didactic purposes (see Chapter 2). Persuasive and didactic goals are not mutually exclusive,

---

[15] Ibid., 486.

of course, but attention to these chapters' rhetorical features raises the question of logic in a different form: how does the presentation of the offerings in these chapters convince hearers and readers that it *is* logical, that is, acceptable, even normative? From this perspective, what was "logical" to an ancient audience may prove to be the same as what was conventional within that culture, and this leads us back to the considerations of convention and innovation above.

3. Ritual Priority: Despite Rainey's argument that the administrative and didactic orders, in which the ʿōlāh comes first, should not be confused with the performative order, in which it did not, several scholars have argued that the ʿōlāh did in fact have ritual priority. Baruch Levine argued that the essential function of the ʿōlāh was to attract the deity; it was a signal to draw God's attention to the worshipper and the other offerings. He concluded that it must therefore be offered first:

> One normally invited the deity to a common, shared sacrificial meal [šĕlāmîm] ... after he had been invoked by means of an ʿōlâ. ... On this basis, it is eminently clear why the šĕlāmîm sacrifice, understood as a gift of greeting, a present to the deity, would follow the ʿōlâ and not precede it. Until the deity indicated his readiness to "come" to his worshipers, it would have been less appropriate to offer such a gift to him.[16]

Levine regarded the ḥaṭṭāʾt that precedes the ʿōlāh to be "a preliminary rite, which did not affect the ʿōlāh-zebaḥ or ʿōlāh-šĕlāmîm dynamic as we have explained it. The actual approach to the deity began with the ʿōlāh, whereas the ḥaṭṭāʾt, in such cases, was a prerequisite to invoking the deity."[17] Milgrom also considered the essential function of the ʿōlāh to be to "entreat" the deity prior to making the other offerings, but he entertained a broader significance for it: "Entreaty covers a wide range of motives: homage, thanksgiving, appeasement, expiation."[18] He put forward a historical hypothesis (see above), in which the ḥaṭṭāʾt was at

---

[16] Levine, *In the Presence of the Lord*, 26.
[17] Ibid.
[18] Milgrom, *Leviticus*, 1:175.

a given point prefixed to the original ritual sequence of *'ōlāh* followed by *šĕlāmîm*. The *'ōlāh*'s priority in most biblical texts reflects its original ritual priority, and this historical memory explains its continuing significance in Israel's later cult.[19]

It is unlikely, however, that every *šĕlāmîm* could have been preceded by an *'ōlāh*. In times and places where any slaughter of livestock from herd or flock was regarded as an offering to be shared with the deity (so Lev 17:1–9), the cost would have been prohibitive. Though most biblical stories that recount temple ceremonies deal with great national events or with individuals afflicted with unusual ailments, in which *'ōlôt* figure prominently, stories that focus on an individual's ordinary worship do not mention the *'ōlāh* (e.g., 1 Sam 1:3–5, 21, 24–25; 2:13–17; 20:6; cf. Judges 13, where an offer of food is turned into an *'ōlāh* on the orders of an angel). Of course, it may be that the function of the *tāmîd* "daily" burnt offerings in the sanctuary at dawn and at dusk (Num 28:3–8) ensured that, every day, an *'ōlāh* preceded (and followed) all other offerings in the temple. In that case, the *'ōlāh* may have had ritual priority in the temple cult (or, at a minimum, in texts intended to govern that cult) though not necessarily in the people's ordinary ritual experience. The question of the *'ōlāh*'s ritual priority then comes down to what one considers the limits of a "complete" ritual. That would have varied depending on who was interpreting the extent of a ritual, and for what purpose.

4. Theological/Symbolic Importance: A fourth explanation for the *'ōlāh*'s prominence in the Bible points to its theological or symbolic importance. Milgrom concisely stated this view: "When the sacrifices are prescribed they are listed in order of their sanctity (i.e., importance), and therefore the ubiquitous and venerable *'ōlâ*, burnt in its entirety as a total gift to God, comes first."[20] However, the observation that the *'ōlāh* is especially sacred and important cannot be found in the biblical texts, except as an inference from the priority it receives there.

19 Milgrom, *Leviticus*, 1:488.
20 Ibid.

Nowhere is the 'ōlāh labeled as any more sacred than the other "most holy" offerings (that is, all of them except the šĕlāmîm). This therefore does not explain its prominence but only points it out.

Milgrom implied, however, that it is the 'ōlāh's character as a whole offering, donated entirely to God (except for the hide, which goes to the priest: Lev 7:8), that singles it out for special treatment. In other words, the biblical writers regarded this offering as most representative of Israel's worship, as best expressing the proper worship of God. It is notable that almost all of the regular temple offerings (morning and evening, Sabbath, new moons, festivals, etc.) mandated in Numbers 28–29 are 'ōlôt accompanied by cereal and drink offerings (occasionally a ḥaṭṭāʾt is added: monthly, 28:15; at festivals: 28:22; 29:11, 16, etc.). Therefore the 'ōlāh exemplifies the temple cult of the priests, apart from the lay people's participation in it, as pure gift to the deity devoid of almost any profit to the priests. The implication of its rhetorical prominence then is that the 'ōlāh represents the purist form of divine service.

That point is underscored by biblical stories of human sacrifice. The stories of Abraham and Isaac (Genesis 22), Jephthah and his daughter (Judg 11:29–40), and King Mesha of Moab and his son (2 Kings 3:27) all describe the offering of one's child as an 'ōlāh. Though the stories' evaluations of such acts are mixed, they underscore the idea that to offer an 'ōlāh is to give up something of great value. The prominence of the 'ōlāh in biblical rhetoric emphasizes this ideal of self-denial, even though it prohibits the specific act of child sacrifice (Exod 13:13; Lev 18:21; 20:3–5; Deut 18:10). The child sacrifice stories suggest that offering an 'ōlāh indicates a willingness to give God much more than just an animal.

The Rhetorical Effect of the 'Olāh's Priority

This ideal of selfless devotion to YHWH could not, however, dictate the actual functioning of the cult because it would have starved the priests and impoverished the laity. The economic backbone of the system had to be the *šĕlāmîm*, whose meat was shared by priests and the lay worshippers, and the grain of the *minḥāh*, which also provided food for the priests (as frequently did the *ḥaṭṭāʾt* and the *ʾāšām* according to Lev 6:18 [LXX 6:24]–7:10; see Chapters 4 and 5). Of these offerings, the deity received only the blood, the fat, and a token portion of the meat or grain. In terms of quantity, the *šĕlāmîm* and *minḥôt* had to provide the bulk of the priests' livelihood, and their regularity was ensured by mandating that firstborn and firstfruits offerings be brought to the sanctuary at various times during the year, as well as tithes to support the Levites (Num 18:8–32). As these texts from Leviticus and Numbers show, the P writers were quite concerned to claim divine authority for the system of priestly and Levitical income.

Thus the rhetorical priority of the *ʿōlāh* in the Bible did not represent the relative economic importance of the kinds of offerings, but in fact inverted it. The *ʿōlāh* came first to emphasize the religious ideal of self-less devotion to God. The biblical and especially the priestly writers did not place the ideal of selfless devotion in opposition to the economic necessities of the temple cult, but they did emphasize the former, which had the effect of downplaying the latter. The prominence given the *ʿōlāh* disguised the priests' self-interest in promulgating these regulations, just as depicting them as divine commands to Moses disguised the priestly authority behind the writing of these texts.[21] Leviticus and Numbers authorized the economic claims and religious authority of Aaronide priests, but they hid this reality by foregrounding the self-less ideal represented by the *ʿōlāh*. They therefore pictured the regular priestly services as consisting mostly of *ʿōlôt* offerings (Num 28–29), though their days must actually have been spent dealing mainly with the people's *šĕlāmîm*.

I do not mean to depict the P writers as especially devious or under-handed, but only to explain how the priority and emphasis that they

---

[21] See Watts, *Reading Law*, 146–7, and Chapter 7 of this book.

put on the ʿōlāh supported the persuasive goals behind Leviticus 1–7 in particular and the P legislation in general. Their strategy resembles the fund-raising appeals of modern congregations: though the bulk of the budget inevitably goes to the payroll and much of the rest to maintaining the buildings and grounds, their appeals usually emphasize the congregation's community and charity programs, because these best represent the congregation's goals and ideals and are most likely to motivate people to provide financial support. Similarly, though P wrote detailed instructions about the priests' income and the šĕlāmîm offerings of the people, it began its instructions with the ʿōlāh and returned to the ʿōlāh repeatedly to emphasize the ideal of selfless devotion to God and to portray the priests as exemplifying that ideal through their service.[22]

The P writers did not invent this strategy. The convention of the ʿōlāh's priority throughout biblical texts demonstrates that it was a commonplace, even a cliché, of Israel's religious rhetoric to give pride of place to the ʿōlāh. In adopting and amplifying this convention, the P writers enhanced the persuasiveness of their instructions and the likelihood that they would be accepted as normative *torah* for Israel's worship, as indeed they were. They also obscured their innovations and drew attention away from how their legislation served priestly self-interests.

The Priority of the ʿŌlāh in the History of Religion

The place of the ʿōlāh in biblical rhetoric in general, and in the priestly rhetoric of Leviticus and Numbers in particular, led to the burnt offerings of the Jerusalem temple becoming representative of the Jewish

---

[22] Bergen compared P's rhetoric to McDonald's advertising (*Reading Ritual*, 19–21), but this choice of analogy led him to conclude that the ʿōlāh offering defies economic sense; in modern economics, "waste is evil because it is bad economics. In Leviticus, waste is a sign of great good" (21). The rhetoric of modern charity campaigns comes closer to P's economic logic than does the advertising of fast-food restaurants.

religion by the Second Temple period, and probably much earlier. Jews, however, were not alone in focusing especially on burnt offerings. In the first millennium B.C.E., the religions of Syria/Palestine, Anatolia, and Greece all featured burnt animal offerings on altars. That, however, had not always been the case. The cultic traditions of Mesopotamia and Egypt, and perhaps also of the Minoans and Mycenaeans, focused on food offerings to the gods to the point of defining the purpose of the human race as the feeding of the gods.[23] They, however, presented cooked food to the deities; they did not roast it on altars in temple courtyards.[24]

The tradition of burnt offerings nevertheless predates Israel. It can be found in the ritual texts from Ugarit and of the Hittites/Hurrians from the latter half of the second millennium B.C.E. Though no ritual text from these cultures describes the precise manner in which they were offered (the Ugaritic offerings were placed on altars, but no text specifies that a burnt offering was entirely burnt), the names of some Hittite and Ugaritic offerings were constructed out of verbal roots in each language meaning "to burn," which suggests that they may have functioned similarly to Israel's 'ōlāh.[25] The Ugaritic ritual and narrative texts already emphasized animal offerings burnt whole or in part over all others, and they paired burnt offerings (šrp) with peace offerings (šlmm), just as biblical texts do. The words šrp and šlmm,

---

[23] See W. G. Lambert, "Donations of Food and Drink to the Gods in Ancient Mesopotamia," in *Ritual and Sacrifice in the Ancient Near East* (ed. J. Quaegebeur; Leuven: Peeters, 1993), 191–201.

[24] B. Bergquist, "Bronze Age Sacrificial Koine in the Eastern Mediterranean? A Study of Animal Sacrifice in the Ancient Near East," in *Ritual and Sacrifice in the Ancient Near East* (ed. J. Quaegebeur; Leuven: Peeters, 1993), 11–43.

[25] For the linguistic comparison, see Moshe Weinfeld, "Social and Cultic Institutions in the Priestly Source Against Their Ancient Near Eastern Background," in the *Proceedings of the Eighth World Congress of Jewish Studies* (Jerusalem: Magnes, 1983), 95–129, esp. 106–9. For a discussion of Ugaritic ritual procedures, see Levine and de Terragon, "The King Proclaims the Day," 76–115; for the text and translation of this ritual (*KTU* 1.41), see Dennis Pardee, *Ritual and Cult at Ugarit* (WAW 10; Atlanta: SBL, 2002), 56–65.

in that order, are regularly paired and sometimes refer to identical amounts of offerings in Ugaritic ritual texts; often a long list of offerings will culminate in the declaration that these are for a šrp; then the declaration that they are for a šlmm begins the following list.[26] Dennis Pardee concluded: "Bloody sacrifice is the *sine qua non* of a complete ritual carried out in the official cult at Ugarit."[27]

The practice of burning offerings gained popularity during the first millennium and spread from its original home in northwest Syria. Burnt offerings clearly played a central role in Phoenician rituals of the early first millennium B.C.E., and they were exported by the Phoenicians to their colonies across the Mediterranean, and perhaps to Greece as well.[28] References to burnt offerings and depictions of burning altars began to appear in Assyrian records and artwork in the eighth or seventh centuries B.C.E., presumably due to Syrian religious influence.[29] Farther east, fire altars had become an identifying feature of Zoroastrian practice as well, though no animals were burnt on them. This may have been an independent cultural development. By the fourth or third centuries, however, burnt offerings on horned altars in the Syrian/Palestinian style had become a feature of many Egyptian temples, along with priests bearing titles such as "superintendent of the burnt offerings of Amon and the slaughterhouse of meat."[30] By the

---

[26] E.g., *KTU* 1.39, 1.41, 1.46, 1.111, 1.148, 1.161, 1.164, 1.168, translated in Pardee, *Ritual and Cult at Ugarit*, 27–9, 48, 63–4, 68, 75, 77, 85, 92.

[27] Pardee, *Ritual and Cult at Ugarit*, 3–4.

[28] On Phoenician/Punic rituals, see E. Lipiński, "Rites et sacrifices dans la tradition Phénico-Punique," in *Ritual and Sacrifice in the Ancient Near East* (ed. J. Quaegebeur; Leuven: Peeters, 1993), 257–81. The influence of Phoenician ritual practices on the Greeks was suggested by Birgitta Bergquist, "Bronze Age Sacrificial Koine in the Eastern Mediterranean? A Study of Animal Sacrifice in the Ancient Near East," in *Ritual and Sacrifice in the Ancient Near East* (ed. J. Quaegebeur; Leuven: Peeters, 1993), 11–43 [42].

[29] Lambert, "Donations of Food and Drink," 194; Bergquist, "Bronze Age Sacrifical Koine," 25–6.

[30] Jan Quaegebeur, "L'autel-à-feu et l'abattoir en Égypte tardive," in *Ritual and Sacrifice in the Ancient Near East* (ed. J. Quaegebeur; Leuven: Peeters, 1993), 329–353.

turn of the era, then, animal offerings on burning altars had become a prominent and ubiquitous feature of the religions of the Near Eastern and Mediterranean world.

Thus the Torah's emphasis on burning animal offerings and on the *ʿōlāh* as paradigmatic of Israel's worship identified Jewish cult practice with a tradition of worship that was gaining popularity in many first millennium cultures. The priority of the *ʿōlāh* in biblical rhetoric is part and parcel of a wider discourse of ritual practice and rhetoric that transcended Israel's boundaries and was reshaping the religious world of antiquity. The biblical writers cannot have been aware of the long-term changes in religious practice that their rhetoric reflected and supported. This development cannot, therefore, be credited to internal religious developments in Israel, and its progression probably cannot be traced redactionally in the Bible, as Levine attempted to do.[31] Israel inherited it along with the practice of burnt animal offerings as the conventional rhetoric and practice of divine worship.[32] The biblical writers then used it to promote an ideal of selfless devotion to God.[33] Nevertheless, the Jerusalem Temple's alignment in this regard with other prominent cult institutions of the Persian and Hellenistic empires must have helped gain it respect from non-Jewish rulers as an ancient (i.e., conventional) institution worthy of respect and support.

The Bible's idealization of the *ʿōlāh* as representing selfless devotion had major ramifications for subsequent religious traditions. Though the destruction of the Jerusalem Temple in 70 C.E. brought to an end, for the most part, the offering of animals among Jews and animal

---

[31] Levine, *Numbers 21–36,* 400–3.

[32] Gerstenberger argued that "The completely burned sacrifice is probably an Israelite peculiarity" (*Leviticus,* 34). Though the Hittite and Ugaritic evidence does not contain proof that he is wrong, the similarities in ritual practices and terminology between the texts of these cultures argue less for discontinuity than for continuity in their treatment of the burnt offering.

[33] Though this ideal may be implied in the older Hittite/Hurrian and Ugaritic rhetoric and practice of burnt offerings, I cannot find any text that makes it explicit.

offerings fell into disfavor among Christians for other reasons, the ideal of the ʿōlāh continued to shape the religious imaginations of Jews and Christians. Rabbinic literature devoted great attention to the details of the Temple service, now existing only in text and memory. Christian theology reinterpreted the execution of Jesus of Nazareth with the imagery of biblical animal offerings and combined it with the typology of Abraham's offering of Isaac to turn the crucifixion into the ultimate ʿōlāh.[34] Both traditions used the same imagery to interpret deaths because of religious persecution as examples of the ideal of total devotion to God.[35] These interpretive applications of the ʿōlāh to noncultic experience gave rise to the idea of "sacrifice" that has shaped Western religious traditions and cultures to the present day. The Muslim practice of *qurban*, the slaughter of an animal as representative of one's submission to God, gives concise expression to this developed symbolism of self-sacrifice here reapplied to animal slaughter (though not as a whole offering). The Qur'an depicts the story of 'Ibrahim's offering his son as illustrating that both of them had "submitted their wills" to God (24.1.5). It gives instructions for animal sacrifice to pilgrims on the Haj and to all Muslims who can afford it (22.28, 30, 34–37). The last of these verses specifies: "It is not their meat nor their blood, that reaches Allah: it is your piety that reaches Him: He has thus made them subject to you, that ye may glorify Allah for His Guidance to you and proclaim the good news to all who do right" (Yusufali translation).

In other words, the word "sacrifice" now means relinquishing something of great value rather than providing food for God. I do not know whether that idea was already attached to the burnt offerings of the late-Bronze Age kingdoms of Syria and Anatolia. What is clear is that

---

[34] Jon D. Levenson, *The Death and Resurrection of the Beloved Son: The Transformation of Child Sacrifice in Judaism and Christianity* (New Haven: Yale University Press, 1993).

[35] See Daniel Boyarin, *Dying for God* (Stanford: Stanford University Press, 1999); George P. Heyman, *Martyrdom and Sacrifice: Roman and Christian Representations of Power* (Minneapolis: Fortress, 2007).

the Bible's rhetorical elevation of the *ōlāh* as the paradigmatic offering of Israel's cult established selfless devotion as the religious ideal. That allowed the idea of "sacrifice" to embark on a cultural career often totally unconnected to the practice of burnt animal offerings. (For more on the meaning of "sacrifice," see Chapter 8.)

4

The Rhetoric of Sin, Guilt, and Ritual Offerings

Contemporary scholarship on Leviticus 4–5 operates under the shadow of an especially contentious history of interpretation. Early Christian rhetoric depicted the *ḥaṭṭāʾt* and *ʾāšām* offerings of Leviticus 4–5 as paradigms of Israel's whole system of worship. The Septuagint, following Hebrew usage, had translated the names of the offerings with common Greek nouns for "sin" (*hamartia*) and "guilt, offense" (*plēmmeleia/plēmmelēma*). On that basis, Christian interpreters regarded atonement for sin and guilt as the essential goal of all Jewish offerings. They also judged them to have failed to achieve complete atonement, which they argued became available only through Jesus' self-sacrifice (e.g., Heb 9:22, 10:1–18).

The rise of critical biblical scholarship gave a historical twist to this thesis. Nineteenth-century scholars such as Julius Wellhausen and William Robertson Smith argued that the concern with sin and guilt represented by the *ḥaṭṭāʾt* and *ʾāšām* offerings was paradigmatic only of exilic and post-exilic Jewish thought and practice (though Wellhausen thought this trend began with the seventh century B.C.E. reforms of Josiah and the book of Deuteronomy). The older cultic worship emphasized celebratory meals in the presence of the national god (a practice not too dissimilar from Protestant celebrations of Communion). They maintained, however, that this tradition degenerated into a theocratic focus on sin and guilt, due to the disastrous national histories of Israel and Judah in the eighth through the fifth centuries and the centralization of power in the hands of the priestly hierarchy.[1]

Jews have always protested such disparaging depictions of worship in the Jerusalem temple, and some Jewish scholars have successfully dismantled these anti-Semitic arguments in modern Christian scholarship. Moshe Weinfeldt challenged them directly by pointing out that cultic concern for purification and atonement was not a late innovation precipitated by Jewish history. It is reflected in many ritual texts from earlier ancient Near Eastern cultures, particularly the Hittite and Ugarit cultures.[2] Jacob Milgrom has reinforced Weinfeldt's thesis, though not every detail of his comparisons, and added arguments for the moral and theological significance of P's ritual regulations.[3] Both scholars have argued repeatedly that P and its ritual regulations date from the pre-exilic period and thus are representative of classical Israelite (or, at least, biblical) religion just as much as any other part of the Hebrew Bible.

Because of these fundamental arguments over Israel's religious history and ideas, debates over the proper translation of two terms for offerings, *ḥaṭṭāʾt* and *ʾāšām*, have attracted a great deal of attention in recent scholarship. Milgrom and others have insisted that they be rendered in English as "purification offering" and "reparation offering," respectively. Others have argued that *ḥaṭṭāʾt* is better rendered "expiation offering" (Gray) or "separation offering" (Marx). The argument revolves around the function of the offerings. Does the *ḥaṭṭāʾt* expiate for sins (so, already in 1925, Gray and recently again Gane) or purify

---

[1] Wellhausen, *Prolegomena*, 59–82; William Robertson Smith, *Lectures on the Religion of the Semites* (2nd ed.; London: Black, 1894 [1st ed. 1889]), 215–16, 237–60, 353, 401.

[2] Weinfeld, "Social and Cultic Institutions," 95–129.

[3] E.g., Milgrom, *Leviticus*, 1:704–42.

from defilement due to sinful and unsinful acts (Milgrom), or both (Levine, Kiuchi, Schenker, Schwartz, Gilders)?[4] Or is it a "separation offering" to put distance between the sinner and pollution (Marx) or an "empowerment ritual" to restore the status of person or altar (Baumgarten)?[5] And is it the sanctuary that is purified (Milgrom) or the worshiper (Marx, Gane) or both (Kiuchi, Schwartz)?[6] Most of these interpreters agree that the *'āšām* is best translated "reparation offering," but does it compensate for damages to YHWH caused by crimes (Marx) or for desecration of the sanctuary and what belongs to it (Milgrom)?[7] And to what degree must the offense be unintentional or not (contrast Milgrom with Schenker)?[8]

Apart from such disagreements over the meaning of the offerings within ancient ritual practices, the debate over the translation of these offering names also has implications for the history of Israel's religion, as Milgrom noted: "The advantage to freeing the *ḥaṭṭā't* from the theologically foreign notion of sin and restoring to it its pristine meaning of purification is that now it is possible to see this sacrifice in its true ancient Near Eastern setting. Israel was part of a cultic continuum that abounded in purifications both of persons

---

4   George Buchanan Gray, *Sacrifice in the Old Testament: Its Theory and Practice* (New York: Ktav, 1971 [1925]), 59–60; Levine, *In the Presence of the Lord*, 103; Nobuyoshi Kiuchi, *The Purification Offering in the Priestly Literature: Its Meaning and Function* (Sheffield: JSOT Press, 1987), 65, 109; Adrian Schenker, "Interprétations récente et dimension spécifiques du sacrifice *ḥaṭṭā't*," *Bib* 75 (1994): 59–70; Baruch J. Schwartz, "The Bearing of Sin in the Priestly Literature," in *Pomegranates and Golden Bells* (ed. David P. Wright, David Noel Freedman, and Avi Hurvitz; Winona Lake, IN: Eisenbrauns, 1995), 3–21; Gilders, *Blood Ritual*, 30–2; Roy Gane, *Cult and Character: Purification Offerings, Day of Atonement, and Theodicy* (Winona Lake: Eisenbrauns, 2005).

5   A. Marx, "Sacrifice pour les péchés ou rites de levee de sanction," *ZAW* 100 (1988): 183–98; Albert I. Baumgarten, "*Ḥaṭṭā't* Sacrifices," *RB* 103 (1996): 337–42.

6   Milgrom, *Leviticus*, 1:254–6; Marx, "Sacrifice pour les péchés"; Gane, *Cult and Character*, 106–43; Kiuchi, *The Purification Offering*, 65; Schwartz, "Bearing of Sin."

7   Marx, "The Theology of Sacrifice," 118; Milgrom, *Cult and Conscience*.

8   Contrast Milgrom, *Cult and Conscience*, 119–24, with Schenker, "Once Again, the Expiatory Sacrifices," *JBL* 116 (1997): 697–9.

and of buildings, especially sanctuaries."⁹ All of the translations suggested by these scholars avoid the traditional formulations "sin offering" and "guilt offering" in order to put the old anti-Semitic polemic to rest.

The odd result, however, is that the translations of contemporary commentators completely obscure the fact that the Hebrew uses the same words, or at least what look and sound like the same words, for two offerings and for the common nouns "sin" and "guilt." No one can tell from, for example, Milgrom's translation of Leviticus 4:3, "he shall offer for the wrong he has done a bull . . . as a purification offering," that the root *ḥṭ'* appears here three times, or from his translation of Leviticus 5:19, "It is a reparation offering; he has incurred liability to the Lord," that three of the five words in this verse employ the root *'šm*. In the effort to reinterpret the ritual function of these offerings and through them a key aspect of ancient Israel's religious practices and beliefs, the actual language of Leviticus 4–5 has been almost completely obscured.¹⁰

This chapter takes a fresh look at Leviticus 4–5 from a rhetorical perspective. The question to be answered is: what effect did the writers of Leviticus 4–5 hope to evoke by repeatedly using in close juxtaposition to each other the words *ḥaṭṭā't* and *'āšām* for "sin" and "guilt" as well as for the names of offerings?

Leviticus 4–5 in Context

Leviticus 4–5's description of the *ḥaṭṭā't* and *'āšām* offerings continues the systematic portrayal of Israel's principal offerings begun in Leviticus

---

⁹ Milgrom, *Leviticus*, 1:254.
¹⁰ This trend has not yet influenced popular translations of the Bible. Robert Alter has also demurred, translating *ḥaṭṭā't* as "offense offering" and *'āšām* as "guilt offering." He summarized Milgrom's arguments about the *ḥaṭṭā't*, but noted that "something is lost by using a designation for this offering that is not cognate with the verb" (*The Five Books of Moses: A Translation with Commentary* [New York: Norton, 2004], 557).

1. Each of the first five chapters of Leviticus details the ritual instructions for a different offering, starting with the *ʿōlāh* and continuing through the *minḥāh* and the *šĕlāmîm* before reaching the *ḥaṭṭāʾt* and *ʾāšām* in Leviticus 4–5. Leviticus 6–7 emphasizes different aspects of these same five offerings and presents them in a different order (see Chapter 2 of this book). Leviticus 8–9 describes the inauguration of the priests in the Tabernacle using these same offerings, priests who then assume their duties in presiding over these offerings. Thus Leviticus logically presents the regulations for the different kinds of offerings immediately before narrating the commencement of the Tabernacle cult that employed them.

The offerings described in Leviticus 1–3 seem to reflect long-established rituals in Israelite culture. The *šĕlāmîm* even appear with that name and with, apparently, the same function in Ugaritic ritual texts.[11] The term *minḥāh* appears in Ugaritic to refer to tribute payments, a meaning it also has in a variety of biblical narratives. P's instructions narrow the definition of this traditional term to nonanimal food offerings (e.g., *minḥāh sōlet*, "grain offering"). The name of the *ʿōlāh* seems to be unique to Israel's traditions, but all historical levels of biblical texts emphasize its role as a whole burnt offering. Precedents for burnt offerings are discernible in Ugaritic and Hittite sources as well. Thus the first three chapters of Leviticus seem to describe long-established practices. By rehearsing regulations for these well-known offerings, the book tries to establish its credibility as the authoritative source of ritual instructions (see Chapter 3) – a point reinforced by the refrain "this is the *torah* for..." in Leviticus 6–7.

Leviticus 4–5 contains several indications, however, that the writers expected their regulations for the *ḥaṭṭāʾt* and *ʾāšām* to be regarded as more innovative and/or controversial than those in the preceding

---

11 For the Ugaritic vocabulary, see Chapter 3. The functional comparison has been challenged by Modéus, who argued that Hebrew and Ugaritic usage shared at most a common pool of technical vocabulary (*Sacrifice and Symbol*, 269–80, 359, 366).

chapters. Unlike Leviticus chapters 1–3, which never mention the occasions for particular offerings, but settle for vague phases like "whenever you bring your offering..." (e.g., 1:2, 2:1), Leviticus chapters 4–5 carefully specify what situations require a ḥaṭṭāʾt or an 'āšām. Leviticus 4 requires different rites depending on who committed the offense (4:3, 13, 22, 27), while Leviticus 5 describes in detail the nature of the offenses (5:1–4, 15, 17, 21–24 [LXX 6:2–5]) to distinguish different ritual requirements. Thus the writers of Leviticus assume that its readers and hearers already know when 'ōlôt, minḥôt, and šĕlāmîm are permissible or required, but the writers think this audience needs to be clearly informed when they must bring a ḥaṭṭāʾt or an 'āšām. The latter information was not common knowledge.[12]

A second indication that the writers have shaped Leviticus 4–5 for a more controversial reception is the increasing number of assertions that God commanded these offerings. That claim appears in the narrative framework at the beginning of the book (1:1–2) but not again until 4:1. Leviticus 5 feels the need to repeat it twice (5:14, 20 [LXX 6:1]), though not as often as in Leviticus 6–7 (6:1, 12, 17 [LXX 6:8, 19, 24]; 7:22, 28). The writers' emphasis on the divine origins of these instructions reflects their increasing anxiety about how readily the regulations would be accepted.[13]

The strongest evidence, however, that the writers expected a contentious reception for these regulations stems from the use of the words ḥaṭṭāʾt and 'āšām in Leviticus 4–5. The chapters play on the ritual and nonritual meanings of these words in a rhetorical crescendo that accelerates throughout its two-chapter span. I turn, therefore, to the nature of these words and their function within these chapters of Leviticus.

---

[12] Milgrom, *Leviticus*, 1:176.
[13] That Leviticus 6–7, which is directed explicitly to priests, shares this anxiety is reflected in the refrain "this is the *torah* for... " that insists on the authority of these regulations over priestly practice, and also in the prominence of negative stipulations in these chapters.

Jargon and Wordplays in Leviticus 4–5

Many contemporary scholars insist that as names for offerings, *ḥaṭṭāʾt* and *ʾāšām*, along with the rest of P's ritual vocabulary, are technical terms with precise meanings for the writers of Leviticus 1–10. This use of technical vocabulary, or jargon, reinforces their view that Leviticus presents a rational and realistic system of worship.[14] As a result of this conclusion, interpreters do not look for rhetorical wordplays in P. So Milgrom, for example, recognized a wordplay on the two meanings of *ḥaṭṭāʾt* in Jeremiah 17:1, but not in Leviticus 4.[15] There are some dissidents who think P's precision has been overrated,[16] but most discussions of Leviticus 1–10 presume that for P, as Adrian Schenker put it, "rhetorical redundancy is foreign to him."[17] Only Meir Paran has called attention to wordplays in P.[18] Milgrom and Israel Knohl have emphasized the precision of P's vocabulary as a criterion for distinguishing P materials

---

[14] For discussion and evaluation of the view that P's regulations are rational and realistic, see Chapter 1 of this book.

[15] Milgrom, *Leviticus*, 1:288.

[16] Helmut Utzschneider argued that the narrative framework and its presentation of Leviticus as public ritual interpretation places the ritual instructions in the context of the larger law, within which it should be interpreted ("Vergebung im Ritual: Zur Deutung des *ḥaṭṭāʾt*-Rituals (Sündopfer) in Lev 4,1–5,13," in *Abschied von der Schuld? Zur Anthropologie und Theologie von Schuldbekenntnis, Opfer und Versöhnung* [ed. Richard Riess et al.; Stuttgart: Kohlhammer, 1996], 107). Gilders called the term *ḥaṭṭāʾt* "complex and multivalent" (*Blood Ritual*, 32). Cf. also the older view of Robertson Smith (*Religion of the Semites*, 424, 439–40).

[17] "Rhetorische Redundanz ist ihnen fremd" – Adrian Schenker, "Der Unterschied zwischen Sündopfer *ḥṭ't* und Schuldopfer *ʾm* im Licht von Lev 5,17–19 und 5,10–6," in *Pentateuchal and Deuteronomistic Studies* (ed. C. Brekelmans and J. Lust; BETL 94; Leuven: Peeters, 1990), 115–23; reprinted in *Recht und Kult im Alten Testament: Achtzehn Studien* (OBO 172; Freiburg: Universitätsverlag / Göttingen: Vandenhoeck & Ruprecht, 2000), 104–12 [106]. See also Rolf Rendtorff (*Leviticus*, 148), whose detailed enumeration of the uses of *ḥaṭṭāʾt* in these chapters led him to conclude that the usage is unambiguous and not colloquial.

[18] Paran, *Forms of the Priestly Style*, vii. He also argued, however, that P uses many words in the distinctive manner of a professional circle, that is, as technical vocabulary (xiv).

from H materials, arguing that H is noticeably looser in its usage.[19] The furthest most commentators are willing to go in recognizing literary concerns shaping Leviticus 4–5 is the common observation that the emphasis gradually shifts from *ḥaṭṭāʾt* ("sin" and the offering by that name) to *ʾāšām* ("guilt" and the offering by that name) over the course of the two chapters.

Comparisons of biblical uses of offering names, however, weigh against the notion that *ḥaṭṭāʾt* and *ʾāšām* were part of a priestly jargon, at least an old priestly jargon. Whereas *ʿōlāh, minḥāh,* and *šĕlāmîm* look like age-old technical terminology, *ḥaṭṭāʾt* and *ʾāšām* do not. They seem to be innovations from the time when this portion of Leviticus was composed, because Leviticus 4–5 labors to introduce the reasons for performing the offerings as well as the means for doing so.

The observation that the terms were newly minted does not, by itself, counter the claim that they are jargon: it is characteristic of technical vocabulary to be constantly expanded with new words. As common Hebrew words whose basic meanings denote "sin" and "guilt," however, *ḥaṭṭāʾt* and *ʾāšām* have strong emotional overtones that would make them poor choices for technical jargon, but excellent rhetorical devices. One usually expects technical vocabulary to eschew normative overtones in favor of the appearance of technical objectivity. Failure to do so can interfere with the vocabulary's precise technical definitions. For example, a recent series of lawsuits in the United States over the right to die became a political *cause celebre* because of the popular associations evoked by a technical phrase, "persistent vegetative state," to describe a medical condition. Far from avoiding such problems, the choice of the words *ḥaṭṭāʾt* and *ʾāšām* to name types of offerings seems to revel in complicating overtones.

Of course, ancient writers may not have shared our cultural presuppositions about how to choose jargon. But at the very least, if the

---

[19] Milgrom, *Leviticus*, 1:15, 2:1327–30; Israel Knohl, *The Sanctuary of Silence: The Priestly Torah and the Holiness School* (Minneapolis: Fortress, 1995), 106–7, who described P's use of language as "fastidious" and "scrupulous."

description as "technical vocabulary" is to mean anything at all, we should expect writers to clearly distinguish technical uses of a word from any nontechnical applications. Words cannot serve the needs of specialists for a concise and precise vocabulary if they constantly run the risk of being confused with other meanings of the same terms. Yet Leviticus 4–5, far from avoiding the common meanings of *ḥaṭṭāʾt* and *ʾāšām*, juxtaposes them directly to the offering names. The chapters seem to intentionally play on the multiple meanings of the terms. This suggests that the names have been chosen to achieve other goals than just the communication of technical expertise.[20]

Leviticus 4–5 clearly focuses attention on the terms *ḥaṭṭāʾt* and *ʾāšām*. It very obviously distinguishes the offerings by those names, and details when they should be presented and how they should be handled. The two chapters, however, also emphasize the cause-and-effect relationship between the verbal roots of these nouns. They describe various people as "sinning" (*ḥṭʾ*) and as a result becoming "guilty" (*ʾšm*) themselves (4:22, 27; 5:17, 23) or, in the anointed priest's case, making the people "guilty" (4:3). (In what follows, I will consistently render all uses of the roots *ḥṭʾ* and *ʾšm* in English as "sin" and "guilt/be guilty" simply to show the frequent usage of these Hebrew roots. I do not intend to suggest that these renderings are, in the end, the best English translations of the meaning of the Hebrew words in context. That issue is discussed later in this chapter.)

Leviticus 4–5 does not stop there, however. These chapters deliberately and repeatedly juxtapose verb, common noun, and offering name of the same root, especially *ḥṭʾ*, in patterns that are quite redundant (contra Schenker). For example, the refrain "sin that he sinned ... as

---

[20] Gilders described Leviticus 4's use of *ḥaṭṭāʾt* as a "sophisticated pun" ("*Ḥaṭṭaʾt* as 'Sin Offering': A Reconsideration," conference paper presented at the International Society of Biblical Literature meeting in Cambridge, July 2003). Paran observed that, in general, "The priestly writer tends to expand, reduplicate and engage in various kinds of word play because of the joy of writing. The priestly writer enjoys playing with words as though they were building blocks which can be put together in a variety of patterns according to the whim of the writer" (*Priestly Style*, vii).

sin" appears eight times (4:3, 14, 23–24, 28, 5:6, 7, 10, 13). The most exaggerated use of redundancy for rhetorical impact appears later in Leviticus 5, where verse 19 consists of only five words and uses the root *ʾšm* three times: *ʾāšām hûʾ ʾāšōm ʾāšam lYHWH* "It is guilt – guiltily he became guilty before YHWH."[21]

Repetitions of the roots *ḥṭʾ* and *ʾšm* in these chapters also introduce variations on the formulas that seem to play intentionally on their multiple meanings and blur distinctions between them. "Sin that he sinned" in 4:3, 14, 28 (twice), 5:6, 10, 13, becomes "his guilt that he sinned" in 5:7 and even the odd "his offering (*qorbānô*) that he sinned" in 5:11. Atonement (*kipper*) is achieved simply for persons (*ʿălēhem*) in 4:20, becomes also "for" and "from his sin" (*ʿālāyw . . . mēḥaṭṭāʾtô*) in 4:26 and 5:6, "from his sin that he sinned" in 5:10, "for the sin that he sinned" in 5:13, "for what he sinned" in 5:16, and finally "for the one of all the things that he did by which he became guilty of it" in 5:26 [LXX 6:7]. (Again, my English rendering of the Hebrew prepositions is intentionally mechanical and nonidiomatic.) These sequences of repetitive variation become increasingly intense and also shift from *ḥṭʾ* to *ʾšm* as one reaches the latter part of Leviticus 5.

The repetition and intensification of these verbal patterns in Leviticus 4–5 suggest intentional plays on the various meanings of *ḥṭʾ* and *ʾšm* for rhetorical effect. I conclude that the offering name *ḥaṭṭāʾt*, which is pointed qal, is not as Levine maintained a Masoretic mispointing for the piel meaning "purification offering."[22] The fact that the chapters intentionally play on and even identify the meanings of *ḥaṭṭāʾt* shows that the similarity between the words was

---

[21] The redundancy of this verse receives remarkably little comment from recent interpreters. In the Middle Ages, however, Rashi felt constrained to rebut the charge that "this is a verse which is not needed" (*The Metsudah Chumash/Rashi* [ed. Avroham Davis; Hoboken: Ktav, 1998], 58).

[22] Levine, *In the Presence of the Lord*, 101–2; idem, *Leviticus* (JPS Torah Commentary; Philadelphia: Jewish Publication Society, 1989), 20. Gilders has recently reexamined this issue ("*Ḥaṭṭaʾt* as 'Sin Offering'").

recognized by the writers who expected readers and hearers also to recognize it. Whatever English words are chosen to render *ḥaṭṭāʾt* and *ʾāšām*, translations should try to present some sense of the Hebrew wordplays between common nouns, verbs, and names of offerings, rather than totally hiding them as most contemporary commentators do.[23]

I do not underestimate the difficulty of this task: wordplays are notoriously untranslatable because words cover different semantic ranges in different languages. Often the best one can do is evoke the impact of the Hebrew with an English phrase that is not strictly a translation. For example, a sentence like "Pay sin taxes on the sins you sin!" reproduces the use of the root "sin" as common noun, verb, and technical term,[24] while also portraying the emotional freight attached to this vocabulary. But the nonequivalence between American sin taxes and ancient Israel's *ḥaṭṭāʾt* makes this rendering only illustrative, and the English phrase is artificial in any case.

In the end, the nuance of the Hebrew may not be translatable into other languages. Nevertheless, it is vital that interpreters recognize and try to understand the Hebrew wordplay. The question of translation is a separate problem.[25] Interpretation of the Hebrew usage of *ḥaṭṭāʾt* and *ʾāšām* has too often been confused with the problem of how to translate the terms.

---

[23] Gilders therefore defended the LXX's rendering of *ḥaṭṭāʾt* with *hamartia*, "sin," noting "what appears to be a deliberate construction of the *texture* (a la Vernon Robbins) of Leviticus 4 directed at identifying the *ḥaṭṭāʾt* offering as a sacrifice for *ḥaṭṭāʾt* ('sin'). This deliberate construction may be characterized as 'midrashic' in quality, in the sense that an intertext(ure) is created through formal juxtaposition of words in a new context" ("*Ḥaṭṭāʾt* as 'Sin Offering'").

[24] "Sin taxes" in American usage are government taxes on alcohol, tobacco, and other commodities with the ostensible purpose of reducing their consumption.

[25] Similarly, Christophe Lemardelé: "La question de la traduction ne doit pas occuper l'essentiel de la discussion; plus important est le sens d'un tel rite" ("Le sacrifice de purification: un sacrifice ambigu?" *VT* 52 [2002]: 284). In fact, the problem of translation does not even exhaust the question of how the words are used in this text, much less what the ritual means.

The Rhetoric of Wordplays in Leviticus 4–5

Why does Leviticus 4–5 play on the meanings of *ḥaṭṭāʾt* and *ʾāšām*? Wordplays are a common feature of Hebrew style, especially poetic style. If this text were found in prophetic literature, we would immediately suspect a polemical intention behind it. Indeed, the idea of naming temple offerings "sin" and "guilt" is reminiscent of Amos's sarcastic call to Israelite worshippers: "Come to Bethel – and transgress; to Gilgal – and multiply transgression! Bring your sacrifices every morning, your tithes every three days . . . " (Amos 4:4 NRSV). Critical sarcasm, however, does not seem to be characteristic of P's offering instructions, to say the least. Leviticus 1–7 works to establish its authority as the normative guide to Israel's tabernacle (i.e., temple) worship. It maintains a tone of serious instruction about important practices that are vital to the covenant relationship between Israel and God. The prophets' polemical satire is quite foreign to Leviticus' purpose.

Yet as we have seen, Leviticus 4–5 does play on the offering names, *ḥaṭṭāʾt* and *ʾāšām*, and their associated common nouns and verbs. Some interpreters have naturally looked for symbolic and theological significance in the choice of this vocabulary. Modern interpreters who have taken the words *ḥaṭṭāʾt* and *ʾāšām* as cues for theological interpretation include Martin Noth, who suggested that the offering names "denoted first of all not a particular kind of sacrifice, but the purpose of the sacrifice,"[26] and Klaus Koch, who argued more elaborately that the sacrificial animal becomes, through the ritual, an "embodied sphere of sin."[27] Because theological interpretation laid the basis for the Christian critique summarized at the beginning of this chapter, however, most contemporary commentators have obscured the verbal connection between offering names and "sin" or "guilt" and have devoted their theological reflections, if any, to the notions of purification and reparation. There are other reasons to avoid theologizing

---

[26] Noth, *Leviticus*, 37.
[27] Klaus Koch, "*ḥṭʾ*," *TDOT* 4:318.

the terminology. The fact is that P shows little inclination for such symbolic interpretation elsewhere and certainly does not elaborate on it in Leviticus 4–5.[28]

Rhetorical analysis looks instead for persuasive purposes behind the choice of vocabulary. In the case of *ḥaṭṭā't* and *'āšām*, they are not hard to imagine. Wordplays on emotionally laden terms like "sin" and "guilt" convey a sense of urgency: these offerings are necessary, essential! The patterns in which Leviticus 4–5 deploys this vocabulary reinforce an impression of urgency: refrains using these terms appear with increasing frequency toward the end of Leviticus 4 and into Leviticus 5, and slight variations on the formulas increase along with their frequency. Add to that the shift in the preponderance of the vocabulary from "sin" to "guilt," that is, from the act to its consequences, and the chapters appear to be carefully crafted to convince their hearers and readers of the urgent necessity of fulfilling their ritual stipulations. In contrast to the methodical, even unconcerned, air of Leviticus 1–3 that finds it completely unnecessary to mention any reasons for bringing the offerings called *'ōlāh, minḥāh,* and *šělāmîm,* Leviticus 4–5 conveys much greater concern and urgency both in style and contents. Naming the offerings "sin" and "guilt" contributes significantly to that rhetorical strategy.

The question remains, however, of why these particular words were chosen as names for offerings. Within that question lies a historical issue: Did P invent these names? I have noted various indications that the writers of Leviticus expected their instructions for the *ḥaṭṭā't* and *'āšām* to meet with some opposition from their intended audience

---

[28] Chapter 9 provides an explanation for the lack of explicit theologizing in priestly ritual instructions. Mary Douglas argued instead that theology permeates Leviticus, but that it is presented in an analogical rather than discursive mode of thinking that discursively oriented interpreters do not recognize (*Leviticus as Literature,* 20–40). Contra the argument being made here, note that one effect of Douglas's theory of Leviticus' analogical mode of thought is to deny any emotion to the language: "The interpreter must not read emotional quality into language which is primarily cast in a spatio-temporal mode" (150). For a critique of Douglas's ideas about Leviticus, see Chapter 1 in this book.

because the chapters are shaped rhetorically to overcome it. I have also repeated the long-standing observation that the *ḥaṭṭāʾt* and *ʾāšām* offerings were not as old as the *ʿōlāh*, *minḥāh*, and *šĕlāmîm* in Israel's religious practice. Together, these observations may suggest that P wrote Leviticus 4–5 to advocate these new rituals and named them *ḥaṭṭāʾt* and *ʾāšām* to make the new legislation more persuasive. Other P texts and Ezekiel, however, do not reflect the same urgency about the *ḥaṭṭāʾt* and *ʾāšām*.[29] If Leviticus 4–5 is the source of this innovation, it must predate Ezekiel, which treats the terms as conventional.

It would, however, be very unwise to establish the dating of P, or even just these two chapters, based on their use of two terms alone. It is not hard to imagine other scenarios. Perhaps P addressed a different or broader audience than did Ezekiel, an audience to whom the older priestly terms and offerings would appear innovative and controversial. This would explain the urgency conveyed by these chapters, but not why "sin" and "guilt" were chosen as the names of offerings in the first place. It is possible that earlier (eighth-seventh centuries?) priestly preaching produced these terms as part of a cultic reform that introduced the *ḥaṭṭāʾt* and *ʾāšām* offerings. Leviticus 4–5 then continued (in the sixth-fifth centuries?) an earlier rhetorical emphasis because P could not yet assume general agreement and compliance with this relatively new ritual program. It is likely that only the growing authority of the Torah in the course of the Second Temple period finally overcame resistance to the innovation of the *ḥaṭṭāʾt* and *ʾāšām* offerings, just as it overcame resistance to the better-known innovations of "biblical religion" such as monotheism and the suppression of private and village cults, though differing views on these points persisted throughout the Second Temple period as well.

Whether or not P in Leviticus 4–5 introduced the *ḥaṭṭāʾt* and *ʾāšām* offerings or simply urged compliance with an earlier innovation of

---

[29] Gray pointed out that Ezekiel is quite capable of noting innovations, but does not do so for the *ḥaṭṭāʾt* and *ʾāšām* offerings (*Sacrifice in the Old Testament*, 64). See also Milgrom, *Leviticus*, 1:288.

the priestly party, the question remains, Why make this innovation? Why introduce these two offerings, and why name them *ḥaṭṭāʾt*, "sin," and *ʾāšām*, "guilt"? It is precisely answers to these questions by both traditional and critical Christian commentators that raised the stakes in current debates over the meaning of these terms and the historical circumstances from which these rituals arose. I do not recommend returning to the kind of theological interpretation of the terms that gave rise to the problem in the first place. A rhetorical perspective can instead suggest answers that recognize how the chapters play on the meanings of *ḥaṭṭāʾt* and *ʾāšām* without making a theology of "sin" and "guilt" the matter of crucial concern.

A focus on persuasion tries to determine whose interests this rhetoric may have served. This naturally leads to considering possible social contexts in which such rhetoric might have been deployed. I will suggest several possible social contexts, first for the rhetoric of Leviticus 4–5 alone, then for the place of these chapters within the rhetoric of the Pentateuch as a whole.

Many interpreters have noted that the common nouns *ḥaṭṭāʾt* and *ʾāšām* carry legal connotations in nonpriestly parts of the Hebrew Bible.[30] The fact that the offering names evoke legal situations suggests that they were introduced because the priesthood and temple were playing, or wished to play, a larger role in legal matters. One can only speculate as to the cause and date of such a change. The destruction of the Judean monarchy, and therefore its legal functions, due to the sixth century Babylonian exile, and the rise of the Jerusalem temple as the only durable central institution of Second Temple Judaism provides one possible context for this development. Earlier events, however, such as the decimation of villages and their legal systems

---

[30]   So Levine: "The term *ḥaṭṭāʾt* reflects an extensive history, as we learn primarily from the Akkadian evidence. It derives from the vocabulary of treaties and legal documents, as well as from cultic terminology. It represents one of a complex of terms appropriated by cultic establishments from other contexts" (*In the Presence of the Lord*, 102); see also Utzschneider, "Vergebung im Ritual," 100, 106, 118–19. On the legal connotations of *ʾāšām*, see Milgrom, *Cult and Conscience*, 13–16.

in the seventh century wars, may also have prompted the Jerusalem temple to take on more legal functions.

The priesthood had an obvious incentive to do so. The imperial wars of the eighth to sixth centuries and the eventual loss of a royal sponsor must have had very negative impacts on temple revenues. Furthermore, the centralization of worship in Jerusalem in the seventh century, though never complete, increased the number of priests and Levites who depended on priestly prebends. According to Leviticus 4–7, priests received most of the meat from most *ḥaṭṭā't* and *'āšām* offerings. Therefore the introduction of these new offerings that supplemented, but did not replace, the *minḥôt* and *šĕlāmîm* from which the priests also derived revenue, served to enhance the temple's economic stability.[31]

Another kind of change may also have precipitated the innovation of *ḥaṭṭā't* and *'āšām* offerings and provided a rationale for their startling names, namely, a new *literary* context. The location of P's ritual instructions within the Pentateuch as a whole places them together with a variety of legal, moral, and religious prescriptions, narratives, and sanctions. The narrative framework that unites the whole composition is invoked three times in Leviticus 4–5 by the comment that YHWH spoke to Moses (4:1; 5:14, 20).[32] More than that, the emphasis placed by these chapters on the situations that require a *ḥaṭṭā't* offering evokes the larger context with the repeated phrase, "doing one of all the commandments of YHWH which one should not do" (4:2, 13, 22, 27). Leviticus 5 substitutes more specific offenses that also echo the wider legislation – failure to testify (5:1), pollution (5:2–3), rash oaths (5:4), and the broad category of offenses against *sancta* (5:14–15) – before returning to the overarching category of "doing one of all the commandments of YHWH which one should not do" (5:17). Its final paragraph turns to specific criminal behaviors – theft and fraud (5:21–24 [LXX 6:2–5]).

---

[31] For more about how financial issues affected P's rhetoric, see Chapter 3.

[32] See Utzschneider, "Vergebung im Ritual," 100; Watts, *Reading Law*, 62–5, 93–102.

Therefore, the use of the terms *ḥaṭṭāʾt* and *ʾāšām* with their legal and emotional overtones evokes the literary context of the larger Torah. The Torah describes social norms and ritual instructions as divine mandates enforced ultimately by sanctions on the people as a whole. The urgency communicated by using these terms in Leviticus 4–5 echoes the Torah's sense of urgency: it argues that the law and the cult that it prescribes are vital to Israel's survival. As Bergen noted, the rhetoric of Leviticus 4–5 encourages readers to be "deeply concerned with sin and its effects." Since it is textual rhetoric that creates this attitude, not ritual practice, "someone can still be concerned about sin even when they cannot sacrifice."[33]

The literary form of P and of the Torah as a whole was, of course, influenced by the same social forces that I described above. The influence of the literary context therefore probably reinforced impulses from the social context to advocate these offerings, but provided additional reasons for calling them *ḥaṭṭāʾt*, "sin," and *ʾāšām*, "guilt." Reference to the literary context of the Pentateuch points out the place of the *ḥaṭṭāʾt* and *ʾāšām* instructions within a larger rhetorical program. The Torah emphasizes drastic consequences if divine laws are not obeyed. Therefore disobedience requires quasi-legal ritual rectification. The *ḥaṭṭāʾt* and *ʾāšām* offerings fill that need, ritually in the temple and literarily in the Torah.

---

[33] Bergen, *Reading Ritual*, 40. He compared the rhetoric of Leviticus 4 with television advertising to note that persuasion may depend more on subconscious associations rather than rational argument, and suggested that this explains how a text mandating ritual offerings has been accepted as normative by communities that do not practice animal sacrifice. "Like ads during a football game, the associations and emotions produced by the ritualized text most likely does not work at the level of consciousness. People are not expected to articulate the dissonance between what they are reading and what they are doing. . . . Yet in both cases the text does work. We know that it does work because millions of people have participated in the ritual in which the text is read yet sacrifice is not performed, and they do not understand this new ritual to be inadequate to address the problem the sacrifice ritual is meant to address" (*Reading Ritual*, 35–6).

The Aaronide priests controlled both Torah and ritual. They made sure that both scripture and temple services emphasized the need for the offerings, and the rituals' names reminded worshippers of the Torah's demands on them. Thus the emphasis on sin, guilt, and ritual offerings in Leviticus 4–5 united text and ritual in a performative discourse in which priests and Torah reinforced each other's authority.

5

The Rhetoric of Ritual Narrative

After seven chapters of ritual instruction whose only narrative features are the framework statements that God spoke to Moses, the words "Moses did as YHWH commanded" in Leviticus 8:4 introduce the first, and only large-scale, narrative in the book of Leviticus. Instruction, though still prominent in Leviticus 8–10, now yields space to stories of how Moses carried out the initiation of the priests and tabernacle (Lev 8) and how Aaron then inaugurated Israel's regular worship services (Lev 9). These same words in 8:4 also announce the theme of the chapters, which frequently repeat this refrain of compliance with divine instructions. One story of disastrous noncompliance (10:1–3) breaks the pattern, but only to have it reinstated in the rest of Leviticus 10. The theme of priestly obedience is reinforced by YHWH's commission of Aaron (10:8–11) as the authoritative teacher and interpreter of the divine instructions.

The narratives of Leviticus 8–10 thus legitimize the ritual authority of the Aaronide priests by telling about their initiation by Moses himself on the basis of divine commands, and ground the high priests' interpretive authority in a divine revelation to their ancestor. The fact that their work, if done incorrectly, places them in mortal danger only emphasizes the priests' dedication and implies that the rarity of such divine outbreaks attests to their competence. In these ways, the rhetoric of the ritual narratives in Leviticus 8–10 legitimates and defends the priests' monopoly over Israel's temple offerings.

Leviticus 8–10 in Contemporary Scholarship

Modern scholars have been aware that these chapters (or, at least, chapters 8–9) serve to legitimate the Aaronide priesthood, but they have focused on other issues. They have devoted much attention to the relationship between Leviticus 8–9 and the instructions for carrying out these rites found in Exodus 29/40 and Leviticus 1–7, respectively. The similarities and differences between Leviticus 8 and Exodus 29 in particular have prompted extensive arguments over the literary and historical relationship between these two texts.[1] Moses' unique role, as inaugurator of tabernacle and priests but not a priest himself, has attracted considerable speculation about its relation, if any, to ancient Israel's religious institutions.[2] The anointing of the high priest (8:12) has stimulated even more historical arguments over the antiquity of this practice and its possible derivation from royal anointings.[3]

Contemporary scholars continue to debate these historical issues but have also given increasing attention to interpreting the text as it is (synchronically). They typically interpret the rituals of Leviticus 8–10 in terms of their presumed social function and symbolic meaning, just as they do the preceding ritual instructions. In the case particularly of Leviticus 8, however, it has become routine to invoke insights from the comparative study of religious rituals, especially Arnold Van Gennep's

---

[1] E.g., Alfred Bertholet, *Leviticus*, KHAT (Tübingen: Mohr Siebeck, 1901), 24–5; Noth, *Leviticus*, 76; Elliger, *Leviticus*, 106–20; Milgrom, *Leviticus*, 1:543, 545–9; Hartley, *Leviticus*, 109–10.

[2] Levine, *Leviticus*, 49; Milgrom, *Leviticus*, 1:555–8; Gerstenberger, *Leviticus*, 112–14.

[3] Gray, *Sacrifice*, 258–60; Roland De Vaux, *Ancient Israel* (tr. John McHugh; New York: McGraw-Hill, 1961), 105, 347, 399–401; Milgrom, *Leviticus*, 1:553–5; Hartley, *Leviticus* 110.

description of rites of passage, to understand the ritual symbolism.[4] The fact that this chapter focuses on the ritual transformation of persons, rather than offerings or ritual objects, makes the comparisons with the anthropological literature more compelling. Jacob Milgrom applied a broad range of functionalist anthropological studies to the chapter.[5] Using more recent theories of ritual, Frank Gorman and Gerald Klingbeil have subjected Leviticus 8 to sustained ritual analyses, giving detailed attention not just to the priests but also to ritual space, time, clothing, and the like.[6] Karen Eliasen has returned attention to the priests, especially the high priest, by using feminist approaches to highlight Aaron's embodied subjective experience as he lived through the rites of chapters 8–10.[7]

These efforts at ritual analysis have been reinforced by parallels from other ancient Near Eastern ritual texts. Baruch Levine used the differences between Leviticus 8–10 and Akkadian, Hittite, and Ugaritic texts to argue that Israel developed the genre of descriptive rituals into true narratives to describe the origins of Israel's cult.[8] Milgrom pointed to similar concerns for fulfilling divine orders in a Babylonian tablet

[4] Arnold Van Gennep, *The Rites of Passage* (tr. M. B. Vizedom and G. L. Caffee; Chicago: University of Chicago Press, 1960).

[5] Milgrom, *Leviticus,* 1:566–9, citing the works of Van Gennep, Edward Leach, and Victor Turner.

[6] Gorman, *Ideology of Ritual,* 103–30; Gerald A. Klingbeil, *A Comparative Study of the Ritual of Ordination as Found in Leviticus 8 and Emar 369* (Lewiston: Edwin Mellon, 1998); idem, "Ritual Time in Leviticus 8 with Special Reference to the Seven Day Period in the Old Testament," *ZAW* 109 (1997): 500–13; idem, " 'Who did what when and why?' The Dynamics of Ritual Participants in Leviticus 8 and Emar 369," in *Inicios, Paradigmas y Fundamentos: Estudios teológicos y exegéticos en el Pentateuco* (ed. G. A. Klingbeil; San Martín, Argentina: Universidada Adventista del Plata, 2004), 105–34.

[7] Karen C. Eliasen, "Aaron's War Within: Story and Ritual in Leviticus 10," *Proceedings – Eastern Great Lakes and Midwest Biblical Societies* 20 (2000): 81–98; idem, "Getting a Feel for a Concept: A Ritual-Critical Reading of the Nadab and Abihu Incident in Lev 10," conference paper presented at the Eastern International Region meeting of the American Academy of Religion in Ithaca, NY, March 30–31, 2001.

[8] Levine, "Descriptive Tabernacle Texts of the Pentateuch," 313–14; for further analysis of this position, see Chapter 2 in this book.

commemorating a temple restoration.[9] Daniel Fleming found for the first time clear evidence for the anointing of a priest in extra-biblical texts in a thirteenth or twelfth century B.C.E. ritual text from Emar.[10] Klingbeil elaborated the ritual comparisons between this same Emar text and Leviticus 8.[11]

While Leviticus 8 has attracted much interest for the rituals it depicts, Leviticus 10 has attracted a different kind of interest because of the ambiguity of its stories. Since antiquity, interpreters have struggled to understand what Nadab and Abihu did so wrong as to prompt instantaneous divine retribution (10:1–3) and how Aaron won the argument with Moses at the end of the chapter (10:16–20). They have also wondered what connection the story has to the stories of Aaron's construction of the golden calf (Exodus 32) and the deaths of the similarly named sons of Jereboam I, also a builder of golden calves (1 Kings 14).[12] Leviticus 10 thus provides ready examples of narrative and contextual ambiguities that a series of interpreters have used to demonstrate the indeterminacy of biblical (and other) texts in general. Edward Greenstein seized on Leviticus 10:1–5 as a "model of undecidability" for his article on "Deconstruction and Biblical Narrative." Using intertextual allusions to the similar story in 2 Samuel 6:1–8 to amplify his theme, Greenstein drew both literary and theological conclusions: "It is not that we can never produce a reading. We can never produce a certain, stable, or impregnable meaning" and "YHWH breaks up the orderliness [of the ritual instructions] to show he is above/beyond the cultic order."[13] Similar means and goals but different intertextual comparisons were employed by Timothy Beal and Tod Linafelt, who pointed

[9] Milgrom, *Leviticus,* 1:550–3.
[10] Daniel E. Fleming, "The Biblical Tradition of Anointing Priests," *JBL* 117 (1998): 401–14.
[11] See note 6.
[12] Modern interpreters who have explored these allusions include R. Gradwohl, "Das 'fremde Feuer' von Nadab und Abihu," *ZAW* 75 (1963): 288–96, and Damrosch, "Leviticus," 70–2.
[13] Edward L. Greenstein, "Deconstruction and Biblical Narrative," *Prooftexts* 9 (1989): 43–71 [56, 62, 64].

to linguistic echoes of child sacrifice in Leviticus 10,[14] and by Benjamin Sommer, who pointed to stories of troubled beginnings throughout the Hebrew Bible.[15] Bryan Bibb used the story as an example of the general problem in biblical narratives of ambiguous gaps that cannot be filled.[16]

Thus unusual features of Leviticus 8–10 – as narrative in a book of instructions, as ritual descriptions rather than prescriptions, as curt ambiguities surrounded by detailed descriptions – have generated a broad range of interpretive approaches. What can rhetorical analysis add to these? Rhetorical analysis focuses first on the text of Leviticus 8–10, as do the self-consciously postmodern interpreters, rather than the situations and rituals it portrays. Its attention to persuasion, however, leads it immediately to ask, "Who is trying to persuade whom of what?" – that is, "Who is being addressed?" "Who is addressing them?" and "Why?"[17]

From such a rhetorical perspective on persuasion, the "meaning" of the text derives from its use in a particular relationship, and the text has no meaning apart from such a relationship. Its meaning necessarily changes whenever the parties to the relationship change: thus in Late Antiquity, Philo used Leviticus 10 to depict heavenly rewards for exemplary worship, early Christians used it to foreshadow the Christian church, and a variety of Jewish and Christian interpreters used it as an object lesson against drunkenness.[18] Moreover, the rhetorical

---

[14] Timothy K. Beal and Tod Linafelt, "Sifting for Cinders: Strange Fire in Leviticus 10:1–5," *Semeia* 69/70 (1995): 19–32.

[15] Benjamin D. Sommer, "Expulsion as Initiation: Displacement, Divine Presence, and Divine Exile in the Torah," in *Beginning/Again: Toward a Hermeneutics of Jewish Texts* (ed. Aryeh Cohen and Shaul Magid; New York & London: Seven Bridges, 2001), 23–48.

[16] Bryan D. Bibb, "Nadab and Abihu Attempt to Fill a Gap: Law and Narrative in Leviticus 10.1–7," *JSOT* 96 (2001): 83–99.

[17] For more discussion of persuasion and audience, see Chapter 2 in this book, and Burke, *Rhetoric of Motives*, 20–38, 49–52; Patrick and Scult, *Rhetoric and Biblical Interpretation*, 104.

[18] For summaries and anthologies of ancient interpretations of these chapters, see Robert Kirschner, "The Rabbinic and Philonic Exegesis of the Nadab and Abihu Incident,"

function of a text may not be simply a matter of its linguistic *meaning*. Particular phrases, sentences, and even stories may be used persuasively more for the connotations that an audience can be expected to associate with them than for their specific contents. For example, allusion to or quotation of the *Kadesh*, the traditional Jewish prayer for the dead, or in some Christian circles the Twenty-third Psalm, can be used to bring to mind ideas of mourning and comfort that long usage in funereal situations have associated with these texts, more than what they actually say.

A rhetorical focus on persuasion points out that the function and meaning of texts change as their readers change and as those readers reconceive the identity of the persons addressing them through those texts. This is nowhere more true than in the interpretation of the Bible, whose message has been reconfigured as addressed to a huge variety of communities and individuals in their particular and distinct situations. To explain the unique form and contents of a particular text, however, one must try to reconstruct what rhetorical relationship its *authors* intended for it: one needs to determine who they were, who they were trying to persuade, and of what, so as to figure out why they shaped the text in this way. Such work is necessarily speculative (and never definitive, as deconstructionists note) for any text, because one cannot know an author's intentions with any certainty. It is even more difficult when, as is the case with most biblical texts, we do not know who the authors and original addressees were, and we suspect that more than one person played a role in writing the texts. Nevertheless, because the text's persuasive function appears only in the context of that speaker/author and hearer/reader relationship, estimating their identities is essential and basic work in order to read any text as a *communication* between people, that is, as persuasive rhetoric. Since

JQR 73 (1983): 375–93; James L. Kugel, *Traditions of the Bible: A Guide to the Bible as It Was at the Start of the Common Era* (Cambridge, MA: Harvard University Press, 1998), 744–7; Joseph T. Lienhard, *Exodus, Leviticus, Numbers, Deuteronomy* (Ancient Christian Commentary on Scripture, Old Testament 3; Downers Grove, IL: InterVarsity, 2001), 172–5; and my discussion in Chapter 7.

biblical texts contain overt evidence of an intention to communicate and persuade, and since they are commonly read that way within the religious traditions that cherish them as scripture, rhetorical analysis proves necessary for understanding both their original and later roles.

The Rhetoric of Leviticus 8–10

In premodern literature, rhetorical effects are produced more by sound than by sight. Readers read texts aloud, even to themselves, and people encountered the contents of texts primarily by hearing them read aloud. Even experts who had mastered particular texts (such as the ancient rabbis) interpreted them from memory rather than by rereading physical manuscripts. Thus oral recitation and aural reception would have been the media by which authors expected their works to be received and for which they shaped them.[19] Rhetorical analysis of premodern texts must therefore pay particular attention to those features designed to affect aural reception, such as refrains, wordplays, sudden juxtapositions, and so forth.

In Leviticus 8–10, the refrain *ka'ăšer tsiwwāh YHWH*, "as YHWH commanded," sounds thirteen times (8:4, 5, 9, 13, 17, 21, 29, 34, 36; 9:6, 7, 10; 10:15) and the same idea in different words or attributed to Moses' command appears nine times more (8:31, 35; 9:5, 21; 10:5, 7, 11, 13, 18). This drumbeat of obedience to divine commandments gives

---

[19] Orality studies has been a growing field for more than a generation now. For a survey of how texts were used orally and aurally in premodern and even early modern cultures, see William A. Graham, *Beyond the Written Word: Oral Aspects of Scripture in the History of Religion* (Cambridge: Cambridge University Press, 1987), esp. 30–48. Studies of orality in ancient Israel have divided between those who find clear development from greater orality to greater literacy (e.g., Susan Niditch, *Oral World and Written Word: Ancient Israelite Literature* [Louisville: Westminster John Knox, 1996]; William Schniedewind, *How the Bible Became a Book* [Cambridge: Cambridge University Press, 2004]); and those like myself who find orality/aurality and textuality intertwined in almost all levels of the biblical tradition (see Watts, *Reading Law*, 15–31, and especially the comprehensive survey by David Carr, *Writing on the Tablet of the Heart*).

the chapters their distinctive flavor and recalls immediately the similar emphasis in Exodus 35–40, which recount Moses' completion of the tabernacle and its contents in accordance with the instructions from God in Exodus 25–31. In the same way, the refrain in Leviticus 8 points back to the instructions for clothing and consecrating the priests in Exodus 29, a reference reinforced by the reuse of much of that chapter's language here. In Leviticus 9 it points to the instructions for conducting the sacrificial service in Leviticus 1–7. Thus the rhetorical effect of the refrain is to unify Leviticus 8–10 under a single thematic emphasis and to connect it to the preceding materials.

These references have been explored by many interpreters. Fewer, however, have noted the refrain's unifying effect on Leviticus 8–10. Gordon Wenham did, because more than most readers he tried to describe the literary effects of the chapters.[20] Milgrom and Gorman also drew attention to the refrain's role in chapter 8 because they discerned a sevenfold repetition that seemed to echo similar patterns in Exodus 39 and 40.[21] Unfortunately, the sevenfold pattern depends on a questionable structural analysis of the chapter divided into seven parts, because the refrain actually occurs nine times in Leviticus 8.

[20] Gordon J. Wenham, *The Book Leviticus* (NICOT; Grand Rapids, MI: Eerdmans, 1979), 130–5.

[21] Milgrom, *Leviticus*, 1:542–3, who drew implications for the history of the chapter's composition from this observation; Gorman, *Ideology of Ritual*, 49–50, who found in it a theological parallel with God's creation of the world in seven speech acts. Helmut Utzschneider (*Das Heiligtum und das Gesetz: Studien zur Bedeutung der Sinaitischen Heiligtumstexte (Ex 25–40; Lev 8–9)* [OBO 77; Freiburg: Universitätsverlag / Göttingen: Vandenhoeck & Ruprecht, 1988], 215) provided a comparative analysis of this phrase throughout P, in which he discerned three distinct uses: as an introductory formula (Exod 25:8; 31:6; 35:1, 4, 10; 36:1, 5; 39:1; 40:16), a concluding formula (Exod 27:8; 31:11; 35:29; 38:22; 39:32, 42–43; Lev 8:36), and as a refrain (Exodus 39, 40, Leviticus 8). Like Milgrom and Gorman, however, he ignored the reach of the refrain into Leviticus 9 and 10. In contrast, Karen Eliasen argued for treating the chapters together because of the cumulative effect of the ritual on Aaron's internal experience ("Getting a Feel for a Concept," 3). Her focus on psychological effect advanced the discussion, but I suggest that it is the story's effect not on Aaron but on the readers/hearers that unifies the three chapters.

A rhetorical analysis of this ancient text should be less interested in how a literary structure appears to the eye than in how a text sounds to the ear and might impact the minds and emotions of a listening audience. In that setting, the exact number of refrains likely has less significance than the emphasis on faithful compliance conveyed by their frequent repetition. Though the plot of Leviticus 8–10 emphasizes inauguration or initiation rituals, repeating "as YHWH commanded" over and over again turns it into a story about the ritual implementation of previously given instructions.[22]

The thematic emphasis provided by the refrain suggests looking for parallels in ancient texts other than just the descriptive or prescriptive ritual texts usually employed for such comparisons. Implementation of previously given instructions is not an emphasis in the descriptive rituals analyzed by Levine or the Emar ritual of the high priestesses' installation discussed by Fleming and Klingbeil.[23] It is found rather in royal inscriptions commemorating a king's achievements or in royal prayers appealing for divine aid, where kings assert their faithfulness by claiming complete adherence to divine instructions. Thus the prayers of a Hittite king claim that "Whatever I, My Majesty, discover now in the written records, I will carry out. When I consult a venerable old man, [as] they remember [each(?)] requirement and report it, thus I shall carry it out."[24] Milgrom pointed to the same concern in an inscription of the Babylonian king, Samsuiluna, which like Exodus-Leviticus presents a detailed divine command to build a temple followed by the story of its fulfillment that echoes the words of the commandment.

---

[22] Levine, "Descriptive Tabernacle Texts," 310; also Gerstenberger (*Leviticus*, 100): "[The authors] are not in the least oriented toward any possible sequence of events, neither in the Sinai period nor at the end of the sixth century, when the temple was rededicated. They are utterly fixed on the written model of the proclamation of Yahweh's will before them, one composed either by others or by themselves."

[23] See notes 6, 8, and 10.

[24] *CTH* 382, translated by Itamar Singer, *Hittite Prayers* (WAW 11; Atlanta: SBL, 2002), 83. See also the Second Plague Prayer of Mursili, §§3–6 (*CTH* 387.II), translated by Singer, *Hittite Prayers*, 58–9.

Samsuiluna claims twice to have fulfilled the god's orders in every respect.[25]

Leviticus 8–10 use the theme of compliance with divine instructions much more often to create a repetitive refrain that drums in its message.[26] Furthermore, the length and detail of Leviticus 8–10's ritual descriptions find better parallels in the prescriptive and descriptive ritual texts of the ancient Near East than in royal prayers and inscriptions. Thus, as we discovered in the ritual instructions of Leviticus 1–7 (see Chapter 2 of this book), the writers of the ritual narratives of Leviticus 8–10 seem to have combined a framework drawn from royal genres with the detailed contents typical of ritual texts. Both have been modified and elaborated to reflect their particular message: it is not a king but rather Moses and the priests, and ultimately all Israel in its role of spectator, who take responsibility for fulfilling the instructions, and the descriptions of the rituals have been worded to echo the instructions (as in Samsuiluna's inscription) even while presenting many ritual details (like Emar 369). Levine then was right to claim that the biblical texts reflect a further development from ancient Near Eastern genres, but the range of genres they evoke is broader than he suspected.

Repetitive refrains lead an audience to expect their exact repetition. Changing or reversing the refrain can then produce a shock that reemphasizes the theme of the refrain through its contradiction. Leviticus, 8–10 produces this effect when, after two chapters of repeating *ka'ăšer tsiwwāh YHWH*, "as YHWH had commanded," 10:1 announces that Nadab and Abihu did *'ăšer lō' tsiwwāh*, "what had *not* been commanded." The intrusion of the negative, *lō'*, "not," in the familiar refrain comes like a thunderclap, an aural shock to a listening audience

---

[25] The Samsuiluna B bilingual (Sumerian-Akkadian) inscription, translated and analyzed by Milgrom, *Leviticus*, 1:550–3.

[26] On the use of repetitive refrains for rhetorical emphasis, see Chapter 2 in this book, and Watts, *Reading Law*, 68–74.

just as YHWH's consuming fire presented a visual shock to the watching Israelites in the story. The endless attempt by interpreters to explain what Nadab and Abihu did wrong is pointless. The story says it explicitly – they did not follow instructions. That phrase qualifies the words "strange fire" to explain that the absence of a divine mandate makes the fire "strange" or "foreign." In the context of twenty-two repetitions of the refrain of compliance with divine instruction, that is quite enough to explain the fatal consequences.[27]

Most interpreters have themselves felt the shock of the inversion so strongly that they separated Leviticus 10 from what comes before it as a separate episode dealing with different issues, or even dealing with the issue of disruption and separation itself, in the case of the deconstructionist interpretations cited earlier. That interpretive move, however, ignores the fact that Leviticus 10 reestablishes the theme of compliance with divine instructions as it progresses. It does so gradually, beginning with two statements of compliance with "the word of Moses" (10:5, 7). Then, breaking every precedent in the Pentateuch up to this point, YHWH addresses Aaron individually and commands him and his sons to teach YHWH's laws to the Israelites (10:9–11). After that, the chapter reasserts active compliance with the commandments of Moses (10:13) and of YHWH (10:15). Thus the rhetoric of Leviticus 8–10 builds the theme of compliance with divine commandments through constant repetition, then emphasizes it with a single example of noncompliance and its disastrous consequences before reasserting the theme in the rest of chapter 10. Of all the commentators, Wenham

[27] Interpreters have, of course, noticed that the noncompliance phrase modifies the description of the fire as strange, but they have usually felt this to be an inadequate explanation. Bibb ("Nadab and Abihu Attempt to Fill a Gap," 87–8), for example, considered whether the "strange fire" might be clarified by "which he had not commanded them," but he argued that this phrase is also vague and differs from other formulas of disobedience, such as Lev 26:14–16. Bibb failed to notice that the positive version of this formula is pervasive throughout Leviticus 8–10, and the negative statement in 10:1 has been formulated precisely to invert it.

depicted the rhetorical drift of the three chapters best:

> Practically every verse in ch. 8 is a quotation or adaptation of commands first given in Exod. 29. In chap. 9, we find rather freer summaries of the laws on sacrifice in Leviticus. 1–7. In this way, Moses' strict adherence to God's declared will is emphasized. . . . Chapter 10 makes plain that the converse is also true. The precise nature of Nadab and Abihu's offense is obscure, save that their action was such as the Lord "had not commanded them." But this transgression was enough to turn the fire of blessing (9:24) into the fire of judgment (10:2). . . . Various features in the rest of ch. 10 recall ideas from the previous two . . . but only slowly does the structure of the narrative revert to the patterns found in chs. 8–9. Like ch. 8, ch. 10 (vv 12–19) ends with instructions about eating the sacrificial meat in a holy place. The old pattern has reappeared, giving the reader a feeling of security and normality, reinforced by the closing remark: "Moses was satisfied" (v. 20).[28]

Wenham did not ask, however, why this rhetoric of compliance should be asserted so strongly in Leviticus 8–10. This brings us back to the central question of rhetorical analysis: who was trying to persuade whom of what by using the refrain of compliance with divine instructions? The story shows the initiation of the priests and the tabernacle by Moses and the inauguration of the tabernacle service by Aaron. The chapters avoid the generic term for "priests" in favor of the genealogically specific phrase, "Aaron and his sons."[29] Clearly, they aim to legitimize the Aaronide priesthood, as many interpreters have observed.[30]

---

[28] Wenham, *Leviticus*, 131, 134–5.

[29] See René Péter-Contesse, "Le Sacerdoce," in *The Book of Leviticus: Composition and Reception* (ed. Rolf Rendtorff and Robert Kugler; VTSup 93; Leiden: Brill, 2003), 189–206, who observed that the word *kōhēn*, "priest," appears 194 times in Leviticus, but never in Leviticus 8–10, where "Aaron" or "Aaron and his sons" are referred to 33 times instead (189).

[30] E.g., N. H. Snaith, *Leviticus and Numbers* (New Century Bible; London: Nelson, 1967), 75; Philip J. Budd, *Leviticus* (New Century Bible; Grand Rapids: Eerdmans, 1996), 129–30; Gerstenberger, *Leviticus*, 105, 113; Walter Kornfeld, *Levitikus* (Die Neue Echter Bibel; Würzberg: Echter, 1983), 35.

It has also been common to assume that the chapters validate the services of the Jerusalem temple as well.[31] The chapters describe a unique event, however, not the regular temple service. Their focus then is not on cult so much as on the priests themselves, and in this they are emphatic. Whereas the refrain of compliance in Exodus 35–40 applies to a long-gone tabernacle and could be applied to Jerusalem's cult only by interpretive derivation, the Aaronide priesthood became or remained a potent religio-political force in Second Temple Judaism. Its scions served to legitimate the temples at Mt. Gerizim and Leontopolis as well as at Jerusalem. Throughout this period, the high priests wore the sacred garments with which Moses clothed Aaron (Exod 28; 39; Lev 8:6–9) and that conveyed such authority that Roman governors insisted on controlling their use.[32] Thus the Torah grounds the legitimacy of the Aaronide priests in divine instructions from Mt. Sinai far more explicitly and repeatedly than it does the Jerusalem temple.[33]

[31] E.g., Gerstenberger, *Leviticus*, 100: Leviticus 8's "purpose is to demonstrate that the sacrificial worship service in the temple of Jerusalem already familiar to its contemporaries was established at Sinai and still proceeds according to the same pattern."

[32] Josephus, *Ant.* 15.402–8, 19.93, 20.6–16. Josephus, Philo, the Letter of Aristeas and Pseudo-Philo give extensive descriptions of the priestly garments, which attest not only to the fascination they aroused but also to the rhetorical function of literary descriptions in furthering the priesthood's mystique. That is also the purpose of the original descriptions in Exodus and Leviticus. For a discussion of the significance of the priestly garments in the Second Temple and rabbinic periods, see Michael D. Swartz, "The Semiotics of the Priestly Vestments in Ancient Judaism," in *Sacrifice in Religious Experience* (ed. Albert I. Baumgarten; Numen 93; Leiden: Brill, 2002), 57–80.

[33] Scholars' preoccupation with the issue of cultic centralization in Jerusalem shows that Deuteronomy has been allowed to determine the agenda for historical inquiry much more than the Priestly source, so much so that there has been an enduring debate about whether P presupposes cult centralization. The fact that P leaves it ambiguous should be taken as an indication that centralization was not a major concern for priestly writers. That impression is reinforced by the cultic history of the Second Temple period, when Aaronide priests in fact inaugurated YHWH temples in at least two locations outside Jerusalem (Mt. Gerizim in Samaria and Leontopolis in Egypt). 1 Chronicles is also unconcerned with cult centralization, going so far as to depict David as maintaining simultaneous cults of the ark in Jerusalem and the tabernacle in Gibeon (1 Chr 16:37–42), until they are united in Jerusalem at the dedication of Solomon's temple (1 Kgs 8:4; 2 Chr 5:5). Even if this tradition is a product of the

Though it is true that Leviticus 8 narrates the initiation of the tabernacle and the anointing of its altar in parallel with the initiation and
anointing of the priests,[34] the latter receives more attention in the text
and created a direct continuity with later cultic officials, unlike the
implicit analogy between tabernacle and temple.

Leviticus 8–10 forms the center of the Pentateuch's argument for
Aaronide legitimacy and authority. The scholarly consensus is no
doubt correct in attributing Leviticus and many other key portions
of the Pentateuch to priestly writers (P). We can conclude then that
Leviticus 8–10 was written to help Aaronide priests convince the rest
of Israel (other priestly classes such as the Levites as well as nonpriestly
Jews) to accept their authority over the conduct of temple offerings
and over the interpretation of the Torah as well. We know that this
claim to authority succeeded, at least in the Second Temple period and
perhaps earlier (see Chapter 7).

Though Leviticus 8–9 obviously supports the claims of the Aaronide
priesthood to a monopoly over Israel's cult, most interpreters have
thought that Leviticus 10:1–3 qualifies that endorsement. The death of
the high priest's oldest sons by divine fire must, in the view of many
commentators from antiquity to the present, reflect a scathing criticism of those individuals' actions and, in the view of many modern
historians, of the priestly families they represented. Interpreters oriented more to literary and theological themes than historical issues
have emphasized this story's radical contradiction of what precedes
it. They have connected it thematically to other biblical stories of
erring sons or sudden divine outbreaks or bungled beginnings. These
interpretations have struggled, however, to understand the nature of
Nadab and Abihu's offence, as well as the relationship of the story to
the authorization of priestly duties in 10:8–11 and the very different

Chronicler's wish to excuse Solomon's worship at Gibeon as many commentators have
maintained, the writer's disinterest in the geographic centralization of the YHWH
cult is nevertheless notable.

[34] Levine, *Leviticus*, 48.

outcome of another story of (apparent) priestly malpractice at the end of the chapter. Deconstructionist critics have emphasized these ambiguities to illustrate the indeterminacy of this text, but since in theory such indeterminacy is a feature of all texts, this approach does not further our understanding of the distinctiveness of Leviticus 10:1–3 very much.

The fact that Leviticus 10:1 characterized Nadab and Abihu's actions with a reversal of the common refrain from chapters 8–9 and that the rest of Leviticus 10 gradually reestablishes the theme of compliance with divine directives, restating the refrain itself in verse 15, indicates that chapter 10 should be interpreted in thematic continuity with the previous two chapters rather than in contrast to them. The story in Leviticus 10:1–3 does not introduce a new theme or subject, but rather the momentary reversal of the theme of compliance with divine instructions that the following verses then reinstate. The writers no doubt meant the story to be shocking: they not only negate the refrain but also follow it with a description of YHWH's fiery outbreak (10:2) using exactly the same words as those used in 9:24: "fire came out from before YHWH and consumed. . . ." The shocking contrast posed by this event is reinforced by the continuity between chapters in the terminology and phrasing of both vv 1 and 2. This shows that the theme remains the same as before: the ritual importance of following instructions.

Many interpreters have recognized the role of the story as an object lesson telling priests to perform their duties with care, but they have nevertheless viewed it as a criticism of priestly performance as well.[35] I disagree. Attention to the likely rhetorical impact of this story on the intended audience in ancient Israel suggests that it would have strengthened the legitimation of the Aaronide priests in Leviticus 8–10,

[35] Noth, *Leviticus*, 84; Snaith, *Leviticus and Numbers*, 75; John C. Laughlin, "The 'Strange Fire' of Nadab and Abihu," *JBL* 95 (1976): 559–65 [562]; Peretz Segal, "The Divine Verdict of Leviticus 10:3," *VT* 39 (1989): 91–95; Levine, *Leviticus*, 58; Lester L. Grabbe, *Leviticus* (Old Testament Guides; Sheffield: Sheffield Academic Press, 1993), 221; Walter J. Houston, "Tragedy in the Courts of the Lord: A Socio-Literary Reading of the Death of Nadab and Abihu," *JSOT* 90 (2000): 31–9 [38–9].

rather than undermining it.[36] This story explicitly emphasizes how necessary it is for priests to comply with the divine instructions through Moses, that is, with Torah. The automatic cost of noncompliance illustrated by 10:1–2 shows not only that the priests must comply (the usual moral drawn), but also implies that their continued survival shows that they usually do comply. This kind of incident, by its very rarity, reinforces an impression of the diligence and competence of the Aaronide priests. Modern corporate rhetoric would have suggested posting a sign in the Temple to make this point: "Serviced by the House of Aaron, injury-free for 310,250 days."

The cryptic oracle reported by Moses in verse 3 wraps priestly responsibility and danger in the mystique of divine presence. The verse reads, "Moses said to Aaron, 'This is what YHWH said: "I will be sanctified by those approaching me, and I will be glorified before all people."'" Interpreters have struggled to understand the meaning of this oracle and its role in this context. When did God say this? (It does not appear elsewhere in the Bible.) How do Nadab and Abihu's deaths "sanctify" and "glorify" YHWH?[37] Inquiries into the verse's precise

---

[36] Christophe Nihan reached a similar conclusion, that the story served to justify the monopoly of the priests, and especially the high priest, over incense offerings ("The Death of Nadab and Abihu and the Priestly Legislation on Perfume Offering: Leviticus 10 in the Context of the Final Editing of Leviticus," conference paper, Biblical Law Section of the Society of Biblical Literature Annual Meeting, 2003; online at http://www.law2.byu.edu/Biblical_Law/annual_meeting.htm).

[37] Philo and Rashi both took the verse to indicate that Nadab and Abihu had been translated to heaven as a reward for their exemplary service, rather than as punishment for some ritual mistake (Kirschner, "Rabbinic and Philonic Exegesis," 390–2). Most moderns, however, along with many ancient interpreters, have understood the incident negatively or ambiguously. Segal repointed the verb "approach" to convey a more antagonistic sentiment ("Divine Verdict," 91–5). Segal also pointed to a similar theme in Ezek 28:22 and Milgrom noted a wider biblical theme of divine glorification through the punishment of infractions by those closest to the divine presence (*Leviticus*, 1:601–4). Bibb suggested that since their punishing deaths serve to sanctify YHWH, "It seems that the deaths of these two priests have not been in vain after all" ("Nadab and Abihu," 90). Nihan explained the verse's ambiguity by arguing that Lev 10:3 summarizes the theology of H (as in 22:32) and P, and is intended to mediate between the two ("Death of Nadab and Abihu," 3).

meaning usually fail to consider its rhetorical impact. In antiquity, oracles were famous (or infamous) for their ambiguity, which served to strengthen their appeal and impact. We should therefore expect that verse 3's ambiguity is intentional, especially since its rhetorical effect is not hard to discern. "Those approaching me" may refer to the priests in general, who legitimately approach the inner sanctum as part of their duties, or it may refer to illegitimate trespass on the deity's sanctum, or both. YHWH may feel honored by their loyal service, or offended by their presumption, or both. The oracle's ambiguity sums up perfectly the narrative context in which the deity requires specific services from the priests that place them in mortal danger from that same deity. Whatever theological confusion may result from this, the rhetorical effect of enhancing the mystique of priestly service is quite clear and is enough to explain the contents and placement of this verse.

In its own way, the story of verses 1–2 demonstrates through the example of Nadab and Abihu that the priests do a dangerous job and almost always do it well. The first nine chapters of Leviticus as a whole argue for the necessity of the priests' service; now 10:1–3 shows that it is also a dangerous job. Juxtaposing the danger of priestly work with the necessity of the Aaronides' monopoly produces a strong argument for the legitimacy of their claims and privileges. In essence, the message from the Aaronide priests to the Israelite congregation was: "We do a dangerous but necessary job, and the rarity of fatalities shows that we do it well! So don't begrudge us its perks!"[38]

---

[38] Other interpreters have summarized the message in a similar way: Milgrom noted the comments of ancient and medieval interpreters that "if such [things happen] to his intimates, others will all the more so have cause to fear" (*Leviticus*, 1:603, citing Bekhor Shor and *b. Zebah*, 115b); similarly, Gorman: "The priests are ritually located in a dangerous place and are called to undertake dangerous activity!" (*Leviticus*, 54); and Houston: "Aaron did not himself seek this dangerous honour, but had it thrust on him as an offer he could not refuse" ("Tragedy," 34). Gorman and Houston reproduced the biblical rhetoric accurately but did not notice its purpose in buttressing the institutional claims of the priestly writers.

The story, nevertheless, does raise a practical problem for Israel's priests. The story of Nadab and Abihu, precisely by not faulting them for intentional malpractice but only for going beyond their explicit instructions, raises the issue of interpretation. Instructions, even the most detailed, require interpretation. No finite set of instructions can anticipate every eventuality or give completely unambiguous directions. An institution that derives its legitimacy and operating procedures from a public oral tradition or text, as the Pentateuch describes the tabernacle and its priesthood as doing, requires procedures for adjudicating interpretive ambiguities and conflicts, all the more so when the cost of mistakes can be fatal. Who can safely wield this interpretive authority?

Leviticus 10:9–11, a divine speech directly to Aaron, grants that authority to the high priest. It begins by enjoining the priests to abstain from alcohol when serving in the sanctuary (10:9). Though interpreters have long struggled to understand why that command should appear here, the emphasis of the following verses on the priests' teaching and diagnostic roles suggests that it is motivated by their need for clear mental faculties. YHWH makes the priests responsible for distinguishing between what is holy and what is common, between what is clean and what is unclean, and for teaching the Torah to the people of Israel (10:10–11). This means that the high priest is granted, among other things, the right to determine correct ritual procedures as well as to carry them out with the other priests. Leviticus 10 emphasizes the dramatic nature of this grant of interpretive authority by casting it as direct divine speech to Aaron by himself, something that otherwise occurs only in Numbers 18.[39] It also sets the speech at the center of a concentric structure (chiasm), consisting of stories of priestly practice on the outer frame (vv 1–3, 16–20) and an inner frame of instructions

---

[39] Rashi suggested that Aaron was rewarded for his obedient response after his sons' death by receiving the divine word directly to him. Eliasen observed that Numbers 18 is also concerned with the priestly vocation ("Aaron's War Within," 84).

from Moses (vv 4–7, 12–15).⁴⁰ The divine grant of interpretive and teaching authority to Aaron thus becomes the literal center and key to the chapter.

Aaron's new power is then demonstrated in the argument at the end of the chapter, when Moses yields to Aaron's interpretation. Commentators have again been puzzled by the text's ambiguity, which does not make clear the nature of the controversy.⁴¹ I suggest that just as at the beginning of the chapter the text's ambiguity indicates that the authors' interests lie elsewhere. The writers of Leviticus 10 did not intend to decide a particular issue of ritual practice by telling this story but instead wanted to demonstrate Aaron's newly granted authority in action. While prior to receiving the divine edict, Aaron was silent in the face of his sons' deaths (10:3),⁴² now Aaron takes it upon himself to respond to Moses' accusation against his remaining sons. Whatever the exact details of the issue may be, it is clear that the controversy concerns how to deal with sanctified meat from the altar. In the language of 10:10, it involves a discriminating judgment about "what is holy" and the levels of holiness, and how they should be dealt with in the specific context of the extraordinary events of that day. Thus it involves exactly the kind of judgment that YHWH assigned Aaron to make. This Aaron now does. The fact that his decision appeared "good in Moses' eyes" (10:20) may have less to do with the specifics of his reasoning than with the fact that Aaron here assumes this high

---

⁴⁰ Hartley, *Leviticus*, 129; T. Staubli, *Die Bücher Levitikus, Numeri* (NSKAT 3; Stuttgart: Kohlhammer, 1996), 85; Nihan, "Death of Nadab and Abihu," 2.

⁴¹ For an exhaustive discussion, see Milgrom, *Leviticus*, 1:635–40.

⁴² Levine ("Silence, Sound and the Phenomenology of Mourning in Biblical Israel," *JANES* 22 [1993]: 89–106), followed by Karen Eliasen ("Aaron's War Within," 85), argued that Aaron was not silent (Lev 10:3) but rather in mourning, deriving the verb from a second root suggesting loud grief, "wailing." The parallel story at the end of the chapter, however, seems to present a deliberate contrast to this one with Aaron's verbal response to Moses' speech. Of course, since both meanings work well in this context, we should probably reckon with intentional double-meaning, a deliberate pun that plays on both the meanings "mourn" and "quiet."

priestly role and therefore his decision (*ex cathedra* as it were) may not be gainsaid. The story validates Aaron's hermeneutical authority with Moses' approval.

This story (10:16–20) gives one final twist to the theme of compliance with divine instructions that has reverberated throughout Leviticus 8–10. After the negation of the compliance refrain in 10:1 and then its gradual reassertion over the next fourteen verses, 10:15 marks its full reestablishment with the refrain "as YHWH commanded," appearing here for the last time in chapters 8–10. Moses' criticism of Aaron's sons, however, asserts the theme again in a variant form that he has used three times before, *ka'ăšer tsiwwêtî,* "as I commanded" or "as I was commanded" (10:18; cf. 8:31, 35; 10:13).[43] This time, however, Aaron contests the issue with Moses by invoking his newly granted authority to discriminate levels of holiness. His decision cites what would be "good in YHWH's eyes" (10:19) on this particular day, perhaps an allusion to the spirit of the law rather than its letter. In this exchange, Moses remains the mediator of the law to Israel, but Aaron assumes the role of authoritative interpreter of that law, and Moses yields to his authority.[44] Leviticus 11:1 reinforces the high priest's new status

---

[43] The verb is pointed piel, active, "as I commanded," in 8:31 and 10:18, but pual, passive, "as I was commanded" in 8:35 and 10:13. The difference is merely a matter of the vowel points added to the original Hebrew consonants, and so is quite open to being revised, as some dictionaries and translations do to make 8:31 (*BHS, HAL,* NAB, NRSV) and sometimes even 10:18 (NAB) passive. See Milgrom, *Leviticus,* 1:535, 626, and Hartley, *Leviticus,* 108.

[44] Eliasen observed correctly that "By the end of Lev 10 . . . Aaron has reached a personal place of ritual authority where Moses has not accompanied him. . . . Aaron has now discerned and acted out of his own divine empowerment" ("Getting a Feel for a Concept," 7). I would only challenge the appropriateness of the word "personal" for this development. Rather than a rhetoric of private psychological and ritual experience that Eliasen finds here, the rhetoric of Leviticus 10 is one of public recognition and honor for an individual who as the priest's ancestor and as the first high priest represents a socio-religious class and institution. The same criticism may be applied to the observations of Damrosch ("Leviticus," 70–71), who also found here a personal focus on Aaron and his lost sons. My approach to rhetoric and ritual lies closer to that of Roy Rappaport, who, referring to ritual, noted: "It is the visible, explicit, public act of acceptance, and not the invisible, ambiguous, private sentiment, which is socially

by depicting Aaron as receiving the regulations for clean and unclean animals alongside Moses. Leviticus 10, then, returns to the priests, and especially the high priest, some of the interpretive control over the cult that they lost through the publication of Torah.[45] Though now all Israel can hear and (if they have the skills and access) read Moses' rules for the cult, that Torah itself grants the high priest the ultimate authority to adjudicate its internal ambiguities.

Narrative ambiguity in Leviticus 10 therefore serves rhetorical purposes. In raising the issue of the necessity of interpreting even the most detailed instructions, the chapter does anticipate a deconstructionist claim about the undecidability of texts. It raises the problem of ambiguity, however, not to discuss epistemology like a deconstructionist but rather to argue more persuasively for the priests' interpretive authority. By combining a story that illustrates the dangers posed by interpretive ambiguity with a story that illustrates the high priest's divinely ordained power to settle such ambiguities and forestall their dangers, the chapter enhances the mystique of the priestly office. To explain exactly why Nadab and Abihu's incense offering was wrong or exactly how Aaron reasoned regarding the eating of the sin offering would spoil the mystery of priestly service. The message from the priests to

and morally binding" (*Ritual and Religion in the Making of Humanity* [Cambridge: Cambridge University Press, 1999], 122).

[45] The amelioration of priestly authority by the publication of the Torah is described in Chapter 2 of this book, and also in a different way in Watts, *Reading Law*, 116–21. The conclusion that Leviticus 10 protects the priests' interpretive authority is at odds with that of many interpreters who think the post-exilic priesthood did not exert teaching authority; e.g., Gerstenberger: "This assignment of Torah instruction to the priests is rather a means of subordinating the priestly class to the supervision of Moses. At least this is how Lev 10:11 is to be understood. This also relativizes Yahweh's unique address to Aaron in the introduction to the section (v. 8). In the end, Yahweh's instructions refer to the commandments given through Moses, and thus subject the priesthood to the supervision of the office of scribe, an office closer to the congregation itself" (*Leviticus*, 125). To reach this conclusion, Gerstenberger must downplay Ezra's identity as priest. This approach dichotomizes the roles of scribes vis-à-vis priests in a way not justified by the evidence from any period in Israel's history prior to the late Second Temple, and the juxtaposition may be questioned even then.

Israel is that "it is enough for you to know that our job is dangerous but God has given us the ability to handle it." Ambiguity is used at both ends of Leviticus 10 for persuasive effect.

To summarize this analysis of the internal rhetoric of Leviticus 8–10: the chapters argue for the authority of the Aaronide priests over Israel's worship practices by narrating their initiation by Moses and their conduct of the cult. They emphasize repeatedly that this was all done in perfect fulfillment of the divine instructions that appear in earlier parts of Exodus and Leviticus. The story of Nadab and Abihu's death illustrates the danger of priestly service and why such compliance with the instructions is necessary. Chapter 10 then presents YHWH as investing Aaron and his successors with the authority to adjudicate ambiguous cases, and ends by showing him doing so. Moses' acceptance of the high priest's ruling clinches the argument for the priest's monopoly over the cult and over decisions regarding its performance.

Parallels and Intertexts of Leviticus 8–10

Interpreters have sought to illuminate the meaning of Leviticus 8–10 by reference to similar stories in other parts of the Hebrew Bible. Some parallel certain themes in these chapters, and others are linked by explicit references to them or implicit allusions. Rhetorical comparison of these stories with Leviticus 8–10 will further specify the persuasive methods and goals that motivated these chapters. Before considering those specific connections, however, it will be worthwhile to compare the rhetoric of Leviticus 8–10 with that of other stories about cult initiations in general.

Cult Initiation Stories

Cult initiation stories appear in several places in the Hebrew Bible, and also in various kinds of sources from other ancient Near Eastern cultures. Comparing these accounts shows that the diversity of their contents clearly reflects the different interests of their writers as much as or more than different ritual practices.[46]

The story of David's installation of the ark of the covenant in Jerusalem appears in both 2 Samuel and 1 Chronicles. Both accounts describe first a ritual disaster in which one man, Uzzah, touches the ark to stabilize it and gets struck dead by YHWH. David then waits three months before trying again. The account in 2 Samuel 6:12–23 focuses on ritual: because a ritual mistake resulted in aborting the initial attempt to move the ark (6:6–10), the second attempt emphasizes scrupulous attention to offerings (vv 13, 17) as well as a very energetic dance led by the king himself (vv 14–16) and public festivities (vv 18–19). His dance, however, prompts ritual criticism from the queen.[47] David's dismissal of the criticism (and the queen) preoccupies the rest of the story (vv 16, 20–23). In this context, David's dance and his rejection of ritual criticism serve to emphasize his zeal. The story uses his ritual innovation to portray his religious character positively and so validate the Davidic dynasty's sponsorship of the Jerusalem temple.

1 Chronicles 15–16 tells the same story but focuses on the songs of the Levites, though offerings, ritual clothing, and proper procedure are also mentioned. The context of the earlier ritual disaster leads 1 Chronicles 15:13 to emphasize the need to do the job "with proper care" (so NRSV; actually *kammišpāṭ*, "rightly, justly"), though what this means exactly is obscured by the preceding phrase: "the first time you did not, so YHWH our God broke out against us" (leaving unspecified

---

[46] Gerstenberger made the same comparison to conclude that the purpose of each text "is to serve as models for certain understandings of the worship service," i.e., the Deuteronomistic prayer services in 1 Kings, Levitical singer guilds in Chronicles, the priestly service in Leviticus (*Leviticus*, 104).

[47] As to the pervasiveness of ritual criticism not just in modernity but throughout human cultures, Ronald Grimes noted that ritual criticism, and criticism by ritual, is as persistent and ubiquitous as ritual itself, and closely related to ritual innovation: "The contradiction between complaining about and revising rites, on the one hand, and treating them as a sacrosanct preserve, on the other, is blatant and persistent" (*Ritual Criticism: Case Studies in Its Practice, Essays on Its Theory* [Columbia: University of South Carolina Press, 1990], 17).

what it was they did not do). The clear interest of the Chronicler, however, is to legitimize the musical role of the Levites on the basis of David's royal edicts, so the chapters give the most space to their commission and the psalm they sing, illustrating their fulfillment of that role.[48]

Both versions set up the situation as a problem of ritual accuracy, as does Leviticus 10, but in such a way that innovation (David's dance in 2 Samuel; David's commission of Levitical musicians in 1 Chronicles) is not only tolerated, it is celebrated. The Samuel account carries this the furthest: here ritual improvisation (David's dance) is evaluated positively (unlike Lev 10:1–3), while criticism of it is decisively overridden (rather more strongly than in Lev 10:16–20). Though Samuel and Chronicles focus on royal and, in the latter case, Levitical interests rather than priestly ones, they share Leviticus' concern for ritual accuracy and the ambiguities encountered in ritual performance.

Texts from other ancient cultures also attest to a concern for ritual accuracy in the founding of cults. In addition to commemorative inscriptions like Samsiuluna's inscription that boast of the founder's fidelity to established procedures (discussed earlier), other texts give detailed instructions for establishing new temple cults. For example, a Hittite prescriptive ritual, titled by the colophon "When someone settles the Deity of the Night separately, for her/it this is the ritual," tells how to establish a new temple, its furnishings and its rituals.[49] It begins by specifying that the new cult statue should be just like the old one and its rituals conducted in just the same way, before describing the necessary materials for the unique rituals that initiate the new cult over five days. Here even the innovations due to new circumstances have been reduced to prescribed formulas that meet the demand for ritual continuity.

[48] On the function of the psalm, and of music in general, in Chronicles, see Watts, *Psalm and Story*, 155–68; John W. Kleinig, *The Lord's Song: The Basis, Function and Significance of Choral Music in Chronicles* (JSOTSup 156; Sheffield: Sheffield Academic Press, 1993).

[49] *CTH* 282, translated by Billie Jean Collins in *COS* 1.70.

Concerns for ritual accuracy do not always figure as prominently in cult initiation stories. The descriptions of the initiation of Solomon's temple (1 Kings 8; 2 Chronicles 5–7) focus on words rather than ritual actions: the bulk of the text presents Solomon's speech, prayer, and blessing (1 Kgs 8:12–61) though enormous offerings are also listed (8:63–64). The latter includes a note about ritual improvisation: the huge number of offerings (22,000 oxen, 120,000 sheep) exceeded the ability of the temple altar to accommodate them all. An emphasis on large amounts of offerings is very typical of ancient Near Eastern descriptions of cult initiations that serve to glorify the wealth and piety of the donor, usually a king but sometimes commoners as well. Thus when the Egyptian king Akhenaton dedicated the new royal city and temples of Akhet-Aten, his inscription reports, "A great offering was caused to be presented – consisting of bread, beer, long- and short-horned cattle, [assorted] animals, fowl, wine, fruit, incense and all sorts of good plants – on the day of founding Akhet-Aten for the living Aten."[50] The account of the installation of a high priestess at Emar also emphasizes the frequency and amounts of offerings, many coming from the high priestess's family.[51] In all these texts, the rituals serve to display and consume the wealth that sponsors the temple or priesthood. The texts describing such rituals focus on the amounts to glorify the donors. The descriptions of Solomon's initiation of the temple share this rhetoric, but their chief interest lies in the king's words.

The reinauguration of the Jerusalem cult by the returning exiles in Ezra 6:16–18 also emphasizes the large number of offerings (100 bulls, 200 rams, 400 lambs, 12 goats) at this event. This text's other interests appear in its emphasis on compliance with the law of Moses (v 18) and the observance of annual festivals (Passover in 6:19–22; the observance of Booths [Succoth] is associated with the earlier reinstitution of offerings in 3:4). The account in 1 Maccabees of the rededication of the

---

[50] William J. Murnane, *Texts from the Amarna Period in Egypt* (SBL Writings from the Ancient World 5; Atlanta: Scholars Press, 1995), 83.
[51] Emar 369 in *COS* 1.122.

temple in the second century (1 Macc 4:42–58) emphasizes compliance with Torah (vv 42, 47, 53) but also dwells on a problem of ritual ambiguity: what to do with a defiled altar? The decision to demolish it and rebuild it from new materials "as the torah directs" (v 47) represents an innovation celebrated for its faithfulness to divine instructions. This account is also concerned with validating festivals, in this case, the new festival of Hanukkah (v 59). 2 Maccabees 10:1–9 tells of the same event but emphasizes the repentance and joyous celebration of the people.

This comparison of biblical and ancient Near Eastern cult initiation rituals brings us to the same conclusion that Buc arrived at by comparing medieval coronation rituals, namely, that ritual texts invariably select what to say based on their own rhetorical interests.[52] Each account of a cult initiation ritual is highly selective, focusing only on the aspect of worship that is at issue for its writers. Rhetoric shapes their contents for particular persuasive goals. They are therefore difficult sources for reconstructing how any particular ritual was conducted, much less for discovering the ritual's "meaning" in and of itself. Gerstenberger noted that we must keep their particular interests in mind when interpreting the cult initiation stories of Leviticus: "In Leviticus 8–9 we are dealing with the claims of priests to their own specific sphere of work and to the special dignity of their office."[53] The priestly writers have included only what serves those interests. Leviticus 8–10 cannot serve as evidence for the ritual use or omission of practices reflected in other texts with other interests, such as verbal liturgies including prayers and blessings, songs and musical accompaniments, and other aspects of ritual practice that none of the biblical writers thought to mention. Nor can we blithely assume that what it includes necessarily reflects actual ancient events or ritual practices.

---

[52] Buc, *Dangers of Ritual*, 4, 259; see quotations at the beginning of Chapter 1 of this book.

[53] Gerstenberger, *Leviticus*, 105.

The comparison does point out a common interest in the problem of ritual innovation among many of these texts. 2 Samuel 6, 1 Kings 8, and 1 Maccabees 4 all make it a point to describe a ritual problem and then to value positively the innovation required to resolve it (in David's dance, in the location of offerings in the temple courtyard, and in the rebuilding of the altar). This contrasts sharply with Leviticus 10:1's harsh description of the fate of priests who do what they "had not been commanded." The interest in ritual innovation in so many of these texts provides an additional argument for reading the end of Leviticus 10 as a response to the beginning with the divine word to Aaron in verses 9–11 as the key that unifies the chapter around the issue of ritual innovation. Like these other stories, Leviticus 10 in the end validates Aaron's ritual innovation. The difference lies in the fact that this chapter gives to the Aaronide high priest a monopoly over such decisions about ritual fidelity and innovation.

Echoes of Nadab and Abihu

Several biblical texts refer explicitly to the story of Nadab and Abihu's deaths. Leviticus 16 dates the instructions for the Day of Atonement after the deaths of Nadab and Abihu (v 1). Numbers 3 describes the family of Aaron, consisting of himself and his four sons, as "anointed priests" and then mentions the deaths of Nadab and Abihu and their lack of descendants, before enumerating the rest of the Levites. In a similar context of enumerating the clans of Levi, Numbers 26:60–61 lists the sons of Aaron and the deaths of the oldest two. 1 Chronicles 24 presents a more elaborate description of the priestly lineage as divided into twenty-four courses derived from the two houses of Eleazar and Ithamar, the younger sons of Aaron. It explains the lack of descendants from his older sons by mentioning their deaths (v 2). Thus Leviticus 16 mentions the two priests' fate in the course of picking up the narrative sequence after the intervention of five chapters of purity regulations (Leviticus 11–15), while the three mentions in Numbers and Chronicles justify the monopoly of the descendants of Eleazar and Ithamar over the priesthood. The latter emphasis has fueled much historical speculation about conflicts between priestly houses and whether the Nadab and Abihu story arose to discredit two of them.[54] Unfortunately, the only evidence (if it can be called that) for such theories are these cryptic texts.

Though these references to the story are too brief to provide any basis for historical reconstruction, their wording does reproduce different elements of the brief story in Leviticus 10. Leviticus 16:1 emphasizes the deaths of Nadab and Abihu (mentioned twice) and their approach to YHWH, while the two texts in Numbers note that they "offered strange fire." Greenstein therefore argued that the Torah itself offers different interpretations of the story, in Numbers "placing the onus on the fire" while in Leviticus 16 "placing the onus on the personnel."[55]

The difference, however, may have as much to do with the thematic interests at work in those particular chapters as with different interpretations of the story in Leviticus 10. The two passages in Numbers reproduce the most distinctive phrase in the original story but do not elaborate on its meaning, so they do not further its interpretation much. The more interesting question is why Leviticus 16 should instead emphasize the priests' "approach" to YHWH. One does not have to go far to find the answer: in prescribing the rituals for the Day of Atonement, Leviticus 16 is chiefly concerned with the nearest, and most dangerous, approach that any priest should ever make to the presence of YHWH. After mentioning that YHWH gave Moses these instructions after Nadab and Abihu's fatal "approach," the divine speech explicitly characterizes what follows as instructions for when and how to enter the divine presence and avoid death (vv 2–3). The

---

[54] Noth (*Leviticus*, 84) postulated the eviction of the clans of Nadab and Abihu from the cult and their replacement by the clans of Mishael and Elzaphan, who carry the bodies out of the temple in Lev 10:4–5. Though this particular speculation has not gained much following, commentators often presume that the story arose out of conflict between priestly families (Bertholet, *Leviticus*, 28; Snaith, *Leviticus and Numbers*, 75; Hartley, *Leviticus*, 130–1; Gerstenberger, *Leviticus*, 116, 118–19).

[55] Greenstein, "Deconstruction," 60.

chapter then is all about "approaching" YHWH and therefore singles out this element from the story of Nadab and Abihu to set up not only the time frame but also the ritual problem to be resolved.

Rhetorically, Leviticus 16 singles out the high priest as the only person who can survive a near approach to the presence of YHWH. It thereby enhances the mystique of the high priestly office and the Aaronides' monopoly over its functions. The latter purpose is also at work in the three paragraphs in Numbers and 1 Chronicles that mention Nadab and Abihu in the course of distinguishing the descendants of Aaron from all other Levites. Thus all four texts make common cause with Leviticus 10 in legitimating the prerogatives of the Aaronide priesthood. Their mention of Nadab and Abihu's fate in this context is less likely due to inner-priestly conflicts than to a uniform rhetoric that justifies priestly privileges by reminding their audiences of the dangerous risks that priests undertake on their behalf.

The story in Leviticus 10 does, however, find strong though implicit links with a story of priestly conflict in Numbers 16. A large group, consisting of Levites led by Korah as well as Reubenites, challenges Moses and Aaron's exclusive claims to leadership. The ritual competition that ensues involves an incense offering, just as in Leviticus 10, and one of the three divine punishments on the rebels consists of "fire from YHWH that consumed" them (v 35), the only other occurrence of this phrase outside Leviticus 9–10.[56] The rhetoric of Numbers 16–18 obviously emphasizes Aaronide preeminence, making common cause with Leviticus 1–16: not only do Aaron and his sons win the incense competition in Numbers 16, but YHWH selects Aaron's rod to show the preeminence of Levi over the other tribes of Israel in chapter 17. These narratives then lead to a detailed enumeration of priestly prerogatives in chapter 18, beginning with the subservience of other Levites to the descendants of Aaron.

The fact that both stories center on incense offerings led Laughlin to postulate their origin in post-exilic polemics against Zoroastrian

---

[56] Gradwohl, "Fremde Feuer," 290.

ritual practices and Milgrom to describe their background in perennial polemics against private incense cults.[57] Both theories are hampered by a lack of clear evidence for the existence of these conflicts. In addition, one should note that the ritual practitioners in these stories are not foreign priests as one might expect if the target was Zoroastrian practices as Laughlin proposed, but rather true Israelites from the lineage of Rueben, Levi and Aaron himself. The illegitimate incense offerings in both chapters are public rituals practiced at the tabernacle, and so poor models for the private cult Milgrom postulates.

The rhetoric of both stories legitimates the Aaronide priests' monopoly over the public incense cult against Israelite rivals, just as the surrounding chapters (Leviticus 8–10; Numbers 16–18) justify the priests' broader powers and privileges. Perhaps the focus on incense in both stories arose from questions about the extent of the priests' cultic monopoly. Granting their exclusive right to officiate at the altar of burnt offering (Leviticus 8–9), ancient hearers and readers of the Torah might nevertheless have wondered if broader participation in nonbloody incense offerings might be permissible. That thesis has been maintained by Christophe Nihan, who observed that incense altars and censors discovered by archeology increase from the eighth century through the Persian period, and continue to be found to the end of the Second Temple period.[58] Leviticus 10 and Numbers 16 present a firm prohibition of popular participation in public incense cults. Leviticus 16 goes on to make an incense offering (vv 12–13) a key part of the holiest priestly ritual on the entire calendar, the high priest's entry into the inner sanctum on the Day of Atonement. Questions as to the exact limits on lay and Levitical involvement in the cult were likely perennial issues around ancient Israel's temples. That is enough to explain their polemical treatment in Leviticus and Numbers without hypothesizing specific historical conflicts.

[57] Laughlin, "Strange Fire," 561; Milgrom, *Leviticus*, 1:599–600.
[58] Nihan, "Death of Nadab and Abihu," 12–14.

Stories of Errant Sons

Interpreters have often sought insight into Leviticus 10 from other stories in the Hebrew Bible of fathers who lose their sons as punishment for their own or their sons' sins. Jereboam and his sons (1 Kings 12–14) are most frequently cited in this regard because the sons, Abija and Nadab, have very similar names to the sons of Aaron. Both fathers, Jereboam and Aaron, are also infamous for building golden calves (Exodus 32; 1 Kings 12:26–33). An oracle (1 Kgs 14:6–16) predicted the deaths of all of Jereboam's family as divine punishment for the father's sins. Abija then died in infancy (14:17) while Nadab, who succeeded his father to the throne, died in a coup d'etat (15:25–30). Gradwohl therefore interpreted Leviticus 10:1–3 as a protest against Jereboam's golden calf cult.[59] Damrosch found here a literary rather than a historical referent: noting that Aaron interprets the event as having happened to him (Lev 10:19), he followed the clue in the names of Jereboam's sons back to the story of Aaron's golden calf to find in Exodus 32:29 ("Today you have consecrated yourselves to YHWH at the cost of a son or a brother") the interpretive key to Leviticus 10:1–3. "Leviticus 8–10 presents the literal ordination, and the literal death of sons and brothers."[60] Beal and Linafelt wondered if the parallel with Jereboam suggests that, in Leviticus 10:1–3, Nadab and Abihu die not for their own mistakes but rather for their father's sin with the golden calf.[61]

These theories do not take into consideration the possibility that the parallel between Aaron and Jereboam might be one of *contrast*: Aaron did not suffer the fate of the idolaters in Exodus 32 nor of his sons in Leviticus 10, and these stories explicitly validate his tribe (the Levites in Exod 32:26–29) and his own descendants in their respective roles. Jereboam's dynasty suffered quite the opposite fate in 1 Kings 14–15. This interpretation finds support from comparing Leviticus 10

[59] Gradwohl, "Das 'fremde Feuer'," 293–5.
[60] Damrosch, "Leviticus," 71.
[61] Beal and Linafelt, "Sifting for Cinders," 27–8.

with other biblical stories of fathers who lose their disreputable sons to calamitous deaths. The priest Eli fell dead at receiving the news that the ark had been captured and that his sons, who had corrupted the priesthood, died in battle in fulfillment of an oracle against his family (1 Samuel 3–4). The corruption of Samuel's sons provoked Israel to ask for a king – a less drastic story than Eli's but nevertheless producing the same result of displacing Samuel's family from leadership. The story of the death of David's son, Absalom, provides the most extensive account of paternal grief, to the point that David is unable to perform his duties as king until Joab, his general, forces him to (2 Samuel 18–19). Like Eli, David suffers this grief in fulfillment of a divine oracle (2 Samuel 12).[62] The calling and performance of Aaron as high priest, on the other hand, proceeds unaffected by his sons' deaths, in notable contrast especially with Eli and David.

The chief difference between these fathers is that, according to the explicit judgments conveyed in these stories, Aaron responds appropriately (today we would say, "professionally") whereas Jereboam, Eli, and David (and even Samuel, at least to the extent of not acknowledging being implicated in his sons' crimes) did not. Aaron's silent grief, as the pun at the end of 10:3 expresses it (see note 42), does not interfere with his other sons carrying out Moses' instructions to the letter (10:4–7). Comparison with the other story of a divine breakout in 2 Samuel 6:1–8 reveals the same point: whereas David's reaction to the sudden death of Uzzah was to leave the ark alone for three months, Aaron and his sons continued their duties without interruption, in accord with Moses' instructions (10:6–7). Leviticus 10 presents Aaron as the model high priest whose training and commitment will not permit even severe personal grief to interfere with the performance of his duties.

---

[62] Gerstenberger compared Leviticus 10 to Eli, Samuel, and David losing their sons, but drew no comparative conclusion (*Leviticus*, 117). Houston, however, argued that the parallels show that Aaron should be interpreted, like these other fathers, as a tragic character: "Aaron maybe suffers more lightly . . . but his tragedy appears to fall into the same category of family dysfunction" ("Tragedy in the Courts of the Lord," 37).

I am well aware that this conclusion conflicts with how most other interpreters understand this story. The reason that others have not read the story this way is that they have been searching for the historical or literary *meaning* of the story rather than its *rhetorical effect*. Asking what persuasive purpose the story of the Nadab and Abihu, and the rest of Leviticus 10, was intended to achieve casts the chapter in a different light. Rather than standing in literary opposition to the celebration of Aaron in Leviticus 8–9, the chapter's shocks and ambiguities turn out to reinforce his prestige. Leviticus 10 demonstrates the dangers to which priests expose themselves and shows God granting them the interpretive authority to perform their duties successfully. The fact that the reader/hearer cannot understand either the nature of the danger in 10:1–3 or the logic of the Aaron's ruling in 10:16–20 only increases the mystique of the priestly office. Summarized in a more modern idiom, the message from the Aaronide priests to the congregation of Israel in Leviticus 10 is this: "We are professionals doing a necessary and dangerous job, and only we can do it right." Rhetorically, Leviticus 10:1–3 does not function deconstructively more than any other P texts but rather reinforces the monopolistic claims of the Aaronide priests.[63] The mistake of both modernist and postmodernist readers of Leviticus 10 has been to assume that the purpose of the story is to promote understanding of the cult. Ritual texts serve a far larger range of rhetorical purposes than just didactic instruction. This chapter, like its context, aims to persuade its audience that the Aaronide priests hold a legitimate monopoly over Israel's cult.

---

[63] Contra Greenstein, 64; Sommer, 35; Bibb, 97–8.

6

The Rhetoric of Atonement

This book has stated many times that the priestly writers of Leviticus give virtually no interpretations of the rituals they describe and prescribe. There is, however, an exception to this generalization. The P writers offer one explanation, or rather one word of explanation, rather frequently. That word is *kipper*, and it appears forty-nine times in Leviticus. It has traditionally been translated "to atone" and its prominence in P has led many ancient and modern interpreters to expound on P's theology of atonement. Any analysis of P's rhetoric would therefore be incomplete without attention to the meaning and uses of this word. Usage in context must play the key role in any rhetorical analysis of *kipper* in Leviticus. Does this one word explain the meaning of the offerings? Is that its purpose, or does it play other rhetorical roles?

The Meaning of Kipper

Modern scholars have argued extensively about *kipper's* meaning. Older scholarship derived it from an Arabic cognate with the basic meaning "to cover." Though translators have applied that meaning literally in some cases (such as Noah's "covering" the ark with pitch, Gen 6:14), they found in P a metaphorical usage referring to "covering" sins and impurities, hence "atone."[1] The derivation from Arabic "cover," however, has been discredited over the last few decades in favor of one from an Akkadian cognate term meaning "to wipe off." In the cultic contexts in which it often appears in Babylonian texts, ritual wiping effects purification, so by extension the verb means "to purify, decontaminate, purge."[2] Milgrom postulated a hypothetical development of *kipper*'s meaning in Hebrew usage from "wipe off" to "expiate" through cult action in some later priestly texts (H), to a sense of moral expiation in other biblical books.[3]

Some uses of the verb *kipper*, however, seem to be derived from a Hebrew noun, *kōper*, that means "ransom" or "payment." Baruch Levine would limit the meaning "ransom, pay" in P to only three appearances of the root (Exod 30:15–16; Lev 17:11; Num 31:50). Hanan Brichto argued to the contrary that this meaning and its derivatives – "compensate, settle a legal claim" – are the best rendering for most appearances of *kipper*.[4] In many contexts, the term seems to move far beyond any substitutionary and legal connotations to more general economic ones, and a better translation would be "pay, make payment, settle matters."[5]

---

[1] The newer dictionaries (*HAL, DCH*) still preserve this derivation from the Arabic "cover," though *DCH* limits this meaning to Gen 6:14 alone. Only here in the Hebrew Bible does the verb appear in the qal stem. The verse also contains a cognate noun, *kōper*, that only here seems to mean "pitch, tar." One could, however, just as well translate that verse on the basis of the Akkadian cognate: "Wipe the ark with pitch . . ." or, to render the Hebrew's use of cognate verb and noun, "Seal the ark with sealant. . . ."

[2] See Gray, *Sacrifice*, 67–73; G. R. Driver, "Studies in the Vocabulary of the Old Testament, VI," *JTS* 34 (1933): 34–8; Levine, *In the Presence of the Lord*, 56–63; Bernhard Lang, "*Kipper*," *TDOT* 7:288–303; Bernd Janowski, *Sühne als Heilsgeschehen: Studien zur Sühnetheologie der Priesterschrift und zur Wurzel KPR im Alten Orient und im Alten Testament* (Neukirchen-Vluyn: Neukirchener Verlag, 1982), 29–60; Milgrom, *Leviticus*, 1:1079–81.

[3] Milgrom, *Leviticus*, 1:1083–4.

[4] Levine, *In the Presence of the Lord*, 67–8; Herbert Chanan Brichto, "On Slaughter and Sacrifice, Blood and Atonement," *HUCA* 47 (1976): 19–55 [27–36].

[5] There is a more specific Hebrew vocabulary for "ransom, redeem" (*pdh;* see Lev 19:20, and cf. *kpr* for the priest's action in v 22). Brichto noted, "The term 'ransom' for *kōper*

P writers do not qualify the verb *kipper* to further specify its meaning. One has to infer its meaning from its use in context. Outside
of P, *kipper* frequently takes a direct object: a face (Gen 32:21; LXX
32:20), disaster (Isa 47:11), the altar (Ezek 43:20, 26), the temple (Ezek
45:20), the ground (Deut 32:43). In P, however, the effects of *kipper*
are usually described by prepositional phrases. The fullest expression
of these phrases appears in Leviticus 19:22: "The priest pays (*kipper*)
on his behalf (*'ālāyw*) with (*b-*) the ram of the guilt offering before
(*lipnê*) YHWH for (*'al*) his sins that he sinned." Though such prepositions seem to specify the action carefully, they do not eliminate all
ambiguity. Like the English preposition "for," Hebrew *'al* can be used
to mean "on behalf of" or "in place of." Both meanings are suitable
after *kipper*, as is clear from this verse: "on his behalf," "for his sins."
The meaning "on behalf of" is sometimes specified more exactly by
bĕ'ad (Lev 9:7; 16:6, 11, 17, 24), but occasionally more loosely without
prepositions and a simple series of direct objects: "When he finished
kippering the sanctuary and the tent of meeting and the altar" (Lev
16:20; cf. v 33). Such transitive usage favors translating the verb as
a ritual action, "wipe off, purify," while the use of the preposition
"on behalf of" favors translating with an economic metaphor, "pay,
compensate."

is a less than satisfactory translation for an institution which has no one-word equivalent in English. The biblical context of *kōper* is most closely approximated by the term
'composition' in its legal sense, the settling of differences. An imbalance between two
parties (individuals, families, clans, or larger social groupings) results from a damage
or deprivation inflicted upon one by the other. Equilibrium is restored by a process
which consists of a transfer of something of value (a person, an animal, or a commu-
tation of such in the form of commodity or currency) from the injured party to the
injured. . . . The *kōper* is the *quid* in the *quid pro quo* of the compository transaction.
Let us render this *quid* as 'the compository element/payment'" ("On Slaughter and
Sacrifice," 27–8). Some of the ritual contexts in which *kipper* appears have a legal or
quasi-legal cast to them (e.g., the "sin" and "guilt" offerings of Leviticus 4–5), but
others emphasize purification (e.g., Leviticus 12–15) and some are indeterminate (e.g.,
1:4). It seems better, therefore, to adopt Brichto's more general term "pay, compensate"
as a translation for *kipper* with the understanding that such payments may compensate
for injuries against the deity, but may also settle debts (paying a vow) or be payments
for services (thank offerings) or outright gifts (free-will offerings).

Thus P's use of *kipper* seems to range between the meanings "wipe off/purify" and "compensate/pay." Though some argue for two distinct Hebrew homonyms with these meanings, P's frequently ambiguous usage suggests that the meanings "pay" and "purify" (derived from the more concrete "wipe") mark opposite ends of a continuous semantic field, rather than separate words.[6] If those two meanings do not seem to share any common ground, that is an observation about English, not Hebrew, vocabulary. The wisest course is therefore not to specify a single meaning or two distinct and differentiated meanings for *kipper*, but to translate contextually within the semantic range between "pay" and "purify."

It may be that "atone" is the only English term that can encompass the semantic range of *kipper*, though it also carries theological connotations that may not be implied by the Hebrew verb. The flexibility of the Hebrew term *kipper*, "atone," suggests that, just as with the offering names *ḥaṭṭā't*, "sin," and *'āšām*, "guilt" (see Chapter 4), the primary goal of the ritual texts and their vocabulary is not to explain the ritual's precise meaning. They were written to serve persuasive purposes instead.

The Rhetoric of Kipper

The priestly writers' rhetorical interests in *kipper*, "atone," are exemplified by the fact that they use the verb with only one real subject: the priests, and Moses functioning as a priest. While in other parts of the Bible the word frequently describes God's actions and occasionally takes humans like David and Jacob as subject (2 Sam 21:3; Gen 32:21), P only uses it as a word to characterize priestly cultic action (as in Lev 7:7; 8:34; Exod 29:36). The frequent repetitions of *kipper* in Leviticus 4–5, 12–15, and 16 emphasize that only the priests can atone and they do

---

[6] For a detailed argument in favor of this position, see Jay Sklar, *Sin, Impurity, Sacrifice, Atonement: The Priestly Conceptions* (Hebrew Bible Monographs 2, Sheffield: Sheffield Phoenix Press, 2005).

so "on behalf of" others and themselves. The verb usually appears near the end of the regulations for a particular ritual. It does not describe a particular act, but rather characterizes the entire set of priestly actions in regard to that offering as *kipper*.[7] The altar of P's tabernacle functioned like the floor of a modern stock exchange to which only stock brokers have access: the priests conducted transactions with God on the people's behalf, taking their cut (literally a cut of meat in this case) along the way. *Kipper*, "pay, purify," is the word that summarizes this activity, just as "brokering" deals describes the work of traders at an exchange.

One effect, then, of the priestly writers' use of *kipper* was to reinforce the priests' monopoly over Israel's cult. Priests and only priests *kipper* according to P. That usage is sufficiently dominant that the involvement of the priests can be safely assumed even when the subject of the verb *kipper* is indeterminate (Exod 30:15, 16; Lev 1:4; 6:23; 8:34; 14:21, 29; 16:10, 27; 34; 23:28; Num 28:22, 30; 29:5; 31:50). The famous statement in Leviticus 17:11, that blood is "for atoning," is no exception to this pattern: the context of this statement insists on slaughtering all domestic animals at the sanctuary and so explicitly reasserts the priestly monopoly. Thus the rhetoric of atonement reinforced the Aaronide priests' legitimacy and exclusive rights over the cult.

What does a priest's cultic activity, his "atoning," achieve? Two sections of Leviticus use repetitive refrains to emphasize that the priest's atoning produces forgiveness and purity for the people of Israel. In the instructions for the *ḥaṭṭā't*, "sin," and *'āšām*, "guilt," offerings (Leviticus 4–5), the conclusion of every section except the first includes the refrain, "the priest atones on his/her behalf and it will be forgiven him/her" (4:20, 26, 31, 35; 5:6, 10, 13, 16, 18, 26).[8] In the same way, the purification rules for severe pollutants (those that require offerings

---

[7] Janowski, *Sühne als Heilsgeschehen*, 252.

[8] The Masoretic Text of 5:6 omits the phrase "it will be forgiven him," but the Samaritan Pentateuch, the Septuagint, and some other Hebrew manuscripts from the Cairo geniza include it.

at the sanctuary, Leviticus 12–15) conclude instructions for successful purifications with the refrain, "the priest atones on her/his/its behalf and she/he/it will be clean" (12:7, 8; 14:20, 21, 31, 53; 15:15, 30).[9] These refrains produce the largest concentrations of the word *kipper* in Leviticus. Their repetition emphatically connects the action of atoning with the themes of forgiveness (in Lev 4–5) and purification (in Lev 12–15). The three ideas interact even more tightly in the instructions for the Day of Atonement in Leviticus 16 that juxtapose sin and impurity in the context of atonement. The ritual achievements of that day are summarized by verse 16: the high priest "will *kipper* on behalf of the sanctuary from (*min*) the impurities of the children of Israel and from (*min*) their transgressions, for (*l-*) all their sins." By their separate treatment in earlier chapters, however, the priestly writers clearly depict forgiveness and purification as parallel but different consequences of atonement, that is, of the priests' presentation to YHWH of offerings on behalf of the people of Israel and of themselves.[10]

Hence the priests' atoning activities are depicted as essential because only in this way are forgiveness from sin and guilt and cleansing from severe impurities possible. According to P, neither offerings nor blood nor even God provide access to forgiveness and purification apart from the atoning action of the Aaronide priests. The priestly writers do not go so far as to equate the priests' ritual behaviors with those of the deity. They rather connect them in a sequence of action and response: the priest *kippers* (active verb) with the result that "it will be forgiven him/her" (passive verb).[11] Nevertheless, P provides no access to such forgiveness except through the priests' ritual mediation.

---

[9] Modified forms of the refrain appear in Leviticus 14:31, "the priest *kippers* on behalf of the purified one," and 15:15, 30, "the priest *kippers* on her/his behalf for (*min*) her/his (unclean) discharge."

[10] For a convincing argument that P does not equate sin with impurity but rather regards them as distinct problems that are dealt with in the same ritual manner, see Baruch J. Schwartz, "The Bearing of Sin in the Priestly Literature," in *Pomegranates and Golden Bells: Studies... in Honor of Jacob Milgrom* (ed. David P. Wright, David Noel Freedman, and Avi Hurvitz; Winona Lake, IN: Eisenbrauns, 1995), 3–21 [6–7].

[11] Janowski, *Sühne als Heilsgeschehen*, 259.

The chapters that emphasize *kipper* may do so because they extend the priest's monopolistic claims into controversial territory. The regulations for the *ḥaṭṭāʾt* and *ʾāšām* offerings in Leviticus 4–5 seem to use emotional terminology to advocate and justify ritual innovations that directed more revenues to the priests (see Chapter 4 in this book). The instructions for being declared clean of impurities in Leviticus 12–15 designate carefully which impurities require priestly inspection and, if clean, atonement by priests to have that cleansing certified. And Leviticus 16, of course, reserves to the Aaronide high priest alone the privilege of entering the inner sanctum of the Tabernacle to make atonement. Thus the rhetoric of atonement clusters around the regulations most concerned with protecting the cultic privileges of the priests.

In this way, the Priestly writers reinforced the priests' control of Israel's offerings by bringing together urgent instructions to compensate for sin and guilt on the one hand with essential guidelines for restoring purity on the other under a single term to describe the priests' cultic action, *kipper*, "atone." Leviticus works out both basic meanings of *kipper*, "pay, compensate" and "purify," in detailed instructions that make the priests' mediation essential. Atonement thus sums up the priests' rhetoric of necessity: their exclusive role in presenting Israel's offerings is vital to the people's well-being.

Kipper *as Leitmotif*

Leviticus does not present the priests' exclusive claims to *kipper*, "atone," as baldly as the above description might suggest. The book announces the theme in more subtle ways. The first appearance of it in the instructions for offerings does not even mention priests, but focuses on worshippers instead.

Leviticus 1:4 contains the first and only appearance of *kipper* in chapters 1–3. It describes the hand-laying ceremony by which worshippers designate a bull as their burnt offering (*'ōlāh*) and explains that "it will be acceptable on their behalf to *kipper* for them." The formula *kappēr 'ālāyw* appears here before the specific instructions on how to offer an *'ōlāh*, unlike its use as a concluding formula in Leviticus 4–5 and 12–15. Verse 4 uses *kipper* to characterize the significance of the animal offering to the worshipper before the priests become involved in verse 5. The position of the formula in 1:4 suggests that the writers used it to announce the theme of the following instructions.

After describing the ritual for the bull *'ōlāh*, Leviticus 1 provides instructions for sheep or goats or turtledoves instead. These regulations present the ritual in abbreviated form, presupposing the pattern described more fully for the bull. Therefore, though the hand-laying ceremony and its interpretation by the term *kipper* is not mentioned again in the chapter, it can safely be assumed to apply to all the *'ōlāh* rituals of Leviticus 1.[12]

The hand-laying ceremony reappears in the regulations for the *šĕlāmîm* offerings in 3:2, 8, and 13. Though the word *kipper* does not appear here, these verses read like abbreviations of 1:4–5 that presuppose that more complete depiction of the ritual. In this case, performance of the *šĕlāmîm* also serves to *kipper*, "atone." Many interpreters have resisted this conclusion on the grounds that of all of Israel's animal offerings, only the *šĕlāmîm* are never explicitly described as being for *kipper*.[13] This argument presupposes a high degree of precision in P's

---

[12] As commentators regularly note: e.g., Levine, *Leviticus*, 3–4; Hartley, *Leviticus*, 15; Milgrom, *Leviticus*, 1:151–2, who argued that because birds (1:14–17) are carried to the sanctuary in one's hands, hand-laying occurs automatically in this case.

[13] This argument has been stated most forcefully by Milgrom, "Prolegomenon to Lev 17:11," *JBL* 90 (1971): 149–56; reprinted in Milgrom, *Studies in Cultic Theology and Terminology* (SJLA 36; Leiden: Brill, 1983), 96–103; idem, *Leviticus*, 1:1082–3. In 17:11, however, Milgrom allowed that the *kipper* function must apply to the *šĕlāmîm* in a context that prohibits eating blood. Here the "atonement" is for the act of killing the animal itself. That conclusion has been contested by those who argue that 17:11 is a more general statement and the *šĕlāmîm* never fall under the category of *kipper*.

use of ritual vocabulary, an assumption that I have already found reasons to question (see Chapter 4). The appearance of the hand-laying ceremony in Leviticus 3 seems to presuppose its description in 1:4, and neither here nor elsewhere in P is the *kipper* function denied to the *šĕlāmîm*. For that matter, nothing excludes the *minḥôt*, "grain offerings," of Leviticus 2 from falling under the category of *kipper* either. Grain may be given as a *ḥaṭṭāʾt*, "sin offering," according to 5:11–13, where it explicitly says that the priest uses it to *kipper* on behalf of the worshipper.

At any rate, it is clear that Leviticus 1:4 announces the theme of atonement at the beginning of the instructions for offerings, but the following two chapters leave its application unspecified. This ambiguity did not pose a problem for ritual performance because the word *kipper* does not describe a particular ritual action but rather interprets it. *Minḥôt* and *šĕlāmîm* were conducted in the same way regardless of whether anyone considered the priests' actions with them to *kipper* or not. The issue of *kipper*'s application is not an issue of ritual, but of rhetoric.[14] Leviticus leaves the theme undeveloped until chapters 4–5 show its importance for achieving forgiveness and chapters 12–15 its role in purification. By the time chapter 16 specifies these results as the achievement of the high priest on Yom Kippur, the rhetoric of atonement has drilled in the necessity for priestly mediation of Israel's offerings.

The undeveloped implication that the priests' role in Israel's other offerings can also be described by *kipper* does not undermine the structure of priestly theology, as many interpreters have maintained, but simply reinforces the persuasiveness of the priests' claim to a cultic

---

For this position, see Schwartz, "Prohibitions," 58–9; and Rolf Rendtorff, "Another Prolegomenon to Leviticus 17:11," in *Pomegranates and Golden Bells: Studies . . . in Honor of Jacob Milgrom* (ed. David P. Wright, David Noel Freedman, and Avi Hurvitz; Winona Lake, IN: Eisenbrauns, 1995), 23–8 [27–8]. Milgrom defended his original position against critics in *Leviticus*, 2:1474–8.

[14] See Bergen, *Reading Ritual*, 40.

monopoly. Announcing the theme initially near the beginning of Leviticus 1, long before the emphasis on the priestly role becomes explicit, disguises the priestly focus of the rhetoric by putting the worshipper first.[15] It plants the notion that most, if not all offerings involve atonement long before it reveals the political ramifications of this idea.

Atonement in Later Religious Rhetoric

The rhetoric of atonement has, of course, grown far beyond its use by the writers of Leviticus to buttress priestly prerogatives. The Day of Atonement, Yom Kippur, is observed as the most holy day in the Jewish calendar, a time for self-reflection, repentance, and renewal. Christian theologians have developed and debated theologies of atonement to explain the effects of Christ's death for humanity. The word "atonement" therefore carries connotations and implications only incipiently present, if at all, in the *kipper* of the Priestly writers of Leviticus. Why has *kipper* generated such strong traditions of religious reflection? What accounts for the ongoing centrality of atonement in Jewish and Christian discourse?

The above description of *kipper's* use in Leviticus has noted two features of this rhetoric. On the one hand, central chapters of the book connect atonement tightly to rituals that produce forgiveness and purification. On the other hand, the book does not define the limits of atonement's application. It implies, but does not specify, that a wider range of offerings function, in the priests' hands, to atone. This cryptic ambiguity served the writers' agenda of enhancing the authority and mystique of the priests. For subsequent interpreters, it has enhanced the term's usefulness for theological development.

---

[15] Some texts in the latter part of Leviticus extend the theme of atonement to particular issues of personal practice (eating meat, 17:11) or legal practice (19:22). Many interpreters, however, consider these verses to be from a different source (H). Their usefulness for understanding P's use of *kipper* is therefore in doubt.

P's association of atonement with forgiveness and purification on the one hand and with most, if not all, of Israel's offerings on the other laid the basis for equating several theological ideas. First, it allowed many interpreters to identify forgiveness with purification. The idea of atonement reinforced and, in turn, derived significance from the fact that concerns with purity/pollution and with guilt/compensation have been powerful parts of Western religious heritage, all the more so because they have often been mixed together in a common concern for moral behavior. Second, the ambiguous limits of *kipper*'s application led many interpreters to characterize the entirety of Israel's rituals as means for gaining divine forgiveness. Thus *kipper*'s semantic range has reinforced the equation, even the reduction, of religion to morality. Atonement has also come to represent the hope for a "second chance" and in later traditions has been joined with themes of cleansing, renewal, and rebirth to offer moral and spiritual reconstitution.

There are good reasons to think that P did not intend these results, but its rhetoric of atonement provided the building blocks for them nevertheless. It is notable that subsequent religious discourse has generally divorced the rhetoric of atonement from claims for leadership authority, which were P's primary rhetorical concern. In this case, the influence of Leviticus has probably been eclipsed by the less priestly oriented uses of *kipper* in prophetic and psalmic texts of the Hebrew Bible. It is nevertheless worth noticing that with the Jerusalem temple still standing or only recently destroyed, the writer of the New Testament book of Hebrews paid more attention to depicting Christ as high priest than as an offering – a more accurate reflection of the concerns, if not the conclusions, of Leviticus than in most subsequent christian theologies of atonement.

Atonement has developed far beyond the rhetoric of priestly legitimacy that made it the only interpretive comment in the ritual texts of Leviticus. Rhetorical analysis will pay as close attention to its meaning for later communities as for the writers of the book, even if it must challenge claims that those later meanings motivated the composition of the original text. Leviticus, however, has left a rhetorical legacy far broader than the language of atonement. In the next three chapters, I consider the persuasive influence of the book on several other significant religious themes: the status and power of priests, the rhetoric of sacrifice, and the authority of scripture.

7

The Rhetoric of Priesthood

The previous five chapters of this book have all arrived at the same general conclusion. Leviticus 1–16 justifies control of Israel's priesthood by Aaron's descendants and their monopoly over most of its duties, privileges, and sources of income.

Various features of these chapters unite in service to this persuasive goal. The instructions of Leviticus 1–7 work to establish themselves as the ultimate guidelines for Israel's cultic practices. Their refrains and repetitions not only encourage the audience to bring YHWH offerings and gifts, but they also insist that such worship be done in strict accord with the stipulations of this text of priestly instructions. The priority of the ʿōlāh, "burnt offering," in Leviticus as well as elsewhere in biblical rhetoric serves to disguise the priests' economic interests in the temple cult behind an ideal of selfless worship. Because no human receives any economic benefit from an ʿōlāh, attention to it at the beginning of the ritual instructions draws attention away from other more numerous and more lucrative offerings. Rhetorical analysis of Leviticus 4–5 discovered here a case for innovating, or at least a defense of recent innovations, in ritual practice: the addition of the ḥaṭṭāʾt, "sin," and ʾāšām, "guilt," offerings to Israel's regular worship. The chapters' frequent puns on the offering names emphasize that when ultimate issues are at stake, hearers and readers need to bring these offerings to the priests, who receive portions of most of them for their own use. Ritual narratives also glorify the priests, not only by depicting their ordination by Moses in accord with divine instructions (Lev 8–9), but also by emphasizing the danger to which their job exposes them and their god-given ability to discriminate between proper and improper cultic procedures (Lev 10). Attention to the theme of atonement showed the same dynamic behind its deployment by P: only the priests by their presentation of Israel's offerings can atone on behalf of the people. The priests' atoning role is essential for both forgiveness (Lev 4–5) and purification (Lev 12–15). The major rhetorical purpose, then, for writing the first half of Leviticus was to provide prescriptive and descriptive justification for the Aaronides' monopoly over Israel's priesthood and cult. When the Pentateuch as a whole is taken into account, it is notable that out of all the positions of authority in ancient Israelite society, only the institution of the priesthood receives such extensive rhetorical support from the Torah. It depicts the high priesthood as the most important office in Israel.

The Aaronide Hierocracy

The Hebrew Bible does not, however, depict Aaronide priests as maintaining such a cultic monopoly, or even holding positions of unequaled prominence, for much of Israel's history. According to the books of Deuteronomy, Joshua, Judges, Samuel, and Kings, political leadership passed from Moses to Joshua, then to a series of warlords ("judges"), and finally to the kings of Israel and Judah. The kings governed national and religious affairs for four hundred years. The priests at the major temples seem to have owed their positions, privileges, and incomes entirely to royal patronage.

A very different situation obtained after the exile. Unfortunately, huge gaps mar our knowledge of the period and we lack any continuous historical account of it earlier than that of Josephus, from the end of the first century C.E. Nevertheless, the main outlines of developments in Judea are fairly clear. The Persian imperial authorities allowed Judeans to return to Jerusalem to, first of all, reestablish its cult and rebuild its temple. Though members of the Judean royal family led the early return parties to Jerusalem, most of the participants were priests and Levites under the leadership of the Aaronide high priest, Joshua. Effective leadership from the family of David faded at the end of the sixth century, but the family of Joshua seems to have controlled the high priesthood in unbroken succession for the next three hundred years. Frank Moore Cross summarized the situation succinctly: "Hierocracy supplants the diarchy of king and high priest."[1]

At this point, I should justify using the term "hierocracy," which means rule by priests, to describe the authority of the Aaronide priesthood. The ancient Jewish historian Josephus invented the related but broader term "theocracy" in order to describe the form of government mandated in the Torah, where Moses instituted the priesthood's control over temple and ritual affairs and mandated various rules governing civil and criminal law as well.[2] But historical evidence for that state of affairs exists only for Judea in the Persian and Hellenistic periods, not in the pre-monarchic and monarchic periods. Modern scholars are therefore more likely to point out that the Pentateuch institutionalizes no government at all for Israel. It mentions the possibility of an Israelite king only in Deuteronomy 17 and then limits his duties to the careful study of the Torah. The Bible consistently describes the institution of monarchy as a later innovation in Israel's history that remained controversial (see 1 Samuel 8, 10) despite the Davidic kings' claims to a divine right to rule (see 2 Samuel 7; Psalms 2, 110). This curious state of affairs is usually explained by the presumption that foreign empires monopolized claims to governmental powers when the early books of the Bible were written or at least edited into their present form. The

---

[1] Frank Moore Cross, Jr., "A Reconstruction of the Judean Restoration," *JBL* 94 (1975): 4–18 [16].

[2] Josephus, *Against Apion*, 2.16.165.

Pentateuch therefore seems to have omitted any significant role for a king in order to avoid antagonizing the imperial overlords.[3]

The history of the Persian period high priesthood has been the subject of intensive historical investigation and debate as to the exact succession of high priests. A list of the high priests preserved in Nehemiah 12 names six generations: Joshua/Jeshua, who oversaw the building of the second temple, and his descendants Joiakim, Eliashib, Joiada, Jonathan/Johanan, and Jaddua. This list is supported by Josephus and, to some extent, by the Elephantine papyri. Josephus attests that the same family controlled the high priesthood for another century: Jaddua was the ancestor of high priests Onias I, Simon I, Manasseh, Eleazar, Onias II, Simon II, Onias III, and his brother Jason. Cross and others have argued that the six names of Nehemiah's list are too few for a period of two hundred years. He suggested that the practice of papponymy, naming a son for his grandfather, led to the omission of several generations from the list.[4] James Vanderkam has defended Nehemiah's list as accurate.[5] This debate does not, however, significantly undermine the testimony of ancient sources that a single family seems to have controlled the high priesthood in Jerusalem from circa 535 until 175 B.C.E.[6] Imperial governors often exerted temporal rule, such

[3] See Watts, *Reading Law*, 137–43; for a full debate over the influence of the Persian imperial context on the Pentateuch's composition and redaction, see the essays in *Persia and Torah: The Theory of Imperial Authorization of the Pentateuch* (ed. J. W. Watts, Atlanta: SBL, 2001).

[4] Cross, "Reconstruction," 4–18; see also de Vaux, *Ancient Israel*, 401–3; Geo Widengren, "The Persian Period," in *Israelite and Judaean History* (ed. John H. Hayes and J. M. Miller; OTL; Philadelphia: Westminster, 1977), 506–9; Hugh G. M. Williamson, "The Historical Value of Josephus' *Jewish Antiquities*," *JTS* 28 (1977): 49–67; Lester L. Grabbe, "Josephus and the Reconstruction of the Judean Restoration," *JBL* 106 (1987): 231–46.

[5] James C. Vanderkam, "Jewish High Priests of the Persian Period: Is the List Complete?" in *Priesthood and Cult in Ancient Israel* (ed. Gary A. Anderson and Saul M. Olyan; JSOTSup 125; Sheffield: Sheffield Academic Press, 1991), 67–91; idem, *From Joshua to Caiaphas: High Priests after the Exile* (Minneapolis: Augsburg Fortress, 2004), 97–9.

[6] Josephus' mention of a Hezekiah/Ezekias in the time of Ptolemy I as *archiereus* "high priest" or "chief priest," and coins listing someone by that name as governor, introduce a puzzling element, but this person's status and role remain unclear

as Nehemiah who rebuilt Jerusalem's defensive walls. Other priests, such as Ezra, played decisive religious roles during the early centuries of the Second Temple period. Yet none rivaled the status of the high priest as the symbolic leader of the Jews.[7] Over time, as Jerusalem's population and economy grew, the high priests accumulated more and more political power to go along with their control over the temple rituals.[8] Thus according to Josephus, when Alexander of Macedon seized the Persian empire, Jerusalem's high priest, Jaddua, negotiated successfully with the new imperial overlord not only on behalf of Judea

(see Lester L. Grabbe, *Judaism from Cyrus to Hadrian, Vol. 1: The Persian and Greek Periods* [Minneapolis: Fortress, 1992], 71; Vanderkam, *From Joshua to Caiaphas*, 95–7, 115–18).

[7] 1 Esdras 9:39, 40, 49 actually grants Ezra the title *archiereus* "chief priest," but no similar title appears in Ezra or Nehemiah. Ezra 7:1 traces his genealogy through the high priestly line back to Aaron, but it does not link up with the line of post-exilic high priests in Neh 12:10–11; see also 12:26. Interpreters are divided over whether he held the post or not; see notes 4 and 5 for reconstructions of a single family's monopoly over the high priesthood, excluding Ezra. For summaries of the debate, see Klaus Koch ("Ezra and Meremoth: Remarks on the History of the High Priesthood," in *"Sha'arei Talmon": Studies in the Bible, Qumran, and the Ancient Near East Presented to Shemaryahu Talmon* [ed. Michael Fishbane and Emanuel Tov; Winona Lake, IN: Eisenbrauns, 1992], 105–10) and Ulrike Dahm (*Opferkult und Priestertum in Alt-Israel: Ein kultur- und religionswissenschaftlicher Beitrag* [BZAW 327; Berlin: De Gruyter, 2003], 83–4), both of whom concluded that Ezra was, in fact, high priest. Gary N. Knoppers has pointed out that the title "the priest" with which Ezra is designated appears also in Chronicles as a common designation for high priests ("The Relationship of the Priestly Genealogies to the History of the High Priesthood in Jerusalem," in *Judah and the Judeans in the Neo-Babylonian Period* [ed. Oded Lipschits and Joseph Blenkinsopp; Winona Lake, IN: Eisenbrauns, 2003], 109–33). The rhetoric of Ezra-Nehemiah, however, weighs against the conclusion that it intends to describe Ezra as high priest (see Vanderkam, *From Joshua to Caiaphas*, 45–8). Not only do the books not explicitly distinguish Ezra in that role, but his reforms do not deal with how priests do their business in the temple, which was the high priest's primary responsibility; rather, the reforms are concerned with their marriages and other relations with foreigners. Contrast this with the contents of *4QMMT*, the letter from Qumran which in the second century B.C.E. questioned the Jerusalem priests' conduct of the offerings precisely in order to challenge their legitimacy, especially that of their high priest.

[8] For reconstructions of the historical situation behind the hierocracy, see Reinhard Achenbach, *Die Vollendung der Tora: Studien zur Redaktionsgeschichte des Numeribuches im Kontext von Hexateuch und Pentateuch* (BZABR 3; Wiesbaden: Harrassowitz, 2002), 130–40; Vanderkam, *From Joshua to Caiaphas*, 99–239.

and its temple, but also on behalf of Jews living in Mesopotamia.[9] The high priest seems to have functioned as the civil authority in Judea in the later Persian period as well as throughout the following Ptolemaic period.[10]

Concentrations of power attract rivals. Josephus records one struggle for succession to the high priesthood in the fifth or fourth century that ended with the high priest murdering his brother in the temple.[11] Such conflicts did not, however, break the hold of the family of Joshua on the high priesthood of the Jerusalem temple until the early second century. Then bribes induced the Seleucid imperial rulers to transfer the high priesthood from one brother (Onias III) to another (Jason), and then finally to a complete outsider, a Benjamenite named Menelaus.[12] The subsequent conflict saw priestly rivals fielding armies and siding with one or another claimant to the imperial throne. They also became embroiled in broader issues having to do with the compatibility of Hellenistic (Greek) culture with Jewish religious traditions and, finally, involving outright religious persecution. That resulted, predictably, in an armed revolt against the Seleucid empire that lasted, off and on, for twenty-five years. It was led by another priestly family, the Hasmonean brothers who earned the nickname Maccabees "hammers." In the course of this conflict, the Hasmoneans appropriated the office of high priest for themselves. It is notable that their accumulation of the secular titles of governance was much more gradual, and only a later generation of the family added the title "king."

[9] Josephus, *Ant.* xi.326–39.
[10] Grabbe, *Judaism*, 192. Vanderkam, however, argued that the admittedly slim evidence indicates that a governor seems to have wielded civil power throughout the Persian period. The high priests of the Jerusalem temple gained secular power only when the Persian overlords were replaced by the Hellenistic kingdoms (*From Joshua to Caiaphas*, 99–111, 122–4).
[11] Josephus, *Ant.* xi.297–301.
[12] 2 Macc 4:23–6; see 3:4. Historians find this tribal identification unlikely, and tend to argue that Menelaus was a priest (i.e., an Aaronide) but not of the Zadokite high priestly family: see de Vaux, *Ancient Israel*, 401; Grabbe, *Judaism*, 1:277–8; Vanderkam, *From Joshua to Caiaphas*, 203–26.

After eighty years of semi-independence under the Hasmoneans, Pompey conquered Jerusalem to incorporate it into Rome's growing empire. The high priesthood became a political appointment of Rome's proxy rulers in the area, whether local kings such as the Herodian family or Roman governors, and was frequently shifted between several prominent priestly families.[13] The Romans tried, in this way, to dilute the power and influence of hereditary priesthoods throughout their provinces.[14] Various sources ranging from Josephus to the New Testament suggest that the Jerusalem priests nevertheless continued to mediate between the Judean populace and the imperial rulers. But when anti-Roman sentiment coalesced behind all-out revolt in 66 C.E., the priests went along with the rebels, as did Josephus himself (though unwillingly, he claimed). The Romans' destruction of Jerusalem's temple in 70 C.E. deprived the Aaronide priests of their power base and their influence. In later Judaism, religious leadership shifted to rabbis who gained authority from their expertise in interpretation and teaching, rather than from a monopoly over ritual performance.

This account of Judea's priests does not describe all of the Aaronides' influence in the later half of the first millennium B.C.E. The Samaritan priesthood also claimed descent from Aaron. The Samaritan high priest at the founding of the temple on Mt. Gerizim was, according to Josephus, the son and brother of high priests in Jerusalem.[15] Aaronide priests thus led not one but two religious and ethnic communities of increasing size and influence in the last five centuries B.C.E. Despite the rivalry and hostility between Jews and Samaritans, the priests seem to

---

[13] For a list of all the high priests of the Second Temple period, as recorded in the various sources, see James C. Vanderkam, *An Introduction to Early Judaism* (Grand Rapids: Eerdmans, 2001), 177–9; idem, *From Joshua to Caiaphas*, 491–3.

[14] For the Roman policy and its application in various provinces, see Richard Gordon, "Religion in the Roman Empire: the Civic Compromise and its Limits," in *Pagan Priests: Religion and Power in the Ancient World* (ed. Mary Beard and John North; Ithaca: Cornell University Press, 1990), 235–55 [240–5].

[15] Josephus, *Ant.* xi.302–3, 321–4.

have mediated between the two communities, often through alliances sealed by marriage.[16] This practice was harshly criticized by more exclusive Jewish leaders such as Ezra and Nehemiah.[17]

Aaronide priests of the same family also founded and directed a Jewish temple in Egypt. After being deposed as high priest, Onias III or his son, Onias IV,[18] founded a temple in Leontopolis modeled on that in Jerusalem. The success of the Jewish community around this temple is attested by the fact that the priestly sons of this founder led large armies in the service of Egypt's Ptolemaic rulers and were able to influence the Ptolemies favorably toward Jerusalem.[19] It seems that the Aaronide priests, or some of them at any rate, were less committed to Deuteronomy's doctrine of the geographic centralization of cultic worship in Jerusalem than they were to P's doctrine of the Aaronides' monopoly over the conduct of all cultic worship, wherever it might take place.

Even this superficial survey of priestly history shows clearly that Leviticus' portrayal of the preeminence of the high priest and the Aaronides' monopoly over the priesthood corresponds historically to the situation of Jewish and Samaritan priests in the Persian and Hellenistic periods. A hierocracy even developed in Second Temple Judaism. It was strongest under the Hasmoneans, but they built on foundations of priestly authority and political influence that had grown steadily over the previous three centuries. It was in this same period that the Pentateuch, with the priestly rhetoric of Aaronide legitimacy at its center, began to function as authoritative scripture in Judaism (see Chapter 9 of this book). It is therefore to this period and this hierocracy that P's rhetoric applies, either by preceding the hierocracy and laying the ideological basis for it (if P dates to the exilic period or earlier) or by reflecting and legitimizing an existing institution as it

---

[16] Cross, "Reconstruction," 6.

[17] Ezra 9–10; Neh 13:23–9.

[18] Josephus' accounts are contradictory, cf. *Ant.* xii.397 and xiii.62–73 with *Jewish War* vii.426–32.

[19] Josephus, *Ant.* xiii.348–55.

began to accumulate religious and civil authority (if P dates from the early Second Temple period).

The preserved priestly rhetoric does not speak in its own voice, which makes the rhetorical situation in the Second Temple period hard to assess. Exodus, Leviticus, and Numbers use the voice of God and the actions of Moses to legitimize the role and authority of the Aaronide priests. The priests thus disguised their role in the arguments of these times by hiding behind God and Moses, and casting their speeches in the distant past. As a result, it may appear that the preserved Second Temple rhetoric tilts against the high priestly family and criticizes their practices (e.g., Ezra, Nehemiah, Malachi, 1 and 2 Maccabees, 4QMMT).[20] That view can only be maintained, however, if one categorizes the Torah as "pre-exilic" and so ignores its rhetorical impact in the Second Temple period. Whatever their date of composition, the Pentateuch's priestly texts functioned with far greater rhetorical power in the Persian and Hellenistic periods than they ever had previously, because they functioned increasingly as scriptures. The reason for their growing authority was precisely the fact that the Torah did express the voice of the Aaronide priests who controlled both the Jerusalem and Samaritan temples and sponsored the scriptures that authorized those temples' rituals.

The early stages of the canonization of scripture depended upon the books' association with the Samaritan and Jewish temples. As the temple law book, the Torah shared the prestige of the Jewish and Samaritan temples and in turn validated the monopolistic claims of the temples and, especially, their priesthoods over the offerings of Israel. It may be that at some times other factions within and outside the priesthood were able to deploy the authority of Torah against Joshua's dynasty, as Ezra seems to have done. The family of Joshua seems to have retained its hold on the high priesthood until the second century,

---

[20] Chronicles presents a more complicated evaluation of priests and Levites; see Gary N. Knoppers, "Hierodules, Priests, or Janitors? The Levites in Chronicles and the History of the Israelite Priesthood," *JBL* 118 (1999), 49–72.

however, and run on the legitimizing rhetoric of the Torah as well. In light of the priesthood's practices, it is therefore not accidental that the Torah contains no general prohibition on intermarriage, as the books of Ezra and Nehemiah think it should. The Aaronide rhetoric of Leviticus at the heart of the newly canonized Torah occupied the most powerful position from which to influence these debates.

The Many Rhetorical Situations of Leviticus

The testimony of two thousand years of commentaries shows that while celebration of the priests is an obvious feature of Leviticus 1–16, most interpreters quickly pass over it to look for other messages.

For example, a survey of some ancient interpretations of Leviticus 8–10 demonstrates that its message mutated when different communities understood themselves as addressed through this text. The Qumran community in the second and first centuries B.C.E. interpreted Leviticus 8 as applying to annual ordination rituals in the functioning Jerusalem temple, whose priesthood they regarded as corrupt. Their Temple Scroll that details disagreements with current ritual practice is therefore an example of polemical ritual criticism.[21] Once the Jerusalem temple was destroyed, ritual analysis lost its practical import but remained a subject of lively speculation in rabbinic circles. The key indicator of Jewish religious authority was no longer a ritual monopoly but rather authority in interpretation, especially legal interpretation (*halakhah*), and this situation was read back into Leviticus. Therefore, the medieval commentator Rashi repeated the earlier opinion of Rabbi Eliezer about Leviticus 10:1 that "The sons of Aharon died only because they rendered halakhic decisions in the presence of their master Moshe."[22]

---

[21] Milgrom, *Leviticus*, 1:558–62; on the nature and cultural function of ritual criticism, see Grimes, *Ritual Criticism*.

[22] Translated by Avrohom Davis in Rashi, *Vayikro*.

Early Christian commentary on Leviticus 8 was fascinated that here, in the Septuagint Greek translation that they used, the word *ekklesia*, "assembly, church," occurs for the first time.[23] The fourth century Christian commentator, Origen, found in Leviticus 8–10 the priest's clothing most interesting, which he allegorized as qualities for Christian leaders. He also focused on 10:9's injunction against strong drink.[24] Origen admitted, however, the need to avoid the plain meaning of Leviticus and look for less obvious significance, because "unless we take all these words in a sense other than the literal text shows, as we already said often, when they are read in the Church, they will present more an obstacle and ruin of the Christian religion than an exhortation and edification."[25]

Implicit in many of these Jewish and Christian interpretations is a recognition that the chapters deal with the general theme of religious leadership in the specific form of the Aaronide priests. Later communities in different circumstances have therefore applied the chapters to legitimize forms of leadership prevalent in their own communities, employing Leviticus as an ally to persuade others to accept the authority of their own kinds of leaders. They ignore major elements of the text, however, such as the actual identity of these priestly leaders, and give originally trivial features (such as the Septuagint's use of *ekklesia*) decisive significance.

These various readings arise from the presupposition that there must be more to the early chapters of Leviticus than merely a justification for priestly privileges. From a rhetorical perspective, when the audience changes, so does the rhetorical situation and therefore

23 See the survey in Lienhard, *Exodus, Leviticus, Numbers, Deuteronomy*, 172.

24 Barkley, *Origen: Homilies on Leviticus 1–16* (tr. Gary Wayne Barkley; Washington, DC: Catholic University Press of America, 1990), homilies 6 and 7.

25 Barkley, *Origen: Homilies on Leviticus 1–16*, homily 5 on Leviticus 6:17–23, p. 88. More generally, Origen argued that mature religious insight must guide interpretation: "These things are less clear to us to the same degree as our conversion to the Lord is less complete" (homily 6 on Leviticus, p. 116).

the message – the "whom" and the "what," and sometimes even the "who" – has changed in the question, "Who is persuading whom of what?" Rhetorical analysis can investigate every subsequent interpreter and interpretive community for which we have evidence to discover how this text, or the whole scripture, was/is used to convey a persuasive message from human and/or divine speakers to particular audiences.

What relationships obtain, or should obtain, between the ever-changing rhetoric of a text that is reread by different communities in different times and places and the persuasive purposes that shaped it in the first place? The original writers and intended audience have no privileged status from a rhetorical perspective, though they may be privileged by the interpretive traditions of particular religious or academic communities. Different interpretive needs drive communities, on the one hand, to make the text meaningful for themselves and lead historians, on the other hand, to try to understand its original purpose.

If one wishes to describe not just the rhetorical effect of a text but also its form, that is, how persuasive goals influenced its contents and shape, then one must focus on the writers and editors who gave it that shape and their intended audiences. They determined the features of the text and any attempt to explain those features must reconstruct their situation as much as possible. My efforts in this book have therefore concentrated on that original rhetorical situation in order to show that Leviticus has not only served persuasive purposes throughout its history, but that it was originally written to serve specific persuasive purposes.

Writers and their intentions are, of course, difficult to specify for any text, especially for ancient biblical texts that speak through anonymous narrators and the voice of God. Recognition of the persuasive character of these texts nevertheless requires some estimation of the identity of the writers and their intentions for their readers because the persuasive function of the text can only be understood in the context of this social interaction. The common designation of its writers as "priestly" reflects the long-standing recognition that Leviticus represents the perspectives and interests of Israel's priests. As this book makes crystal clear, that means specifically the families descended from Aaron's two younger sons, Eleazar and Ithamar, who, according to 1 Chronicles 24:1–19, rotated duty in the temple in Jerusalem between themselves. The audience addressed by P with the goal of persuading it to accept the Aaronides' authority is only slightly less certain: it was the people who called themselves "Israel." The date and specific historical situation that Leviticus 1–16 addressed are considerably more in doubt, with many scholars maintaining that P was written in the period of the divided monarchy (probably eighth-seventh centuries B.C.E.) against many others who defend the position that P was a product of the exile and post-exilic periods (sixth-fifth centuries B.C.E.). This debate, however, makes only a small difference to the rhetorical analysis of the first half of Leviticus. Whatever the date, in the rhetorical situation between priests and people, the message of Leviticus 1–16 can only have been intended to buttress the privileges and rights of the Aaronide priests, as the preceding chapters have shown.

Priesthood in Later Religious Rhetoric

The unease of later interpreters (especially but not exclusively Christians) with Leviticus' pro-priestly message is reflected in many sources from the last two millennia. It has frequently taken the form of critiques of "empty" ritualism. Phillipe Buc pointed out:

> The opposition between practices empty of any spirit and those that have a transcendental content or referent is a root dichotomy in European political culture. In its more extreme form, it is simply a dichotomy between pure, spiritless practice, and pure spirit unencumbered with material form. Originally . . . the opposition served claims of superiority. It was harnessed to successive theological causes, first to establish Christianity's superiority over Judaism, then to evacuate paganism of its religious substance, then in the age of the Gregorian Reform to

the benefit of newer religious orders and movements, and finally during the sixteenth-century Reformation for the Protestant critique of Roman Catholicism.[26]

Christian rhetoric has routinely attacked ritual performances like those described in Leviticus 1–16 as opposed to the gospel's "spiritual" message.

More specifically, the priestly rhetoric of Leviticus has received a hostile reception from audiences over two millennia who were imbued with religious and political antipathies to rule by priests or, more broadly, rule by any religious institutions. This heritage was produced by a long series of political struggles around several related issues, such as conflicts between secular states and European churches over their tax-exempt property holdings (in one memorable sixteenth-century episode, King Henry VIII of England used his schism with the Roman Catholic Church to seize the properties of monasteries) and over the claims of many popes to exert direct rule over parts of Europe (the Vatican ruled central Italy, including Rome, until the mid-nineteenth century) and over the rights and monies received by politically established religious institutions in many countries of the world still in the twenty-first century (a prominent feature of many political revolutions has therefore been the violent disestablishment of the church, such as in France in the late eighteenth century and in Russia and Mexico in the early twentieth century). In Western Europe, these struggles have tended to pit nationalism against the international political influence of the Roman Catholic Church, and so have generated deep distrust of the political roles played by religious institutions. That distrust has been fueled by legends of priests manipulating politics, such as are associated with the names of the French cardinal Richelieu (seventeenth century) or the Russian monk Rasputin (early twentieth century), even though they each advanced nationalistic interests. And beneath it all lies an abiding anti-Semitism that associates religious manipulation

---

[26] Buc, *The Dangers of Ritual*, 251.

of politics with secret Jewish conspiracies involving religious, financial, and political institutions. All in all, Western civilization has produced a culture very suspicious of Leviticus' rhetoric of priestly preeminence and of Second Temple Judaism's hierocracy.

The political climate of the early twenty-first century is no different in this regard. Fear of theocracy is once again a prominent feature of Western political culture. With so-called "fundamentalists" of various religious traditions bidding for political power and Western military deployments defined frequently in terms of a struggle between liberal democracy and militant religious fanaticism, many public statements voice concern about the growing influence of religion and of religious leaders on political affairs.

One might expect the more theocratic parties in these same conflicts to have celebrated Israel's ancient priests, such as Jesus Ben Sira and Josephus did in the Second Temple period,[27] but that has rarely happened since then. When it has, its persuasive power has been undercut by contradictory tendencies within the same movements. Rabbinic Judaism and its later offspring carried on the heritage of the Pharisees of the Second Temple period. This party of scholars contested the legal interpretations of their rivals, the Sadducees, who usually controlled the high priesthood and the temple. Rabbinic Judaism was therefore conflicted in its estimation of the priesthood of the Second Temple period, despite its fascination with the conduct of the Temple rituals. The high priest of the Second Temple period is remembered and celebrated in the Mishnah and in the medieval liturgy for the Day of Atonement, and descendants of the priests retain the honor of pronouncing the priestly blessing (Numbers 6:24–25) in synagogue worship. Authority over the tradition, however, passed irreversibly into the hands of rabbinic scholars.

The Christian churches of Late Antiquity elevated the office of priest over lay people in an explicit analogy with the biblical precedent. The

---

[27] See the Wisdom of Jesus ben Sira (Ecclesiasticus) 50; Josephus, *Ant.* xi. 329–39.

Christian priesthood, however, was traced from Jesus and his apostles, not from Aaron. It was presented as superseding the role and functions of the Jewish priesthood, whose lineage and function were rendered obsolete for Christian tradition. Therefore neither Judaism nor Catholicism in the medieval and modern periods celebrated Israel's priesthood enough to offset the anti-theocratic ideologies of the times. Even modern scholarship on the Second Temple period has tended to interpret it as background for later developments. As Jonathan Klawans has pointed out, "It is all too easy for the temple to play the role of antagonist in the drama of the development of whatever phenomenon primarily interests the scholar, be it rabbinic Judaism, the New Testament, or the Dead Sea Scrolls."[28]

As a result of this political history, modern scholarship has been prone to celebrate Israel's prophets and to be fascinated with its kings, but not with its priests.[29] Prophets have been embraced as ancient individualists who stood in opposition to idolatrous worship of religious images and political power. Even though sociological research has shown that Israel's prophets were imbedded in social and religious institutions whose interests they represented,[30] the prophets still appear to many modern readers as prototypes of religious reformers and political revolutionaries. Modern fascination with Israel's kings has roots in both Christian messianism and secular nationalism. Christian proclamation that Jesus is the Messiah depends on the royal rhetoric of Judah's kings, especially David, even when it transforms the implications of those claims. Fascination with kingship has therefore been a major theme in Christian imagination. In the late Middle Ages and

---

[28] Klawans, *Purity, Sacrifice, and the Temple*, 104. See also Cothey, "Ethics and Holiness," 133.

[29] It is amazing to realize that, despite the plethora of scholarly publications in the fields of biblical and ancient Jewish studies, the first and so far only history of the high priests of the Second Temple period was published only in 2004 (Vanderkam, *From Joshua to Caiaphas*).

[30] See Robert R. Wilson, *Prophecy and Society in Ancient Israel* (Philadelphia: Fortress, 1980); Thomas W. Overholt, *Channels of Prophecy: The Social Dynamics of Prophetic Activity* (Minneapolis: Fortress, 1989).

the modern period, that theme was reinforced by the literary genre of romance and by the political celebration of kings as symbols of national sovereignty. The waning of monarchy as a political institution simply transferred the fascination to the sovereign state itself (note the lingering royal overtones in the adjective "sovereign"), not least in the modern state of Israel. Christian doctrine, romance literature, and nationalist ideologies have therefore combined to fuel interest in David and the other kings of biblical literature as prototypical nationalist figures in Western cultural imagination.

The writings of Julius Wellhausen, the nineteenth-century German scholar whose analysis of the Pentateuch continues to be influential today, exemplify how these value judgments have biased historical assessments of the priestly literature and the Second Temple priesthood. Wellhausen viewed P's rituals as reflecting spiritual decline: "Worship no longer springs from an inner impulse, it has come to be an exercise in religiosity. It has no natural significance; its significance is transcendental, incomparable, not to be defined; the chief effect of it, which is always produced with certainty, is atonement."[31] He celebrated the pre-exilic period, and especially the prophets, for creating room for individualism, in contrast to the post-exilic period, which "left no free scope for the individual."[32] Wellhausen viewed the state and temple as rivals: "The weaker the state grew, . . . the higher became the prestige of the temple in the eyes of the people, and the greater and the more independent grew the power of its numerous priesthood,"[33] but he gave priority to the state in doing theology: "Now we must acknowledge that the nation is more certainly created by God than the Church, and that God works more powerfully in the history of the nations than in Church history. The Church, at first a substitute for the nation that was wanting, is affected by the same evils incident to an artificial cultivation as meet us in

---

[31] Wellhausen, *Prolegomena*, 424.
[32] Wellhausen, *Prolegomena*, 412.
[33] Wellhausen, *Prolegomena*, 420.

Judaism."[34] His nationalism was linked to anti-Catholicism: the Judaism of the Second Temple Period was, he asserted, "an unpolitical artificial product created in spite of unfavorable circumstances by the impulse of an ever-memorable energy: and foreign rule is its necessary counterpart. In its nature it is intimately allied to the old Catholic church, which was in fact its child."[35] Many readers have noticed that he expressed his anti-Semitism at the end of his encyclopedia article, "Israel," in his expectation that Judaism must inevitably become extinct.[36]

All this is well known and has long been repudiated by most biblical scholars. Newer ideologies of the nineteenth and twentieth centuries, however, have not been any more sympathetic to the rhetoric of priestly hierocracy. Neither proponents of Marxism nor of liberal capitalism look favorably on aristocratic oligarchies, which in economic terms is what the Jewish priesthood became. Norman Gottwald reflected this continuing bias against priestly literature when he wrote, "The view of history and social order in P and Chronicles largely lacks a sense of the contingency and ambiguity of events and institutions that evokes flexibility and humility of mind and calls for continuous critical assessment of oppressive or outmoded power."[37] It would, of course, be unreasonable to expect feminist critics to celebrate the priests' patriarchal hierarchy that systematically excluded women from Israel's positions of institutionalized religious leadership.

Nevertheless, over the last four decades, a cadre of mostly Jewish scholars have worked to rehabilitate P's reputation. They have adopted two basic tactics to achieve that end. On the one hand, they have redescribed P's ritual texts in theological terms to make them more palatable to modern audiences. For a methodological critique of this

---

[34] Wellhausen, "Israel," *Encyclopaedia Britannica*, 9th ed.; reprinted in *Prolegomena*, 429–548 [513].

[35] Wellhausen, *Prolegomena*, 422.

[36] Wellhausen, "Israel," 548.

[37] Norman Gottwald, *The Hebrew Bible: A Socio-Literary Introduction* (Philadelphia: Fortress, 1985), 463.

approach, see Chapter 1. On the other hand, they have argued that the priestly writings should be dated to the monarchic period, rather than after the exile, so that they are represented as part of the mainstream of Israel's history rather than appearing as a supplement to it. The irony of the latter approach is that it places P's rhetoric in a historical context in which, according to the biblical history books, priests did not enjoy the autonomy that they claimed for themselves but were instead dominated by the kings who patronized their temples and appointed them to their offices.

Despite these recent efforts, most audiences in the last two millennia have encountered the priestly rhetoric of Leviticus with more hostility than sympathy. Though ideological critics are no doubt correct that the Bible is usually read much *too* sympathetically, that has not been the case with the priestly literature of the Pentateuch, especially with its rhetoric of priestly privilege. Readers have been shaped by their own histories and experiences to be suspicious of claims that God granted Aaronide priests special rights and privileges. Such readers have then either rejected this rhetoric out of hand, as well as the book that contains it (Leviticus, or the Old Testament, or the Bible), or they have transformed its message into something more palatable, such as advice for religious leaders or spiritual allegories or theological analogies. Thus priestly rhetoric has routinely been criticized and dismissed, or defended only by turning it into something that it originally was not. For those readers, this becomes the message of the text, more than the text's original message of acquiescence to priestly direction in first millennium B.C.E. temples in Jerusalem and on Mt. Gerizim.

Since the force of the text's rhetoric changes with every change of audience, rhetorical analysis can only note the effects of the latter on the former, not argue against them. These later experiences and presuppositions, however, place stumbling blocks in the path of studies of the origins and nature of priestly rhetoric in its original historical situation, that is, as used by priests to influence their listening and reading audiences in ancient Israel, either before or after the exile. Interpreters with such historical goals cannot avoid bringing our own culture and ideological commitments into our work, but we can become conscious of the effects of such biases and begin to imagine other interpretive possibilities. Reading, just like theater, requires a conscious suspension of disbelief, not just in order to accept (momentarily) the imaginative worlds that books can present but also to accept (momentarily) the ideologies that they reflect and project. What is needed to advance our understanding of the origins of P's literature are new imaginative construals of the *values* in priestly rhetoric that consciously try to avoid the biases inherited from later religious and political commitments.[38]

The distinction between contemporary meaning and original purpose is not easy to maintain in practice. A long history of religious and political movements colors all interpreters' evaluations of the rhetoric of Leviticus. Though value judgments cannot be avoided in historical inquiry, bringing the influence of this history to conscious awareness may allow us to reevaluate the pro-priestly rhetoric of Leviticus on a more dispassionate basis.

Reevaluating Hierocracy in Second Temple Judaism

If we can momentarily bracket some of the negative value judgments about ancient priests with which modern history and tradition have indoctrinated us and try to evaluate the ancient Jewish priesthood in its own religious, political, and historical context, this would make possible a more sympathetic evaluation of the ancient Jewish hierocracy. That seems to be what the priestly writers hoped would result from their legitimation and celebration of the Aaronide priesthood.

There is solid evidence in Second Temple period literature that the Torah achieved that, and more. Though P extends the priests' authority beyond ritual procedures only to matters of teaching Israel the distinction between clean and unclean and holy and common

---

[38] Cothey has also recently argued for the necessity of more sympathetic readings of priestly rituals ("Ethics and Holiness," 135).

(Lev 10:9–11) and Deuteronomy extends their authority only a little further to the extent of staffing a high court of appeal (Deut 17:8–13) and teaching the Torah as a whole (31:9–13), P's elaborate descriptions of the vesting and anointing of Aaron and his sons (Lev 8–9; also Exod 28, 39) distinguishes the priesthood as the most celebrated office of leadership in the Torah.[39] It is not surprising then that the Torah's unparalleled celebration of the priests gave them increasing political influence as the Second Temple period progressed. The Wisdom of Jesus Ben Sira (second century B.C.E.) shows clearly the influence of P's rhetoric on Jewish political ideals. In his "praise of famous men" (44:1), Ben Sira gives Aaron (45:6–22) greater space than Moses (44:23–45:5), lingering over the high priest's vestments (cf. Exod 28). He then concludes his book with a paean of praise for the high priest Simon, son

---

[39] Much of the scholarly discussions of the offices of Israel have focused on Deuteronomy's descriptions of prophets, priests, and kings. In comparison with P's elaborate celebration of the Aaronides, however, Deuteronomy's treatment of these offices is very utilitarian and limited. The king, famously, has no duties but to copy and read Torah (17:14–20). Prophets receive a more positive commission, but the text's chief concern has to do with the validity of the prophet's message, which must be determined by its accuracy (18:15–22) and its accord with the henotheistic teachings of Deuteronomy itself (13:2–6, LXX 1–5). Bernard M. Levinson has recently described Deuteronomy's program as a utopian constitution that designates separate spheres of judicial, cultic, and monarchic authority under the governance of a legal text, which is Deuteronomy itself ("The First Constitution: Rethinking the Origins of Rule of Law and Separation of Powers in Light of Deuteronomy," *Cardozo Law Review* 27 [2006]: 1853–8). Ancient Israelite society never actually operated in such a fashion, as Levinson is the first to admit. One should note, however, that Deuteronomy's program of cultic centralization in the Jerusalem temple did not produce a balance of power even in theory so much as tilt power toward the temple's hierarchy: "levitical priests" must supervise the king's copying of the scroll of law (17:18) and rule on judicial cases "too difficult" for local courts (17:8–13), and it is they, of course, who control the reading and teaching of Torah itself (31:9–13). So despite their very many differences from each other, Deuteronomy supports P's privileging of priests. Deuteronomy's focus on Levites rather than P's Aaronides would hardly have impeded the Torah's pro-priestly function in the Second Temple period when priestly genealogies harmonized both groups into one family (see Otto, *Das Deuteronomium im Pentateuch und Hexateuch*, 260, who argues for the priestly, specifically Zadokite, interests behind both Deuteronomy separately and the hexateuchal and pentateuchal redactions that combined it with other books [248–62])

of Onias. He first celebrates Simon's construction projects and political achievements like a king (50:1–4) before lavishing much greater attention on his appearance "when he put on his glorious robe and clothed himself in perfect splendor" (vv. 5–11) and officiated over the temple offerings (vv. 12–21). It is no wonder that later Roman governors insisted on controlling the use of such politically potent clothes.[40]

The ability to imagine a sympathetic reception for this rhetoric is therefore a precondition for understanding it, as Jonathan Klawans has recently emphasized.[41] A rhetoric of the divine right of priests to control Israel's offerings will, however, not carry much weight with modern audiences for whom such rituals are little more than historical curiosities or religious symbols. More plausible will be a reevaluation of the ancient hierocracy on the basis of its historical effects rather than its supposedly divine origins. Its value needs to be judged against the achievements of the priestly dynasty whose rule it legitimated. It is against the background of priestly history in this period, therefore, that the rhetoric of Leviticus should, in the first instance, be judged.

---

[40] Josephus, *Ant.* 15.402–8, 19.93, 20.6–16. The Letter of Aristeas (96–99), Philo (*Vita Mosis* 2.109–35; *Spec. Leg.* 1.82–97), and Josephus (*Ant.* 3.151–78; *Jewish War* 5.227–36) also give extensive descriptions of the priestly garments that echo through rabbinic literature, and that attest not only to the fascination they aroused but also to the rhetorical function of literary descriptions in furthering the priesthood's mystique and power. See Michael D. Swartz, "The Semiotics of the Priestly Vestments in Ancient Judaism," in *Sacrifice in Religious Experience* (ed. Albert I. Baumgarten; Numen 93, Leiden: Brill, 2002), 57–80.

[41] Klawans summarized the theme of his book in explicit contrast to the biases that he documented in much traditional and contemporary scholarship: "The effort has been made here to understand the temple, its practices, and its priests with a reasonable degree of sympathy" (*Purity, Sacrifice, and the Temple*, 248). This point has been emphasized over the last forty years through the detailed explication of priestly rituals by, especially, Jacob Milgrom and Baruch Levine in their monographs and commentaries. They have defended the rationality and realism of priestly rituals against the old and widespread tendency to disparage them as primitive and superstitious (see Chapter 1 of this book). This trend has not yet, however, led to reevaluations of the religious achievements of the Second Temple priesthood itself, though the methodological case for interpretive sympathy when reading about priests has recently been argued by Cothey and Klawans.

By what standards should we judge the priests' effectiveness? There are many possibilities, running the gamut of our contemporary religious and political opinions. I suggest starting with two criteria that balance ancient and modern sensibilities. The first should consist of the religious standards set forth by the Hebrew Bible itself, because they represent values to which the priests themselves subscribed and that their contemporaries expected them to epitomize, and because they remain potent religious ideals in the modern world. Though the contents of the Hebrew Bible are diverse and express multiple opinions on various issues, they nevertheless for the most part subscribe to a common ideal of how Israel's religion should be expressed. Included in that ideal is loyalty to YHWH, the god of Israel, expressed in some texts by pure monotheism, and also by a commitment to fulfilling the ethical and religious stipulations of Torah, conceived either as oral divine instruction in earlier texts or as the written laws of the Pentateuch in later texts. Evaluating the priest's leadership against such standards typical of biblical literature can help us avoid complete anachronism. Our judgments will employ values that the ancient priests most likely subscribed to themselves, since they wrote a significant part of the Hebrew Bible and championed the written Torah's authority.

How well does the Aaronides' record stack up against broad biblical ideals? The Aaronide priests oversaw the establishment of cultic worship in Judea at Jerusalem, in Samaria on Mt. Gerizim, and in Egypt at Leontopolis on the basis of the Torah's ritual instructions.[42] Furthermore, it was in this period that the Torah as written text began

---

[42] The orthodoxy of the Samaritan's practice was contested by ancient Jews who derided it as idolatrous (see 2 Kgs 17:24–41; Josephus, *Ant.* 13.3), but it is difficult to take this criticism seriously. Samaritans, like Jews, revere the Torah and its laws. Though interpretive and textual differences, as well as ethnic rivalries, separated the two communities, and though there is evidence of vast variations in the nature and degree of religious observance within both communities in the Second Temple period, these aspersions against the Samaritan cult reflect polemics rather than historical practices; see Pieter W. van der Horst, "Anti-Samaritan Propaganda in Early Judaism," in *Persuasion and Dissuasion in Early Christianity, Ancient Judaism, and Hellenism* (ed. Pieter W. van der Horst et al.; Leuven: Peeters, 2003), 25–44.

to function normatively for temple practice both in Jerusalem and on Mt. Gerizim, and probably in Leontopolis as well. The Torah was officially recognized as Jewish temple law by the Persians (according to Ezra 7) and was sufficiently respected by the Hellenistic rulers of Egypt, the Ptolemies, for them to sponsor an official Greek translation of it (according to the Letter of Aristeas). Whether or not such official recognitions were really as significant as these Jewish texts make them appear, it is clear that as the Second Temple period progressed, the Torah became increasingly recognized as a symbol of Samaritan and Jewish religious distinctiveness. Accompanying the Torah's elevation to iconic status was the establishment and growing recognition of monotheism as normative for Jews and Samaritans. Though in the late fifth century, the existence of a polytheistic Jewish temple in Elephantine, Egypt, passed without negative comment in the correspondence of that community with authorities in Judea and Samaria, such a situation is unlikely to have been tolerated in the second century and later.

In other words, as Joshua's Aaronide dynasty gained first religious preeminence and then civil power in the Second Temple period, increasing numbers of Jews and Samaritans seem to have conformed to the Bible's most basic notions of proper religious practices and beliefs.[43] This was the case to a much greater extent than at any time previously, according to the Bible's own account of the religious standards of the monarchic period and by most modern historical accounts of that period as well. It can safely be said then that on the basis of the Bible's own standards, the priestly hierocracy of the Second Temple period produced markedly better religious results than did the monarchs of the pre-exilic period, most of whose religious policies

---

[43] My blithe reference to "the Bible" in this paragraph is, of course, anachronistic since at the beginning of the Second Temple period there was no canon to speak of, the Torah became increasingly authoritative through the middle of the period, and the full Tanak gained recognition only late in the period, if then. I use the term here intentionally, however, to emphasize the convergence between priestly influence and the ideals of the emerging scriptures.

are repudiated by biblical writers as rejections of God's covenant with Israel.

It is, of course, hardly surprising that the priests led Jews and Samaritans in basic accord with the Torah's teachings: they wrote and edited much of it, and probably played a decisive role in canonizing it. The surprise comes rather from noting the failure of modern commentators to point out the correspondence between biblical ideals and the achievements of the Aaronides' hierocracy. Even studies of priestly roles and the history of Israelite/Judean priesthoods tend to focus primarily on the pre-exilic and immediately post-exilic priesthoods and limit the priests' influence to the "theological" ideas contained in P, giving little or no attention to their influence on the later political and religious development of Second Temple Judaism. The heritage of later religious and political struggles against theocratic institutions continues to weigh heavily on how the religion of the Second Temple period is portrayed in scholarship, especially in broader treatments of biblical theology or religion.[44]

Take only one prominent example of this nearly universal tendency in modern biblical studies: Walter Brueggeman's *Theology of the Old Testament* (1997) categorizes the Hebrew Bible's means for mediating the divine presence as "Torah," "King," "Prophet," and "Sage," but where one would naturally expect to see "Priest," he lists "Cult" instead.

---

[44] See, for example, Joseph Blenkinsopp, *Sage, Priest, Prophet: Religious and Intellectual Leadership in Ancient Israel* (Louisville: Westminster John Knox, 1995) 113–14, despite his astute description of the effects of anti-priestly biases in scholarship (66–8); see also Lester L. Grabbe, *Priests, Prophets, Diviners, Sages: A Socio-Historical Study of Religious Specialists in Ancient Israel* (Valley Forge, PA: Trinity Press International, 1995). One significant effort to rectify this imbalance was written by Richard D. Nelson, *Raising Up a Faithful Priest: Community and Priesthood in Biblical Theology*, (Louisville: Westminster John Knox, 1993). He chronicled the bias in biblical scholarship against priests, which he blamed primarily on Protestant thought, and wrote positive theological reflections on the priesthood (101–5). Though Nelson recounted the glorification of the high priest in Second Temple literature, his own evaluation of Joshua's dynasty remained muted. His final list of priestly heros – "Ezekiel, the Priestly Writer, Ezra, and the Maccabees" (105) – omits the high priestly line entirely, except insofar as it is represented by P.

His discussion under that heading marks a major advance over most other theologies that give ritual worship much shorter shrift.[45] Like the rest of the field, however, Brueggeman hid the political implications of the Pentateuch's Aaronide claims by focusing on rituals and shrines rather than on priestly personnel.

I turn therefore to a different, more secular standard for evaluating the priests' effectiveness, namely, the practical effects of their rule. What were its consequences for the people of ancient Israel, Judea, and Samaria? This evaluation imaginatively poses a question common in modern political campaigns: were Samaritans and Judeans better off due to priestly leadership and rule, or not? Though political expediency is no virtue according to many biblical texts, political success garners respect from most ancient and modern historians. From the long perspective of two millennia, it is easier to reach a consensus on what counts as "successful" leadership than it is for more contemporary events. The Judean kings who revolted against Babylon in the early sixth century B.C.E. and the Jewish rebels who fought against Rome in 66–70 C.E. were obvious failures, as the disastrous effects of their policies for the people of Judea make clear.

How effective was the hierocracy in promoting the survival and welfare of Jewish and Samaritan peoples? To answer this question is to judge the leadership of the Aaronides on the basis of political pragmatism, or on "the artfulness of cultural persistence" to use Steven Weitzman's more attractive phrase.[46] The political tendencies

---

45 Walter Brueggemann, *Theology of the Old Testament: Testimony, Dispute, Advocacy* (Minneapolis: Fortress, 1997), 567–704. It should be noted that Brueggemann's discussion of the cult highlights the theological stereotyping that has bedeviled Christian biblical theologies and works hard to avoid it by devoting thirty pages to its theological implications. Nevertheless, discussion of the priesthood receives only one page of that (664–5).

46 Steven Weitzman, *Surviving Sacrilege: Cultural Persistence in Jewish Antiquity* (Cambridge, MA: Harvard University Press, 2005), who presents a series of vignettes into strategies for cultural survival and persistence in order to revalue more positively a history that has often suffered from historian's neglect and disdain. Weitzman's focus on literary evidence leads him to ignore the history of the period of the rise of the

of the Aaronide hierocracy, as attested by a variety of sources over six centuries, are fairly clear and relatively consistent. The high priests in Jerusalem maintained accommodationist policies toward imperial overlords (Persia, Alexander, the Ptolemies), resulting in three centuries of largely peaceful relations with them.[47] They oversaw the reconstruction or, at least, the reorganization of the Jewish community in Jerusalem and Judea and its gradual growth in population and wealth. The same period of time witnessed the growth in wealth and political influence of Jewish communities in Babylon and especially in Egypt, where Jewish priest/generals sometimes played major roles in Ptolemaic politics. Though the extent of Aaronide influence in Babylon is unknown, priests and Levites made up the bulk of returning exiles from Babylon in the sixth and fifth centuries. Later, Aaronides founded and maintained a Jewish temple in Egypt for almost three centuries. The Samaritans also recovered from the catastrophes of the Assyrian wars and, like the Jews, solidified their religious and ethnic identity at least partly under the religious leadership of Aaronide priests.

One might well ask whether the various governors of Judea and Samaria in the Persian and Ptolemaic periods should get some of the credit for these political and religious accomplishments. It is, of course,

---

Aaronide hierocracy (sixth to second centuries B.C.E.) for the very good reason that there are few literary sources for this period. My own less subtle analysis of broad political trends uses other means to make a case similar to his for reconsidering the values that guide historical depictions of this period.

[47] The fact that one fourth-century governor of Judah and, perhaps, high priest minted coins with inscriptions in paleo-Hebrew script led William Schniedewind to see their origin in "a nationalist Jewish movement led by the priests" (*How the Bible Became a Book*, 174). That is possible, but the coins still bear the title "governor," which hardly suggests outright rejection of the empire. A more likely setting for this development has been suggested by David Carr. He described the increasing valuation of the Hebrew language in the Second Temple period as an act of cultural resistance against Hellenistic influences (*Writing*, 253–62). Hellenism was already making inroads in the area of Judea in the mid-fourth century and the date of this coin may show that using the Hebrew language as a strategy of cultural resistance originated before the Hasmonean period.

the job of governors to accommodate imperial interests, so such policies no doubt reflect their influence. With the exceptions of Zerubbabel and Nehemiah, however, no governor of these territories gets significant recognition in the surviving rhetoric from the period (except in the Elephantine papyri). By the Ptolemaic period if not before, the office itself seems to have been dispensed with in Judea as the Temple's high priests took over greater political functions, culminating eventually in the hierocracy of the Hasmoneans. Even Nehemiah's text (together with Ezra's) was relegated to the canonical backwater of the *Ketubim*, while P's celebration of the Aaronide priesthood took pride of place at the center of the Torah. Later Second Temple literature allows one to estimate their literary influence: Nehemiah (person and book) does not appear in 1 Esdras or among the Dead Sea Scrolls; the latter include one fragmentary manuscript of Ezra, who, however, does not appear in Ben Sira's review of "famous men," while Nehemiah does (49:13). By contrast, the Qumran library contained at least fifteen manuscripts of Leviticus in three different languages (Hebrew, Greek, and Aramaic) and countless references and allusions to its contents in other works. Many Second Temple period books include celebration of the priesthood as a major theme (e.g., Ben Sira, Jubilees, Testament of Levi, Aramaic Levi, etc.).[48] Though the books of Ezra-Nehemiah rightly play a decisive role in modern historical reconstructions of Persian-period Judea, their value as historical sources should not obscure the fact that, as texts, they seem to have had relatively little rhetorical influence in the Second Temple period itself. Most of the rhetoric preserved from the period does not celebrate the roles of governors and other imperial officials.

Aaronide priests led Samaritans and Jews from catastrophe and devastation in the sixth century B.C.E. to become populous, increasingly wealthy and influential temple communities by the late third and second centuries. The Seleucids and Romans would find Jews

---

[48] See James Kugel, "Levi's Elevation to the Priesthood in Second Temple Writings," *Harvard Theological Review* 86 (1993): 1–63.

and Samaritans to be militarily troublesome, which is itself testimony to their power and how far Aaronide leadership had brought these communities in the preceding period. This record of accommodationist policies is in marked contrast to the nationalistic policies of Israel's and Judah's kings, and of the later Hasmonean dynasty, which took the high priesthood and, eventually, the royal title as well in its pursuit of independence. Though successful in the short term, that policy would fail to preserve Judea's independence and their dynasty in the first century B.C.E. In the following century, it led to national catastrophe. Contrary to modern presuppositions about the typical tendencies of theocracies, many powerful Aaronides showed considerable tolerance for foreigners and foreign ways, as exemplified by their intermarriage with Samaritans and interest in Hellenistic culture.[49] These policies came under withering criticism from those advocating more exclusive perspectives.

Of course, some of the high priests were complicit in nationalistic movements as well, and the more exclusive policies of leaders like Ezra and Nehemiah did not preclude their close cooperation with the Persian overlords. So the distinction I am drawing is not hard and fast. It is nevertheless notable that the priests' pursuit of a *modus vivendi* with imperial powers and/or ethnic neighbors earned them sharp criticism from those, like Ezra, Nehemiah, the Maccabees, and the Zealots, who claimed a divine mandate for policies of separation and exclusion. In the long run, however, the priests' pragmatism produced better results for the material and political welfare of Jews and Samaritans than

---

[49] It was not just Jewish and Samaritan priests that consolidated their grasp on their offices and incomes by accommodating imperial overlords politically. A single Egyptian family controlled the high priesthood of Ptah in Memphis throughout the Ptolemaic period – a span of thirteen high priests over ten generations. By its loyal support of the Ptolemaic monarchs, this family capitalized on its strategic position near Alexandria in a historic capital of Egypt to monopolize this supreme office and its incomes. See Dorothy J. Thompson, "The High Priests of Memphis under Ptolemaic Rule," in *Pagan Priests: Religion and Power in the Ancient World* (ed. Mary Beard and John North; Ithaca: Cornell University Press, 1990), 95–116.

did more confrontational policies, the military successes of the Hasmoneans not withstanding. Though one looks in vain for an explicit defense of such accommodationist policies toward imperial powers in the Pentateuch or other Second Temple literature before Josephus, the Aaronides' policies are probably responsible for the prominent preservation in the biblical canon of antinationalistic oracles by pre-exilic prophets like Isaiah, Jeremiah, and Ezekiel.[50] They almost certainly account for the absence of royal institutions and rhetoric from the Torah itself.

Obviously, I do not advance these reevaluations of the Aaronide record in hopes of reviving an outdated and discredited model of religious and political leadership. I share the critical perspectives of many modern ideologies on the dangers of theocracies. These critiques become anachronistic hindrances, however, when they subconsciously color historical evaluations of the Second Temple period. The Aaronides' record of promoting biblical religious standards and of using relatively tolerant policies to improve the well-being of their communities compares favorably with all of Israel's other leadership models and experiences of that period and earlier. Histories of the period and readings of Leviticus need to reflect that record in order to produce more balanced interpretations of Aaronide rhetoric and its significance for religious history.

Though priestly self-justification has not been received very well in later millennia, other aspects of Leviticus' rhetoric have done better. The next two chapters will explore two cultural themes that seem likely to reflect the rhetorical heritage of the early chapters of Leviticus.

---

[50] Klawans noted, however, that Second Temple priests maintained a more inclusive cult than that advocated by Ezekiel and that this played a role in the relative importance of the latter's texts in this period: "We can safely assume that early Second Temple priests played some role in the canonization – and centralization – of Leviticus and Numbers and the relative ostracizing of Ezekiel 40–48." Contrary to the prevailing assumptions of biblical interpreters, he argued correctly that "here we find anonymous priests defending what would strike us as just and good – openness and inclusion – against the vision of an exclusivist prophet" (*Purity, Sacrifice, and the Temple*, 74).

Chapter 8 examines the theme of sacrifice in Western culture and tries to explain why Leviticus has not been more influential on later sacrificial rhetoric. Chapter 9 addresses the theme of scripture and argues that Leviticus and the rest of P's ritual instructions in the Torah proved to be the decisive factor in creating the idea of authoritative scriptures.

The Rhetoric of Sacrifice

The early chapters of Leviticus are commonly referred to as instructions for making sacrifices. In this book, I have discussed various aspects of these instructions as pertaining to "offerings," but I have rarely used the term "sacrifice." Though Leviticus appears to be more concerned with sacrifice than any other part of the Bible, that term turns out, on closer analysis, to have less to do with this book than most people think. A survey of the rhetoric of "sacrifice" in the contemporary world as well as in antiquity will explain my reticence in using the word, as well as point out the curious disjunction between Leviticus' instructions for offerings and later sacrificial rhetoric.

The language of sacrifice pervades our contemporary rhetoric of politics, religion, and popular culture. References to sacrifice and depictions of sacrifice can be found in music lyrics, movies, political speeches, and news stories about sports, economics, and biomedical research. It is, of course, ubiquitous in the rhetoric of war. Fascination with the idea of sacrifice is also reflected in the large number of academic theories about its nature and origins. For the past century and a half, scholars of religion, sociology, psychology, and anthropology have advanced theories to explain how sacrifice works religiously and why its practice and effects are so widespread.[1] Yet every attempt to describe and explain "sacrifice" always fails to encompass the whole range of ritual and nonritual behaviors called sacrifices.

The entanglement of theory and ideology in discussions of sacrifice has led some to conclude that the word "sacrifice" describes nothing at all but is rather an evaluative term. The classicist Marcel Detienne argued:

> The notion of sacrifice is indeed a category of the thought of yesterday, conceived of as arbitrarily as totemism – decried earlier by Levi-Strauss – both because it gathers into one artificial type elements taken from here and there in the symbolic fabric of societies and because it reveals the surprising power of annexation that Christianity still subtly exercises on the thought of these historians and sociologists who were convinced they were inventing a new science.[2]

Wilfred Lambert, in describing the religions of ancient Mesopotamia, also avoided the term "sacrifice" because it "is so loaded and ambiguous a term that it is best not to use it. In modern usage 'sacrifice' is too dependent on Biblical institutions and concepts to be a suitable vehicle to express ancient Mesopotamian practices."[3] A survey of recent theoretical discussions of sacrifice led Ivan Strenski to conclude that "sacrifice is what might be better called a syndrome, rather than an objective 'thing' with its name written on it."[4] Such skepticism has found a foothold in biblical scholarship as well: in his commentary on Leviticus, Erhard Gerstenberger concluded, "Our attempts to delineate the three notions of offering, community,

---

[1] Anthologized by Jeffrey Carter, ed., *Understanding Religious Sacrifice: A Reader* (London: Continuum, 2003).
[2] Detienne, "Culinary Practices and the Spirit of Sacrifice," 20.
[3] Lambert, "Donations of Food and Drink," 191.
[4] Ivan Strenski, "Between Theory and Specialty: Sacrifice in the 90s," *Religious Studies Review* 22/1 (1996): 10–20 [19].

and atonement as the comprehensive motives represent merely modern rationalizations, and function only in a limited fashion as aids to understanding that cannot completely illuminate the mystery of sacrifice."[5]

These negative judgments can be generalized to say that "sacrifice" is an evaluative term rather than a descriptive one.[6] It expresses value judgments about behaviors rather than describing a distinct form of behavior. An unusual feature of the term "sacrifice," however, is that it conveys not just one but rather several contradictory evaluations of actions. The following survey will show that evaluations of particular ritual and nonritual acts as "sacrifices" depend on analogies with stories of sacrifice. Such narrative analogies ground the idea of sacrifice, which is meaningless without them, and they account for the opposite valuations that it can convey. Comparative analyses of sacrificial rituals have confused the narrative analogy ("sacrifice") with the rituals to which it is applied.

I will defend these claims by categorizing the major theories about sacrifice in modern scholarship on the basis of their use of rituals and narratives. This categorization shows that the ritual/narrative distinction lies at the heart of the theoretical confusion over sacrifice. I will then turn to the problem of ritual interpretation as it impinges on the debates over sacrifice before concluding with a brief analysis of the principal narrative traditions that have shaped the idea of sacrifice in both popular and academic culture.

---

[5] Gerstenberger, *Leviticus*, 20.

[6] The English term "sacrifice" is itself problematic for cross-cultural comparisons, because classical languages (Sanskrit, Hebrew, Greek) and contemporary non-Western languages do not necessarily contain a term that covers the same range of meanings. Even Latin *sacrificium*, a compound of *sacer*, "sacred," and *facem*, "to make," thus "to make sacred, to sanctify, to devote," leaves us, as Carter noted, "with a rather general, somewhat vague definition we could call 'religious action,' which is not really a definition at all" (*Understanding Religious Sacrifice*, 3). The classical languages do, of course, each contain rich technical vocabularies describing ritual offerings and their performance, much of which is obscure to modern interpreters.

Theories of Sacrifice

Modern theories of sacrifice fall rather obviously into two groups based on whether their explanations emphasize *human* or *animal* sacrifices. Of course, most theorists discuss both, but they inevitably explain one in terms of the other, which is more fundamental for their theories.

Theories based principally on animal offerings have been espoused throughout the last century and a half. W. Robertson Smith, for example, traced the origins of sacrifice to a community's consumption of the totem animal in a festival meal. He considered other kinds of sacrifice, including human sacrifice, to be corrupted forms of this original communion meal. So for him eating animals lay behind all traditions of sacrifice whether they involve animals or not.[7] Many other theorists have also emphasized the primacy of animal offerings, though in very different ways from Smith and each other. Thus Edward Tylor's gift theory of sacrifice defined the offering of humans as a version of cannibalism, that is as an alternative food offering to animal meat.[8] Henri Hubert and Marcel Mauss based their sociological theory on the most complete descriptions of sacrificial rituals available to them, the animal offerings of the Vedic (Indian) and biblical (Jewish) traditions. Human offerings, even "the sacrifice of the god," derive from older animal rites.[9] Walter Burkert traced sacrifice back to the hunting of animals, Jonathan Z. Smith to the domestication of animals, and Marcel Detienne to the cooking of animals.[10] And Nancy Jay, though focusing on sacrifice as a patriarchal rite bent on expelling symbols

---

[7] William Robertson Smith, *The Religion of the Semites* (2nd ed.; London: Black, 1907), *passim* but especially 222–7, 245, 353, 361–7.

[8] Edward B. Tylor, *Primitive Culture* (New York: Brentano's Books, 1871), 375–410.

[9] Henri Hubert and Marcel Mauss, *Sacrifice: Its Nature and Function* (Chicago: University of Chicago Press, 1964; French original, 1898).

[10] Walter Burkert, *Homo Necans: The Anthropology of Ancient Greek Sacrificial Ritual and Myth* (Berkeley: University of California Press, 1983); Smith, "The Domestication of Sacrifice," 191–205; Detienne, "Culinary Practices and the Spirit of Sacrifice," 1–20.

of "femaleness," followed Hubert and Mauss in seeing animals as the principal vehicles for such expiation.[11]

Over the same time period, other theorists have focused first on human sacrifice. James G. Frazer collected a wide variety of rituals into a theory of sacrificial kingship, in which the ritual sacrifice of kings undergirds most forms of traditional ritual expression.[12] Though few have followed Frazer's theory, many have seen the killing of humans at the heart of sacrifice. Sigmund Freud postulated a primordial patricide at the root of human culture and religion: a band of brothers murdered their father because of his sexual monopoly of the women of the community. But they were horrified by their crime and repressed the memory of it through incest taboos and ritual reenactment of the murder in the form of animal sacrifice.[13]

The theories of Frazer and Freud grew out of, and in turn fed, a nineteenth- and twentieth-century fascination with human sacrifice as a, or even *the*, fundamental human experience. Nobody took this tendency further than George Bataille, who described sacrifice as the most profound, if ultimately futile, attempt by which humans try to reestablish intimacy with nature. Human sacrifices are, he thought, the most extreme and revealing form of this attempt.[14] But the view that human sacrifice is basic to society has circulated more widely in the form developed by René Girard, who changed Freud's thesis into a general theory of violence. When rivalry threatens to destroy a community, Girard argued, sacrifice diverts the rival's aggression onto a victim who cannot retaliate, thus ending the cycle of violence for the time being. Though animal sacrifice performs this function, Girard's more obvious and effective examples of such violent scapegoating involve human

---

[11] Jay, *Throughout Your Generations Forever*, 1992.

[12] James George Frazer, *The Golden Bough: A Study in Magic and Religion* (abridged ed.; New York: Macmillan, 1922, 1960).

[13] Sigmund Freud, *Totem and Taboo: Resemblances between the Psychic Lives of Savages and Neurotics* (tr. A. A. Brill, New York: Vintage, 1918).

[14] Georges Bataille, *Theory of Religion* (tr. R. Hurley, New York: Zone, 1992; French original, 1948).

victims, and range from witch trials to pogroms to the crucifixion of Jesus.[15]

Many recent writers have continued to give priority to human sacrifice. Bruce Lincoln interpreted human and animal sacrifices as symbolic justifications for the violence deemed necessary to maintaining archaic Indo-European society.[16] Maurice Bloch argued that "rebounding violence" underlies not just sacrifices but almost all religious and political rituals, and leads to the symbolic or actual domination of others through violence.[17] J. C. Heesterman reconstructed the history of Vedic rituals that transformed life-and-death contests between warriors into ritualized expressions of interior self-sacrifice.[18] And Barbara Ehrenreich, combining elements drawn from Burkert and Bloch, suggested that the primordial experience of *being* hunted by large predators conditioned humans to accept the deaths of individuals for the sake of the larger community, a conditioning ritualized both in sacrifice and in war.[19]

This distinction between theories based on animal offerings and those based on human executions not only points to fundamental disagreements among interpreters about sacrifice. It also highlights the failure of all modern interpretations to deal adequately with the ancient and traditional sources that tend *not* to make the same distinction. In fact, one of the curious features of sacrificial traditions (at least to modern interpreters who often remark on it) is their tendency to view humans and animals as, at some level, interchangeable. The modern

---

[15] René Girard, *Violence and the Sacred* (Baltimore: Johns Hopkins University Press, 1977; French original, 1972).

[16] Bruce Lincoln, "Sacrificial Ideology and Indo-European Society," in *Death, War and Sacrifice: Studies in Ideology and Practice* (Chicago: University of Chicago Press, 1991), 167–75.

[17] Maurice Bloch, *Prey into Hunter: The Politics of Religious Experience* (Cambridge: Cambridge University Press, 1992).

[18] J. C. Heesterman, *The Broken World of Sacrifice: An Essay in Ancient Indian Ritual* (Chicago: University of Chicago Press, 1993).

[19] Barbara Ehrenreich, *Blood Rites: Origins and History of the Passions of War* (New York: Metropolitan, 1997).

insistence that one must be historically or symbolically prior to the other does not correspond with this animal-human equivalence in much of the evidence.

The disagreement over the logical and/or chronological priority of animal and human sacrifices can be explained by making another distinction among theories of sacrifice, this one involving their sources of information. We have, on the one hand, descriptions of sacrificial rituals from ancient texts (such as Leviticus) and from modern ethnographers; on the other hand, we have stories – myths, legends, and historiographic accounts – in which sacrifices play a prominent part. Though most theorists invoke both kinds of sources, their theories of sacrifice do not account equally well for both: some theories work better for ritual descriptions than for stories about sacrifices, while others are more apt for stories about sacrifices than for rituals. Furthermore, this distinction among modern theories of sacrifice is congruent with the previous one: theories of sacrifice that view animal offerings as primary work best on ritual texts, whereas those that give primacy to killing humans apply best to stories.

For example, Girard's best evidence for his theory that the sacrifice of scapegoats diffuses violent tensions within a community comes from stories of executions, lynchings, and pogroms, including Jesus' crucifixion (which for Girard exposes scapegoating to criticism and resistance). These stories are only distantly associated with ritual acts, if at all. The application of his theory to temple rituals is strained, and he explicitly disassociates it from the Bible's description of the role of the original "scapegoat" (Leviticus 16), which is after all not even killed.[20] An underlying concern with communal violence also motivates the theories of Frazer, Freud, Lincoln, Bloch, Heesterman, and Ehrenreich, who must turn to myth, legend, and drama for stories of ritual human sacrifice.

[20] Girard disassociated his use of the term from that of Leviticus: see Girard, "Generative Scapegoating," in *Violent Origins* (ed. R. G. Hamerton-Kelly; Stanford: Stanford University Press, 1987), 73–8.

Conversely, Burkert's idea that sacrificial rituals reflect the primordial hunt and the celebratory meal that follows it applies well to the rituals of many cultures but cannot adequately explain the interchange of animal and human offerings in many of the stories, as he himself has admitted.[21] The emphasis on rituals over stories is even more pronounced in the theories of Hubert and Mauss, J. Z. Smith, and Detienne.

These congruent dichotomies among theories that set animals versus humans and rituals versus stories do not simply reflect different evaluations of the same evidence. They rather point out the fact that sacrificial rituals and stories about sacrifice really are about different things: the rituals usually involve eating food, often animals, while the stories almost always revolve around the killing of humans. They are different enough that using the same term, "sacrifice," to *describe* both is untenable. Rather, the correlation of stories with rituals under the category of sacrifice represents a second-order interpretation that is not intrinsic to the rituals. Such correlations serve to *evaluate* a ritual on the basis of a story, and do so for purposes of persuasion. "Sacrifice" then is best understood as a normative, rather than descriptive, term.

Theories of "sacrifice" thus turn out to be about two different things. Some deal principally with narrative traditions about killing people and are therefore concerned with normative evaluations of killing and murder. Others deal principally with the ritual killing of animals and are therefore concerned with the social functions of ritual and religion. The two are related only by analogies derived from the normative traditions themselves.

Ritual Practice and Ritual Interpretation

Why has so much effort gone into trying to explain sacrifice? Theorists have been frustrated by the fact that traditional practitioners offer few

---

[21] On this, see Burkert, "The Problem of Ritual Killing," in *Violent Origins* (ed. R. G. Hamerton-Kelly; Stanford: Stanford University Press, 1987), 173.

explanations for sacrifice. That is not for lack of discussions about it in traditional sources. But ritual texts like those in Leviticus, sermons like those in Deuteronomy, or votive inscriptions like those found throughout the ancient world are more likely to describe and commend a ritual than to explain it.

For example, some of the best-known descriptions of ancient sacrifices can be found in the Hebrew Bible. It contains many stories involving sacrifice, such as Noah's sacrifice of animals after being saved from the flood (Genesis 8:20) and Abraham's near-sacrifice of his son Isaac (Genesis 22). But it also contains detailed instructions on how and when to offer animals at Israel's sanctuary (Leviticus 1–7, 16). Yet the stories and even the instructions do not explain *why* one should offer butchered animals to the deity, except in the most cryptic and ambiguous terms. The effect of burnt offerings is often described as an odor pleasing to God (Gen 8:21; Lev 1:9, 13, 17, etc.), which seems to invoke ideas of feeding the deity, while other texts strenuously deny that interpretation (Ps 50:8–14; Isa 1:11). The deity's claim on firstborn humans and animals, the latter substituting for the former, seems to involve demonstrations of divine ownership (Exod 13:1, 12–15). But no text systematically elaborates on the symbolism of a rite's offerings or other ritual elements. That has been left for interpreters, who since ancient times have quarried the possible symbolism of these rituals.

This failure to explain sacrifices is typical of many traditions. Thus animal offerings were central rites for ancient Roman society, yet this highly literate culture produced little speculation about their meaning.[22] When explanations were offered for traditional Greek rites they seem to be rationalizations of existing practice, usually in the face of criticisms, or rationalizations for changing the tradition.[23] In every case, the ritual action seems to be demonstrably older than the interpretations offered for it by the religious traditions in which it is practiced. Thus Muslim sacrifices for Eid adapt pre-Muslim Arab rites

---

[22] North, "Sacrifice and Ritual: Rome," 981–6.
[23] Detienne, "Culinary Practices," 5.

to symbolize the submission to God that is at the heart of Islam. The Christian Eucharist that memorializes the sacrifice of Christ adapts the Second Temple Jewish Passover sacrifice that memorialized the Exodus from Egypt, which itself was an adaptation of older rites associated with the traditional agricultural cycle of Syria-Palestine. In the process of adaptation, traditional interpretations of sacrifice tend to emphasize motivations for performing the rite, usually grounded in the imitation of a story – whether of Abraham/Ibrahim and Isaac/Ishmael, the Exodus, or the Last Supper and Crucifixion – rather than explaining why the ritual takes the particular form that it does. The goal of such stories is to motivate worshippers to preserve past traditions through present practices.

On the other hand, some traditions distinguish themselves by their preoccupation precisely with the question of ritual meaning. The Brahmanas propose elaborate interpretations of Vedic rituals. The Talmud subjects Israel's offerings to minute investigation and debate. Christian theology has often been obsessed with understanding Christ's atonement and the Eucharist that commemorates it. These traditions for interpreting the *meaning* of sacrifice derive from similar historical settings: they all reflect on ritual slaughter as a practice of the past *no longer* enacted, or which *should* no longer be enacted, or which should *only* be enacted in a very *different* way. Sacrifice must then be interpreted because of the discontinuity between past and present practice. The Indian ritualists prescribed rules to control ancient rites and internalized sacrifice as self-sacrifice.[24] The rabbinic tradition debated the meaning of offerings in the aftermath of the Temple's destruction that prevented their enactment.[25] Christians declared Christ's death the final sacrifice that precludes other sacrifices and struggled with how to understand its nonviolent ritual reenactment with bread and wine.[26]

---

[24] See Heesterman, *Broken World of Sacrifice,* 3–5, 53ff.
[25] See the discussion of Jonathan Z. Smith, "Trading Places," in *Ancient Magic and Ritual Power* (ed. M. Meyer and P. Mirecki; Leiden: E. J. Brill, 1995), 13–28.
[26] See Heyman, *Martyrdom and Sacrifice.*

The quest to understand the meaning of sacrifice arose in each case out of the consciousness of sacrifice as a thing of the past that needs to be replaced with ritual and/or interpretation. The same is also true of academic theories of sacrifice that, like their predecessors in Hindu, Jewish, and Christian cultures, often seem to be preoccupied with the reasons for sacrifice's disappearance and the conditions for its replacement or even revival.[27]

Symbolic interpretations thus seem to multiply around *unperformed* rituals, at least those not performed by the interpreter. Of course, almost everyone both performs and interprets rituals, but often not the same ones. We usually do not interpret our own rituals, but only those of others, because we need explanations only for activities foreign to us. Our own rituals are "obvious" and as a result receive little if any interpretation. Thus Western university professors have spent far more time and effort interpreting sacrificial rituals, and many others that they rarely, if ever, participate in, than they have explaining the graduation rituals of commencement and convocation that their colleges and universities perform at least annually.

Sacrifice complicates the problem of interpretation, because people use the word "sacrifice" for both ritual and nonritual acts, and for behaviors both native and foreign to modern interpreters. That is because "sacrifice" gets applied through a particular kind of interpretation, one always based on stories.

---

[27] In addition to the theorists already mentioned who display this tendency, one should mention Wolfgang Giegerich. He proposed that sacrifice should be regarded by Jungian depth psychology as a fundamental archetype. Giegerich argued that the practice of ritual sacrifice provided the only "mode in all of known history by which the soul was truly able to access or generate actuality," an access that has been missing in the last two millennia ("Killings: Psychology's Platonism and the Missing Link to Reality," *Spring* 54 [1993], 5–18 [16]; see the critique by James Hillman, "Once More into the Fray: A Response to Wolfgang Giegerich's 'Killings,'" *Spring* 56 [1994]; 1–18; and Giegerich's response, "Once More the Reality/Irreality Issue: A Reply to Hillman's Reply," online at http://www.rubedo.psc.br/reply.htm). Giegerich developed his thesis at greater length in *Tötungen: Gewalt aus der Seele* (Frankfurt: Lang, 1994).

Stories of Sacrifice

The religious motivations behind Hindu, Jewish, and Christian discussions of sacrifice explain readily why they have developed so far beyond the explanations of ancient ritual practitioners. They do not, however, explain their preoccupation with sacrifice in the first place. That emphasis stems not from the ritual traditions they study, but rather from narrative roots. The need to explain certain paradigmatic stories is what motivates the concern with sacrifice. A fascination with ritual has confused the discussion of sacrifice, however, because the two topics are not intrinsically connected, despite what most religious traditions and academic theorists assume.[28]

The meaning of the English word "sacrifice" derives entirely from narrative traditions, and mostly from specific narratives reinterpreted continuously over the millennia. Most important to its definition have been a small group of stories: the Hebrew Bible's story (called the *Aqedah* in Jewish tradition) of Abraham's near sacrifice of his son, Isaac, and its variant in the Qur'an; the Greek tragedies' depictions of ritual and nonritual sacrifice; and the New Testament's portrayal of Jesus' execution by Roman soldiers as a divine sacrifice atoning for human sin.

These stories are all notable for their *lack* of ritual contents. Jesus' crucifixion was obviously not a sacrifice to the soldiers who performed it nor to those who witnessed it, though both first-century Romans and Jews were active participants in blood rituals on other occasions. Only religious reflection on this political execution transformed the evaluation of it by labeling it a "sacrifice," in fact the ultimate and final sacrifice.[29]

---

[28] Bergen, to mention only one example, charted the changing meaning of sacrifice from Leviticus to its modern application to acts of war under the heading "the afterlife of Leviticus 1–7 in the Church" (*Reading Ritual*, chap. 6). I suggest instead that such modern uses of the word reflect the persistent influence, not of Leviticus' ritual instructions, but rather of stories of ritual slaughter, most especially Genesis 22.

[29] Heyman, *Martyrdom and Sacrifice*.

I believe a similar claim can be made about the prominence of sacrificial themes in Greek tragedies. They portray human sacrifice as extraordinary and perverse when practiced by Greeks (e.g., in Euripides' *Iphigenia in Aulis*), and routine only when practiced by barbarians where it attests to their depravity (as in Euripides' *Iphigenia in Tauris*). They cast the motif of sacrifice over the theme of murder with which the plays are principally concerned. In these plays, ritual offerings come to represent the reciprocity and equivalence that characterize violence spiraling out of control. But it is the plays that make this identification; there is nothing to suggest that Greek temple rituals usually conveyed such ideas to their participants.

The *Aqedah* (Genesis 22; Qur'an 37) does depict a ritual, but as in the Greek tragedies here human sacrifice is clearly portrayed as an aberrant act: that is what gives the story its tension. The story depicts the rite and its meaning as turning on the interchangeable nature of human and animal offerings, precisely the feature of these traditions that modern theories have such trouble coping with. But this crucial feature of this narrative tradition *introduces* substitutionary ideas into the interpretation of sacrificial practice. The story's emphasis on this point shows that such ideas were not necessarily part of the ritual practices themselves; they had to be introduced by an interpretive overlay of stories.[30] Such an overlay is even more explicit in the Passover story and ritual instructions (Exodus 12–13) that transform the old agricultural festival of Unleavened Bread into a commemoration of the exodus from Egypt and, specifically, the escape of Israel's firstborn from death by the substitutionary slaughter of lambs. The story thus overlays an old ritual meal consisting of animal meat, among other things, with the themes of human sacrifice and salvation.

---

[30] For some of the same reasons, Carol Delaney challenged the notion that "sacrifice – whether human or animal, ritual practice or theoretical discourse – is the most appropriate context for the interpretation of the story" (*Abraham on Trial: The Social Legacy of Biblical Myth* [Princeton: Princeton University Press, 1998], 70; see 70–104).

These stories have wielded enormous influence over Jewish, Christian, Muslim, and academic thought about ritual and sacrifice. The *Aqedah,* and especially speculation about Isaac's voluntary role in it, played a key role in Christian reinterpretation of Jesus' crucifixion as (self-)sacrifice.[31] Both stories' elevation of the ideal of self-sacrifice fueled traditions of martyrs in ancient Judaism and Christianity.[32] The Qur'an's version of the story explicitly grounds the practice of Muslim *qurban,* the ritual slaughter of camels, cattle, sheep, or goats in symbolic imitation of 'Ibrahim's submission to God. And controversies over the meaning of the Christian Eucharist, the ritual meal that commemorates Jesus' sacrifice interpreted in light of both Passover and the *Aqedah,* foreshadow in form and sometimes substance contemporary academic debates over the meaning of sacrifice generally.[33]

It is this narrative tradition, rather than ritual practices, that determines how and when the word "sacrifice" is applied. Thus ritual

[31] See Levenson, *Death and Resurrection of the Beloved Son*; Delaney, *Abraham on Trial,* 107–85; Ed Noort and Eibert Tigchelaar (eds.), *The Sacrifice of Isaac: The Aqedah (Genesis 22) and Its Interpretations* (Leiden: Brill, 2002). The abiding interest in this story in Jewish and Christian scholarship, not to mention broader religious culture, is attested by the large number of recent books devoted to it. In addition to the three above, see Louis A. Berman, *Akedah: The Binding of Isaac* (Boulder: Rowman & Littlefield, 1997); Mishael Maswari Caspi, *Take Now Thy Son: The Motif of the Aqedah (Binding) in Literature* (North Richland Hills, TX: Bibal Press, 2001); Jerome I. Gellman, *Abraham! Abraham! Kierkegaard and the Hasidim on the Binding of Isaac* (Aldershot: Ashgate, 2003); Edward Kessler, *Bound by the Bible: Jews, Christians and the Sacrifice of Isaac* (Cambridge: Cambridge University Press, 2004); and the reprinting in 1993 of Shalom Spiegel's *The Last Trial: On the Legends and Lore of the Command to Abraham to Offer Isaac as a Sacrifice: The Akedah 1899–1984* (trans. Judah Goldin; New York: Schocken, 1967).

[32] Boyarin, *Dying for God*; Heyman, *Martyrdom and Sacrifice.*

[33] For example, the theories of Tylor, Hubert and Mauss, Jay, and Ehrenreich clearly emphasize the propitiatory function of sacrifice in making conditions more favorable, like the "ransom" theory of the atonement. The theories of Freud, Burkert, Girard, Lincoln, Bloch, and Heesterman point to its expiatory role in ridding the individual and society of the effects of violence, similar to the "satisfaction" theory of the atonement. Girard's notion that the New Testament Gospels' account of Jesus' death serves to expose and counter sacrificial violence clearly reproduces, in an appealing sociological form, the "moral influence" theory of the atonement.

slaughter may or may not be a "sacrifice" depending on how a tradition applies the stories of sacrifice. For example, the regulations governing Jewish *kashrut* slaughter, limited to religiously licensed professionals and inspected by rabbis, are far more rigorous than the minimal instructions for Muslim *qurban*, which any man may perform simply by slitting the animal's throat while invoking the name of 'Allah. Yet the latter is a sacrifice according to Muslim teachings because it imitates the sacrifice of 'Ibrahim, while the former is not a sacrifice in Jewish tradition. Jewish sacrifices that imitate Abraham, Moses, and Aaron cannot be performed outside the long-since destroyed Jerusalem Temple. Imitation of stories of sacrifice also permits the application of the term to rituals in which there is no slaughter (e.g., the Catholic Mass, pilgrimages, ascetic disciplines for spiritual attainment), to slaughter that involves no religious ritual (e.g., the deaths of martyrs and soldiers, laboratory animals killed in medical experiments), and to a vast array of behaviors that involve neither ritual nor slaughter (e.g., gifts to religious organizations, labor on others' behalf, any kind of self-denial for the sake of a common good, etc.). What unites all of them is the claim, either by an interpreter or by the actors themselves, that the action imitates a story of heroic sacrifice. Sometimes the story is quite explicit, such as when Christian martyrs or ascetics claim to imitate Christ. At other times, the narrative connection is implicit in substitutionary themes derived from religious tradition, such as the claim that "they died so that others may live" to validate the deaths of soldiers or laboratory animals.[34] But the theme of substitutionary sacrifice is enough to ground the moral evaluation in ancient narrative traditions.

[34] Robert N. Bellah noted that Abraham Lincoln introduced nonsectarian Christian symbolism into American political discourse when he commemorated dead soldiers in the Gettysburg Address with the words "those who here gave their lives, that the nation might live." He then demonstrated the ways in which memorials to the "sacrifices" of war dead have evolved into central shrines and rituals of the American civil religion ("Civil Religion in America," in *Beyond Belief: Essays on Religion in a Post-Traditional World* [New York: Harper & Row, 1970], 168–89; see also Carolyn Marvin and David Ingle, *Blood Sacrifice and the Nation: Totem Rituals and the American Flag* [Cambridge: Cambridge University Press, 1999], 69).

"Sacrifice" is not, however, an unequivocally positive term. It can convey strong condemnation rather than praise. Such negative usage appears frequently in political rhetoric, such as the charge that someone is sacrificing people or principles for personal gain. Religious rituals may also be condemned as "sacrifices": in Florida, local laws banning ritual animal sacrifice and their enforcement against Santeria priests generated a long legal struggle that illustrates a profound animosity to such rituals in modern American culture.[35] To some degree, such aversion reflects the fact that powerful stories about sacrifice in Western culture involve, first, the limitation of legitimate sacrifice to scripturally ordained rites and, second, the *end* of all such sacrifices, either in the destruction of Judaism's ancient Temple or in Christian emphasis on the finality of Christ's sacrifice. These stories therefore render all contemporary ritual slaughter unnecessary and even idolatrous.

Sacrifice has long been a site of interreligious conflict. Greco-Roman rulers persecuted Jews and Christians by forcing their participation in pagan rites. This history and the belief in the finality of Christ's sacrifice prompted concerted efforts by later Christian rulers to suppress ritual animal slaughter in Late Antiquity and the Middle Ages. Such experiences have given the idea of animal sacrifice connotations that evoke horrified antipathy in Western culture.

This horror also grows out of a deeper narrative root: stories of human sacrifice have terrified and fascinated cultures from the ancient Greeks and Israelites to contemporary Europeans and Americans. The Bible, besides emphasizing the substitutionary theme in the *Aqedah*, Passover, and Crucifixion stories, polemicizes against the ritual slaughter of children (Lev 18:21; 20:3–5; Deut 18:10) while also preserving ambiguous stories of its practice by the patriarch Abraham (Genesis 22), the Israelite judge Jephthah (Judg 11:29–40), and the Moabite king Mesha (2 Kgs 3:27). The same tension appears in Greek religious traditions (contrast the tragedians' nuanced treatment of

---

[35] For the U.S. Supreme Court's decision in the case of the *Church of the Lukumi Babalu Aye, Inc., et al. v. City of Hialeah*, see http://www.religioustolerance.org/santeri1.htm.

violence with the Athenians' maintenance of the human *pharmakos*, to be exiled or executed in times of crisis) and Roman historiography (contrast, for example, Livy's admiring account of the Roman consul Decius who sacrificed himself to guarantee the gods' favor on Rome's armies with Roman horror over stories of human sacrifice among the Celts).[36]

The disparity between legends of human sacrifice and ritual animal offerings have led some scholars to wonder if the ritual slaughter of humans was ever regularly practiced in the ancient world. There is far less archeological and textual evidence for it than the narrative traditions would have us believe.[37] Yet there is enough to show that the phenomenon was not entirely imaginary. The strongest archeological evidence comes from the Punic *tophets*, graveyards of Carthage that contain votive inscriptions with burials of children, often a two- and four-year-old together in the same grave. Votive offerings of animals also appear in the same graveyard, showing that the substitution theme did work its way into ritual practice in the Phoenician/Punic tradition.[38] Later textual evidence for the ritual slaughter of humans includes the orders of Pope Gregory III to the Archbishop of Mainz (in 731 C.E.) that Christians not be allowed to sell slaves to non-Christians for use as sacrifices.[39] Of course, this case is mediated through Gregory's Christian definition of "sacrifice," but presumably ritual slaughter is what the German buyers had in mind. Yet we do well not to assume too much: anti-Jewish and anti-Christian polemic in antiquity already featured the "blood libel," the completely unfounded charge that Jews and Christians mixed the blood of slaughtered prisoners or babies into

---

[36] Livy, *Hist.* 8.9; for Roman views of the Celts, see Julius Caesar, *Gallic Wars* 6.16 (tr. W. A. McDevitte and W. S. Bohn; New York: Harper & Brothers, 1869).

[37] For a convenient, and skeptical, summary of the ancient evidence for human sacrifice, see Delaney, *Abraham on Trial*, 71–86.

[38] See Lipiński, "Rites et sacrifices," 279–80.

[39] See Roy C. Cave and Herbert H. Coulson, *A Source Book for Medieval Economic History* (Milwaukee: Bruce, 1936; reprinted, New York: Biblo & Tannen, 1965), p. 284.

the unleavened breads eaten at Passover and in the Eucharist.[40] Thus human sacrifice loomed much larger in ancient imagination, especially when it involved distant ancestors or contemporary enemies, than it did in any ancient ritual practice that we can clearly document. And when the rituals did involve human victims, narrative's priority over ritual is clearly expressed in the *imitatio dei* theme (hence *imitatio narratio*) at work in ancient child sacrifice. Parents sacrificed their children in imitation of myths of divine sacrifices of deities.[41] The same motivation still plays a part in religiously motivated killings of both children and adults.[42]

Charges of human sacrifice have remained a favorite way of vilifying enemies ever since. For example, the blood libel resurfaced as a pervasive expression of anti-Semitism in modern Europe from the fourteenth through the twentieth centuries. The accusation of human sacrifice becomes even more powerful when it can claim some justification in fact. In the sixteenth century, the Aztec's ritual slaughter of prisoners horrified the invading army of Cortez, though these men were quite accustomed to slaughtering people themselves. It was their

---

[40] The earliest reference to and refutation of the blood libel against Jews appears at the end of the first century C.E. in Josephus, *Against Apion* 2:80–III.

[41] See Levenson, *Death and Resurrection of the Beloved Son,* 25–35; Delaney has extended the analysis and critique of the mimetic influence of this story to the modern day (*Abraham on Trial,* 5–68, 233–50).

[42] Recent examples of killings motivated by the murderer's perception of divine orders include the cases of the Mormons Ron and Dan Lafferty, who killed their sister-in-law and her 15-month-old daughter in 1984 (for a detailed account, see Jon Krakauer, *Under the Banner of Heaven: A Story of Violent Faith* [New York: Anchor, 2003]), of the Catholic/Charismatic Christos Valenti, who killed his youngest daughter in 1990 in California (a trial chronicled in detail by Delaney, *Abraham on Trial,* 35–68), and of the Jewish Richard Rosenthal, who after murdering his wife in 1995 in Massachusetts, impaled her organs on stakes in an altar-like pattern (see Susan L. Mizruchi, "The Place of Ritual in Our Time," *American Literary History* 12/3 [2000]: 474–76). Perhaps the case of the evangelical Andrea Yates, who drowned her five children in Texas in 2001 on the orders, she stated, of the devil, should also be counted as a "sacrifice." The cases are united, however, only by the religious element of claims of supernatural prompting. But this, like the broader cultural notions of sacrifice generally, is established in people's minds by narrative examples.

recognition of the Aztec ritual as not just an execution but a "sacrifice" that first horrified the Spaniards and then became their justification for conquering and converting the peoples of Central and South America.[43] Nor did the eighteenth-century Enlightenment put an end to such thinking. Sacrificial rhetoric, both positive and negative, played a powerful role in nineteenth-century French politics and contributed to the war fever in most European countries before World War I.[44]

Yet beyond such polemics, the theme of human sacrifice has remained an abiding source of reflection in literature, art, and political culture: for example, consider the human sacrifice that begins the spiral of violence in Shakespeare's *Titus Andronicus*, the frequent paintings of Jephthah's sacrifice of his daughter by Renaissance and Baroque artists, and the preoccupation with sacrifice in nineteenth-century academic research and American novels of the same period.[45]

The rhetoric of sacrifice alternates between praise and blame, admiration and horror because its underlying narratives explore the ambiguous boundaries between the legitimate and illegitimate killing of human beings. That is its natural subject. Its application to animal slaughter depends on making some equivalence with human stories, either positively through a substitutionary theme – usually animal in place of human, but also human/god in place of all animals and humans – or negatively by implicating animal slaughter in stories of human martyrdom, for example, the hero chose martyrdom rather than sacrificing animals to idols. Theories of sacrifice that try to treat it as descriptive of rituals will always founder on the normative and narrative nature of their subject.

---

[43] The reactions of the Spanish soldiers were recorded in the eye-witness account of Bernal Diaz del Castillo (*The Discovery and Conquest of Mexico* [tr. A. P. Maudslay; New York: Farrar, Straus & Cudahy, 1956]).

[44] For the situation in France, see Ivan Strenski, *Contesting Sacrifice: Religion, Nationalism, and Social Thought in France* (Chicago: University of Chicago Press, 2002). For the rhetoric before World War I, see also Allen J. Frantzen, *Bloody Good: Chivalry, Sacrifice, and the Great War* (Chicago: University of Chicago Press, 2004).

[45] Susan L. Mizruchi, *The Science of Sacrifice: American Literature and Modern Social Theory* (Princeton, NJ: Princeton University Press, 1998).

Thus "sacrifice" is a value-laden term whose meaning is determined by stories, not by rituals. Calling some act a "sacrifice" is to claim that the act is comparable to some paradigmatic action in a hero's or villain's story. It is the rhetoric of sermons and didactic texts that connects the term "sacrifice" to specific rituals. In these contexts, it is clearly an evaluative label, not a descriptive one, which undermines its descriptive use in academic theories. It is, therefore, inappropriate to describe the offerings of Leviticus as "sacrifices" unless one intends to make a normative claim by doing so.

It might seem odd to argue that a word does not mean what everyone thinks it means. After all, does not usage determine meaning? Yes it does, but words can carry connotations that native speakers do not think about explicitly, despite the fact that they may use those connotations regularly and expertly. My point is that, by missing or ignoring the normative connotations of "sacrifice" that derive from narrative analogies, scholars of religion have confused rituals of eating with controversies over killing humans. Only by separating the two can they be clearly analyzed for what they are, and only then can we begin to understand how they came to be related in normative applications of the word "sacrifice" to ritual practices involving food.

It turns out, therefore, that Leviticus has played relatively little role in shaping the rhetoric of sacrifice. The decisive role has been played instead by biblical and nonbiblical stories about killing humans, as well as the interpretive debates that they have generated. The rhetorical legacy of Leviticus 1–16 has instead been felt in another religious arena entirely. Despite the fact that Leviticus has often been treated as a backwater of biblical influence and interpretation, in the Second Temple period its ritual instructions and narratives played a decisive role in the development of the idea of scripture. That is the subject of the next chapter.

9

The Rhetoric of Scripture

Western culture has traditionally drawn a dichotomy between rituals and texts, usually favoring texts over rituals. We tend to associate this bias particularly with Protestant polemics aimed at Catholic rituals, but it was already quite strong in the Middle Ages, as Phillipe Buc has shown.[1] The elevation of text over ritual has served to distinguish "true" religion from ritualized "magic" throughout much of Western history.

Contemporary scholarship has given new attention to ritual to reverse this traditional privileging of text. Theorists of ritual have tried to understand rituals for their own sake. Ronald Grimes, for example, declared, "Ritual studies, unlike liturgics, does not begin with a consideration of traditions and texts. It begins by attending to gesture and posture, the actual comportment of the body in interaction."[2] Ritual studies have therefore grown into a subdiscipline within the study of religion.

The academic dichotomy between text and ritual remains entrenched, however, as witnessed by the different (sub)disciplines and

---

[1] Buc, *Dangers of Ritual*, 6–7, 251.
[2] Ronald L. Grimes, *Beginnings in Ritual Studies* (rev. ed.; Studies in Comparative Religion; Columbia: University of South Carolina Press, 1995), 91.

their associated journals dedicated to each subject even within a given religious tradition. In this chapter, rather than playing down either ritual or text in favor of the other, I want to point out and explain the *interdependence* of texts and rituals. That interdependence is readily apparent in contemporary religious liturgies and governmental ceremonies that highlight the reading and manipulation of texts. For example, processions with Torah scrolls and Gospel books utilize texts as ritual objects, as do many political and judicial oath ceremonies. William Scott Green explored the historical origin of these practices and observed that scripture took the place of the lost temple in Rabbinic Judaism. It was therefore sanctified as a religious object more than as a text.[3] Building on Green's work, Thomas Driver concluded:

> The point is not that scripture took the place of ritual, as some might imagine, but that ritual was modified so as to embrace the Torah texts and exalt them as sacred.... Ritual guides hermeneutics. In Judaism and in many other religions, certain rituals conceptualize the text and secure its place within the ordered world.... Among Protestants also, the scriptures are defined by the protocols (mostly unwritten and passed along by tradition) concerning their use. It is these protocols, not the scriptural words per se, that order Protestant life and give it the character that it has.[4]

Though Driver understates the role that some of the contents of scripture play in Protestant (and Jewish) life, his point is nevertheless well taken. The influence of ritual on beliefs about scriptures has received far too little attention in the scholarship.

The observations of Green and Driver leave open, however, the question of how texts and rituals came to be associated in the first place. What ritual benefit accrued from using texts in this way? I will

---

[3] William Scott Green, "Romancing the Tome: Rabbinic Hermeneutics and the Theory of Literature," *Semeia* 40 (1987): 147–68.

[4] Tom F. Driver, *The Magic of Ritual: Our Need for Liberating Rites that Transform Our Lives and Our Communities* (New York: Harper San Francisco, 1991), 141–2.

argue that old texts were used in antiquity to validate the forms of important rituals. The rituals in turn lent their cultural influence to the texts that prescribed them. The textual authority of Western scriptures has ritual origins.

Scriptural Authority

The problem of how some texts acquired such a high degree of religious authority in ancient Judaism is complicated by the fact that interpreters tend to make a number of unexamined, and unjustified, assumptions about scriptural authority. The first is simply to take scriptural authority as a matter of course and not realize that the Jewish (and later Christian, Manichean, Muslim, Sikh, etc.) reverence for an authoritative book was unusual in the context of ancient Near Eastern and Mediterranean religions.

The second assumption was that scriptural authority is an outgrowth of the text's status as "law." Because the first Jewish scripture, the Torah/Pentateuch, contains several codes of civil law and religious instructions, people easily conclude that the Bible gained its status by virtue of its legal authority. Contrary to modern conceptions of law, however, study of ancient Near Eastern law codes and legal procedures has shown that law codes were not cited as authoritative guides to legal practice. The Code of Hammurabi, for example, which was recopied and distributed through much of the Middle East in the second millennium B.C.E., is never cited nor are its provisions followed in the many court documents that have survived from those same times and cultures.[5] Though the *idea* of law functioned as a pervasive social

---

[5] As observed famously by F. R. Kraus, "Ein zentrales Problem des altmesopotamischen Rechts: Was is der Codex Hammu-Rabi?" *Genava* 8 (1960): 283–96; see also Hans Jochen Boecker, *Law and the Administration of Justice in the Bible and the Ancient Near East* (tr. Jeremy Moiser; Minneapolis: Augsburg, 1980), and the essays in Bernard M. Levinson, ed., *Theory and Method in Biblical and Cuneiform Law: Revision, Interpolation and Development* (JSOTSup 181; Sheffield: Sheffield Academic Press, 1994).

ideal whose normative claims should govern people's behavior, *written collections* of laws did not function as especially authoritative guides for such behavior.

Other models for the origins of scriptural authority have been identified in treaties, which were expected to be publicly read and their provisions followed,[6] and bureaucratic documents that, in Egypt at least, were consulted to guide the decisions of administrators.[7] Treaties did influence the literary form of the covenant in the books of Exodus and Deuteronomy, so these practices may indeed have had some influence on the Torah's authority. Unlike texts revered as scriptures in Judaism and later "religions of the book," however, the ancient use of treaties, bureaucratic records, and royal decrees did not usually emphasize the *antiquity* of the documents to be consulted and followed.[8] In fact, in most such cases authority lay in the most recent treaty or decree (though it was common to appeal to old royal grants to justify land and tax claims).

---

[6] See Dennis J. McCarthy, *Treaty and Covenant: A Study in Form in the Ancient Oriental Documents and in the Old Testament* (2nd rev. ed., AnBib 21; Rome: Pontifical Biblical Institute, 1981).

[7] Donald B. Redford, "The So-Called 'Codification' of Egyptian Law under Darius I," in *Persia and Torah: The Theory of Imperial Authorization of the Pentateuch* (ed. J. W. Watts; Symposium 17; Atlanta: SBL, 2001), 151. Redford notes that this was especially the case during the first millennium B.C.E. in Egypt: "Osorkon, the high priest of Amun during the ninth-century civil war, could boast (probably quite honestly) that 'regular decisions in the Privy Chamber were taken [through] his knowledge of all the pol[icy decisions] which had accumulated throughout the generations of former kings.' [Footnote: punishment of the rebels was meted out 'according to a charter of the ancestors.'] Similarly the worthy Hory (ca. 800 B.C.E.) was 'skilled in the laws of the palace, the regulations of the ancestors'" (ibid.).

[8] A vivid depiction of the politico-religious use of a treaty text can be found in the Assyrian Tukulti-Ninurta Epic (13th century B.C.E.), which depicts the Assyrian king making a legal case before the gods against his Babylonian rival: "I raise aloft, therefore, the tablet of oath between us, and call upon the Lord of Heaven []! . . . [Kashtiliash] was appalled on account of the appeal to Shamash and became fearful and anxious about what was laid before the gods. . . . 'You have entered in evidence against me an unalterable tablet with the seal impression of m[y forefather]s, They too have intro[duced evidence] before me, a [] whose wording cannot be changed!'" (translation by Benjamin Foster, *Before the Muses*, 308–9).

Another apparently obvious source for scriptural authority lay in divinatory consultations of oracular/prophetic texts. The Zoroastrians of Persia, as well as the Greeks and Romans, gave great importance to the correct interpretation of oracles and literary texts by professional exegetes for purposes of divination. Their methods and results bear many similarities to the work of Jewish and Christian interpreters of sacred texts.[9] Though the influence of divinatory methods on later scriptural interpretation cannot be denied, such concerns cannot have been the source of the Bible's religious authority in the first place. The most obviously oracular books of the Hebrew Bible, such as Isaiah, Jeremiah, Amos, and other prophetic books, were not the first to achieve scriptural status. Nor do biblical narratives reflect any interest in ancient Israel in the reading and interpretation of oracular texts.[10] When they mention texts at all, they are rather concerned with the reading and application of Torah. The Bible's canonization began with the Torah, not the prophets as one would expect if divinatory concerns were the primary motive.[11]

The origins of scripture have also been sought in the educational curriculum of ancient Judaism. David M. Carr has recently argued the case for viewing the Hebrew Bible as an educational curriculum promulgated by Second Temple period Jews in conscious rivalry with Hellenistic education. His encyclopedic survey of the function of such "cultural texts" showed how they shaped bureaucratic and social elites in ancient Mesopotamia, Egypt, and Greece. In a similar way, learning to read and memorize the Hebrew Bible provided Jewish elites a distinctive collective identity.[12] Carr's convincing case for the literate-oral

---

[9]   See John F. A. Sawyer, *Sacred Languages and Sacred Texts: Religion in the First Christian Centuries* (London: Routledge, 1999), 152–61.

[10] The one exception is Jeremiah 36, which describes the scribe Baruch reading a scroll of Jeremiah's oracles in the Temple. But the text here was simply a stand-in for the prophet, who could not preach because he was under threat of arrest.

[11] The priority of the Pentateuch (Torah) in the history of canonization is undisputed, even if the rest of the history is less evident.

[12] Carr, *Writing on the Tablet of the Heart.*

dynamic in ancient education and its influence on shaping ancient literatures, including the Hebrew Bible, cannot explain, however, the distinctive authority of Jewish scriptures in Second Temple Judaism in comparison with the roles of cultural texts in Mesopotamian, Egyptian, and Greek literatures.[13] The Torah functioned (and continues to function) simultaneously as cultural text and religious icon, a combination unparalleled in the other cultures of the Near East and Mediterranean before the beginning of the Common Era. The contents of that Torah, with ritual texts at its center, also distinguish it from the narrative, hymnic, and wisdom literatures that tended to dominate other ancient people's cultural texts, as well as the rest of the Hebrew Bible.[14] While the development of a Jewish educational curriculum may well explain the contents and use of the other sections of the Hebrew Bible in later Second Temple Judaism, it leaves unanswered crucial questions about the distinctive contents and role of the Torah.

Thus neither individually nor together do laws, treaties, bureaucratic regulations, oracular texts, and educational practices provide a sufficient explanation for the origins of scripture in ancient Judaism, though they all exerted some influence on the way in which scriptures came to be interpreted and used. The reasons for scripture's developing authority must be sought elsewhere. In antiquity, claims for the

[13] Carr characterized the distinctiveness of the Torah as a "supraroyal constitution" for Judaism (*Writing*, 290).

[14] Carr addressed the issue by pointing out that Israelite/Jewish education became increasingly dominated by temple priests in the middle and latter part of the first millennium B.C.E., just as it did in first millennium Mesopotamia and Egypt, and used this situation to explain the centrality of priestly texts in the Torah (*Writing*, 27, 80–1, 152, 169–72, 194, 197, 202–14). Mesopotamian and Egyptian priests, however, did not revise their curricula to place ritual texts at their center. Carr explains the radical revisions of the old royal Judean curriculum as due to the political convulsions that the country suffered (*Writing*, 162–70), but that still does not explain the ritual contents of the Torah and the unique treatment it received. My argument in this chapter does not challenge Carr's description so much as supplement it by pointing out the crucial contribution of ritual texts to shaping an idea of scripture that incorporated but went beyond the role of classical texts in education and enculturation.

authority of old texts were more frequently made for *ritual* texts than for any others. Rather than law or diplomacy or bureaucracy or divination or education, the use of texts for and in ritual explains more plausibly the origins and development of book religion.

Ritual Accuracy and Ritual Legitimacy

Many students of ritual have noted that a concern with "doing it exactly right" typifies many ritual performances, though such concerns for accuracy in some aspects of a ritual do not preclude the freedom to improvise others.[15] But how does one know if one is doing it right? How can priests be sure that their tradition of performance is correct? How can participants know that the priests are competent? Concerns for correct performance generate an interest in validating the authority of the ritualists. In antiquity, old ritual texts provided one means of validating or invalidating ritual performances.

There are several explicit examples from different cultures and times of using old texts to revive ancient ritual traditions. Livy, the first-century Roman historian, describes a Samnite ritual that was performed circa 300 B.C.E.:

A space, about 200 feet square, almost in the centre of their camp, was boarded off and covered all over with linen cloth. In this enclosure

---

[15] Sigmund Freud noticed the similarity in this regard between obsessive-compulsive behavior in individuals and the ritual behavior of groups ("Obsessive Actions and Religious Practices," in *Readings in Ritual Studies*, 212–17). Fritz Staal went so far as to argue that ritual consists of nothing but close attention to repetitive actions ("The Meaninglessness of Ritual," 2–22). Cf. the more nuanced appropriation of these ideas by Jonathan Z. Smith ("Domestication of Sacrifice," 191–235). Others have documented the prevalence of ritual change and, frequently, the lack of standardization in ritual practice: see Ronald Grimes on the ubiquity of ritual criticism and innovation (*Ritual Criticism*, 17–18), Roy A. Rappaport on the ritual criterion of invariance and the inevitability of both historical change and individual choice in all ritual performances (*Ritual and Religion*, 36–7, 124–6), and Buc on the textual reinterpretation of rituals in the Middle Ages (*Danger of Ritual*, 9–12, 249).

a sacrificial service was conducted, the words being read from an old linen book by an aged priest, Ovius Paccius, who announced that he was taking that form of service from the old ritual of the Samnite religion. It was the form which their ancestors used when they formed their secret design of wresting Capua from the Etruscans.[16]

Livy emphasizes the antiquity of the rite that was being revived for this occasion. The priest read the old linen scroll aloud to ensure that the correct words were recited and to validate the accuracy and therefore efficacy of the whole ritual. Livy does not provide sufficient information to allow us to evaluate the priest's honesty, but his use of the old book suggests that his authority to conduct this ritual or to conduct it in this way may have been contested. The rite required an oath of service in the Samnite army. Refusal meant execution as an offering to Jupiter, a threat actually carried out, according to Livy. So the ritual was clearly performed in the face of considerable social conflict, and reading the old book aloud helped the priest and his supporters to keep the upper hand.

The Samnite's use of a book to revive a ritual is reminiscent of a scene in Jerusalem approximately 150 years earlier, as narrated in the book of Nehemiah. Ezra took "the book of the law of Moses" that he had recently brought from Babylon and read it to the assembled people (Neh 8:1–12). As a result of this reading, the people discovered how to celebrate properly the festival of *Sukkot* (Booths or Tabernacles; Neh 8: 14–17). The story claims that the feast had not been celebrated in this way since the days of Joshua, some eight centuries earlier (though Ezra 3:4 claims that the returning exiles celebrated *Sukkot*).[17] Again, the situation was highly conflictual, in this case having to do with

---

Livy, *History of Rome* (ed. Ernest Rhys; trans. Canon Roberts; Everyman's Library; New York: E. P. Dutton, 1912), 10:38.

Commentators take the reference here to the days of Joshua as involving only the manner in which the festival was celebrated (see David J. A. Clines, *Ezra, Nehemiah, Esther* [NCB; Grand Rapids: Eerdmans, 1984], 186–8; Hugh G. M. Williamson, *Ezra, Nehemiah* [WBC 16; Waco: Word, 1985], 296–7). Perhaps the claim in Nehemiah 8

the ethnic boundaries of the community and the legitimacy of mixed marriages. Ezra used the authority of the book to bring about a mass divorce and the expulsion of foreign wives and their children from the Jerusalem community (Ezra 9–10).[18]

Jerusalem witnessed a similar scene even two centuries earlier, when an old book was discovered in the temple.[19] According to 2 Kings and 2 Chronicles, King Josiah read it to the assembled people and on its authority ordered them to celebrate Passover properly, as it had not been celebrated since the time of the Judges. In this assertion in 2 Chronicles 35:18, the Chronicler seems to forget that in its account (2 Chr 30), though not in 2 Kings, King Hezekiah had celebrated such a Passover two generations earlier. The amnesia here and in Nehemiah 8 (see above and n. 17) suggests that ritual books were conventionally associated with claims for reestablishing discontinued festivals. Josiah also celebrated a covenant renewal ceremony and launched an attack on various ritual objects and sacred sites that he regarded as foreign or idolatrous. The literary context in 2 Kings 23 indicates that this took place as a result of reading the book, so in that case the book invalidated

---

about *Sukkot* intentionally mimics the remark about Passover in 2 Kgs 22:23 to draw parallels between Josiah's and Ezra's book-based festival reforms.

[18] The chronological relationship between the reading of the Torah and the mass divorce is not clear because of the confusing arrangement of the Ezra materials in the books of Ezra and Nehemiah. Ezra, at least, certainly presents the ban on mixed marriages as a commandment of God (Ezra 9:10–12), though the Pentateuch itself is not so clear on the issue. For a political explanation of these divergent views about mixed marriages, see Chapter 7 of this book.

[19] Unlike Livy ("old linen book") and Nehemiah ("the book of the *torah* of Moses, which the YHWH commanded Israel" 8:1), 2 Kings does not describe the age of this "book of the *torah*" (22:8). But Josiah's concern that "our ancestors did not listen to the words of this book" (22:13) and the narrator's claim that the Passover prescribed by the book had not been observed since the time of the Judges (23:21–3) clearly are meant to indicate the book's antiquity. Gary N. Knoppers pointed out that the phrase "book of the covenant" (23:2, 21) connects this book to the Mosaic covenant at Sinai (*Two Nations under God: The Deuteronomistic History of Solomon and the Dual Monarchies. Volume 2: The Rise of Jeroboam, the Fall of Israel and the Reign of Josiah* [HSM 53; Atlanta: Scholars Press, 1994], 131 and n. 20).

certain ritual practices while it validated others.[20] Here again a book is invoked in a situation of conflict, this time explicitly ritual conflict. The account of these events in 2 Chronicles 34–35, however, has the cult reform precede the discovery of the book, which prompted the covenant renewal and Passover observances only.[21] Interpreters remain divided on the relative historical merits of the two versions.[22] But the link between the book and festival reform is explicit in both 2 Chronicles and 2 Kings, as it is in Nehemiah and Livy.

Thus each of these three cases (Livy, Nehemiah, 2 Kings/2 Chronicles) presents a situation of ritual discontinuity lasting centuries. The gaps exceeded the life span of even the oldest ritual specialists and so raised the problem of ritual accuracy in an acute form for those proposing to revive the ancient rituals. Each ritual also took place in the context of considerable social conflict: over soldiers unwilling to fight in an upcoming war against the Romans in Livy's account, over

[20] Knoppers argued that 2 Kings "employs the story of the torah scroll to justify and explain Josiah's unprecedented intrusion into the religious affairs of his people" (*Two Nations under God*, 2:139).

[21] Modern interpreters and historians have focused their attention primarily on the centralization of worship in Jerusalem and the destruction of rival sanctuaries and cult practices, because of the priority they receive in the text of Kings and also because of the effect such "reforms" probably had on the development of Israel's distinctive religious traditions, especially the Hebrew Bible itself (for a thorough review and evaluation of these issues, see Marvin K. Sweeney, *King Josiah of Judah: The Lost Messiah of Israel* [Oxford: Oxford University Press, 2001]). King Hezekiah, however, initiated somewhat similar reforms almost a century earlier (2 Kgs 18:3–6), but no explicit reference to a book appears in that account (Hezekiah is said only to have "kept the commandments that YHWH commanded Moses," v 6). Chronicles' version of Josiah's reform, as well as the parallels from Nehemiah and Livy, suggest that the book's role in this episode was primarily to validate the revival of the ancient rituals of covenant renewal and of Passover.

[22] Some have favored Chronicles' chronology (G. H. Jones, *1 and 2 Kings* [New Century Bible; Grand Rapids: Eerdmans, 1984], 602–6, who reviews the issue and research), but others have argued that Chronicles was entirely dependent on Kings (J. W. McKay, *Religion in Judah under the Assyrians* [Naperville, IL: Allensen, 1973]); H. G. M. Williamson, *1 and 2 Chronicles* [NCB; Grand Rapids: Eerdmans, 1982], 397–8) and many have noted how the stories have been shaped by the thematic interests of both writers (e.g., T. R. Hobbs, *2 Kings* [WBC 13; Waco: Word, 1985], 315–21).

the definition of the Jewish community in Jerusalem and intermarriage with outsiders in Nehemiah, and over correct ritual practice and sacred space in 2 Kings/2 Chronicles. Though in each case the ritual specialists were priests (led by a king in 2 Kings/2 Chronicles) who could claim positional authority to prescribe the manner of the ritual, they felt the need to buttress their authority in these extraordinary circumstances.[23] They used ancient books to provide such reinforcement, because texts have the unique property of appearing to "speak" from the distant past.[24] In each case, reading the texts helped sway many, though not all, of the assembled people to acquiesce to both the ritual and political agendas being advanced by the priests who controlled the texts.

[23] Concern to understand the source of authority behind books and scriptures has led interpreters to emphasize the human authorities who manipulate the book. So, to cite a recent example, Hindy Najman remarked on 2 Kings 22–23 that "the priest, scribe and king are ultimately sufficient to authorize a text, be it new or old" (*Seconding Sinai: The Development of Mosaic Discourse in Second Temple Judaism* [JSJSup 77; Leiden: Brill, 2003], 29). It is true that books by themselves are mute and are made authoritative only by the people who read them and control their use. However, this sociopolitical observation reverses and obscures the claims of the stories themselves, in which priests and kings derive *their* authority from the book (which in 2 Kings is, in turn, validated by inspired prophecy). Thus, though Najman intended to reconstruct the conceptions of textual authority operating in Deuteronomy, her reconstruction (which also relegates the prophet to a later editor) actually reversed the rhetoric of authority in the text of 2 Kings 22–3.

[24] Katherine Stott has recently pointed out the tendency of Greco-Roman histories and novels to gain verisimilitude by claiming to be transcripts of ancient lost texts ("Finding the Lost Book of the Law: Re-reading the Story of the 'Book of the Law' (Deuteronomy–2 Kings) in Light of Classical Literature," *JSOT* 30 [2005]: 145–69). Her useful survey should, however, be contextualized by recognizing the politico-religious uses of the motif of lost-and-found books in many other forms of ancient literature, classical and pre-classical. Broader comparisons with accounts of *ritual* books casts Josiah's book in a somewhat different light: unlike the historiographic and novelistic examples that Stott cites, 2 Kings and 2 Chronicles do not invoke the book to authorize their own narratives, but rather to legitimize ritual innovations on the basis of a different book (or, at most, a different part of a very long multiscroll work, if one counts Deuteronomy through 2 Kings as one work). Though the motif may well be a fictional device in a ritual as well as in a historiographic context, as Stott argues, its appearance here nevertheless attests to the *existence* of a scroll of Torah at the time that 2 Kings was written, since there would be little point in validating the authority of a nonexistent book.

Ritual Text and Ritual Performance

In all three cases described, the public display and reading of the text played a key role in stimulating the ritual acts that followed. Some ancient texts mandated that they be used in this way. The text of the Samnite ritual has not survived, so we cannot know what its contents were like. Most interpreters think that Josiah's and Ezra's books corresponded more or less to Deuteronomy and the whole Torah (Pentateuch), respectively. Deuteronomy mandates public recitation of the book (Deut 31) and many pentateuchal passages command performance of their prescriptions as written. Jewish scriptures are by no means unique in this regard. In cultures across the ancient Near East and eastern Mediterranean, there is evidence that ritual texts mandated that their stipulations be followed exactly as written and that priests and kings were concerned to do so, even to the point that reading and manipulating the ritual texts became part of the rituals themselves.

A number of Egyptian texts mandate verbatim repetition of their contents. For example, the prayers of Pahery, on the walls of Pahery's tomb (Eighteenth Dynasty, ca. fourteenth century B.C.E.), request that those passing by make offerings and recite the prayer for the deceased also recorded on the stela: "say, 'An offering, given by the king,' in the form in which it is written; 'An invocation offering,' as said by the fathers, and as it comes from the mouth of god."[25] Other Egyptian

---

[25] Translated by Miriam Lichtheim (*Ancient Egyptian Literature*, 2:20), showing the citation of the first lines of the prayers (the first written on the tomb, the second not and apparently conveyed by oral tradition "as said by the fathers"). Other translations: "Ye shall say the *htp-di-nsw* exactly like that which is in writing, the invocation in the speech of the ancestors, like that which emerged from the mouth of god. . . . it is to be done as it should be, as that which is according to the *hpw* [law, customary rule, prescription] attested on this stela" (Redford, "So-Called 'Codification,'" 139, who notes that in many contexts, "like that which conforms to the law" parallels "like that which is in writing" [140]); "Just so, may you recite the offering prayer in the manner found in the writings, and the invocation offering as spoken by those long dead just as it came from the mouth of God" (John L. Foster, *Ancient Egyptian Literature:*

texts link exact repetition of spells and prayers with detailed ritual instructions, such as an Osiris ritual from the Ptolemaic period (third to first centuries B.C.E.). It records an elaborate liturgy and then ritual instructions that begin, "Now when this is recited the place is to be completely secluded, not seen and not heard by anyone except the chief lector-priest and the *setem*-priest."[26]

Even more than specific recitation instructions, texts from many ancient cultures prescribe the details of various rituals. These include instructions for the proper sequence of rites, for the performance of individual rituals, for the amounts of offerings for various rituals, and for the celebration of special festivals. In some cases, we have clear indications of how such texts were used. The texts from Ugarit (thirteenth or twelfth century B.C.E.) contain not only a number of rituals but also lists of gods and former kings that were used literally to "check-off" that the rites were performed for the deities and ancestors in the proper order. The cuneiform equivalents of check-marks remain in the margins of the tablets.[27] One Ugaritic omen text, a lung model, specifies the need to eat the sacrifice *dbḥ k. sprt,* "in accordance with the documents."[28] Some Hittite texts witness to acute concerns to perform rituals exactly as "is written in the old tablets" and "on account of the old tablets, they do it in exactly that manner."[29] Hittite kings cited their examination of written documents as proof of their ritual fidelity: "And whatever I, My Majesty, discover now in the written records, I

An Anthology [Austin: University of Texas Press, 2001], 176–7). Several lines further, reward is promised for the recitation: "Goodness is yours when you perform it, for [you] discover [that it earns] you favor" (Foster, *Ancient Egyptian Literature,* 177).

[26] "Lamentations of Isis and Nephthys," translated by Lichtheim, *Ancient Egyptian Literature,* 3:116–21.

[27] Pardee, *Ritual and Cult at Ugarit,* 12–13, 200.

[28] *KTU* 1.127, line 9; translated by Pardee, *Ritual and Cult at Ugarit,* 130; also Weinfeld, "Social and Cultic Institutions," 99.

[29] *CTH* 382, translated by Weinfeld, "Social and Cultic Institutions," 98–9; cf. Singer, *Hittite Prayers,* 83. A large number of Hittite ritual tablets like those referred to here have been discovered. For translations of representative samples, see *COS* 1.60–70, 1.83 or *ANET* 346–61.

will carry out."[30] During a long-drawn-out plague, searches of archives turned up old ritual and treaty texts whose provisions had fallen into abeyance. When oracles confirmed that failure to follow these texts had brought the plague on Hatti (cf. the oracular check performed on Josiah's law book, 2 Kgs 22:13–20), the rituals were reinstated and offerings were made to compensate for the treaty violations.[31]

As other evidence for the use of such texts, inscriptions at or near temples often contained instructions on how to make offerings and, especially, how much to offer. For example, city authorities in Carthage in the late fourth century B.C.E. set up the so-called Punic Tariffs to regulate the amounts of temple offerings.[32] Such public inscriptions were clearly intended to regulate the ritual practices of the general public, not just priests. Greek legal sources confirm the public function of such inscriptions. Thus a speech by the orator Lysias circa 400 B.C.E. accused Nicomachus of falsifying legal inscriptions that he was supposed to transcribe:

> I am merely claiming that he should obey the code established and patent to all and I am surprised at his not observing that, when he taxes me with impiety for saying that we ought to perform the sacrifices named in the tablets and pillars as directed in the regulations, he is accusing the city as well: for they are what you have decreed. And then, sir, if you feel these to be hard words, surely you must attribute grievous guilt to those citizens who used to sacrifice solely in accordance with the tablets. But of course, gentlemen of the jury, we are not to be instructed in piety by Nicomachus, but are rather to be guided by the ways of the past. Now our ancestors, by sacrificing in accordance with the tablets, have handed down to us a city superior in greatness and prosperity to

---

[30] *CTH* 382, translated by Singer, *Hittite Prayers*, 83. The Hittites apparently regarded texts as interchangeable with oral tradition as a means to validate rituals, for the passage goes on to state: "When I consult a venerable old man, [as] they remember [each(?)] requirement and report it, thus I shall carry it out."

[31] The Second Plague Prayer of Mursili, §§3–6 (*CTH* 378.II), translated by Singer, *Hittite Prayers*, 58–9.

[32] Translated by Dennis Pardee in *COS* 1.98.

any other in Hellas; so that it behooves us to perform the same sacrifices as they did, if for no other reason than that of the success which has resulted from those rites.[33]

In ritual matters, the Greeks and Romans and many other cultures usually regarded the ancient local traditions as normative for that place.[34] Old texts provided a public means of validating the accuracy of those local traditions.

It is harder to come by explicit descriptions of rituals that actually incorporated the display and public reading of their ritual texts. The clearest examples are biblical: Moses and Joshua (Exodus 24; Deuteronomy 31; Josh 8:34–35) as well as Josiah and Ezra read books of laws to public assemblies. These early books presumably included ritual regulations like those in the finished Pentateuch that are addressed formally to "all Israel" (e.g., the provisions regarding offerings and the Day of Atonement in Leviticus 1–7, 16). Such public instructions therefore appeared not only on monumental inscriptions but also on scrolls that could be carried about and read aloud. Of course, other kinds of ancient texts were used or even designed for ritual application: execration texts were covered with curses and then smashed to put them into effect; prayers were written in letter form and deposited in temples;[35] offensive letters could be displayed before the deity to plead for protection or revenge against the writer (2 Kgs 19:14–19).

The Egyptian "Opening the Mouth" ritual provides more concrete evidence of how ritual texts were sometimes used. This rite for (re-)vivifying divine statues and, in Egypt, also the dead, is known to us in variant forms from both Akkadian and Egyptian sources. In the Egyptian version, one of the officiants at the rite is, according to David

---

[33] Lysias, *Against Nicomachus*, 17–19, in *Lysias* (trans. W. R. M. Lamb; Loeb Classical Library; London: Heinemann; New York: G.P. Putnam's Sons, 1930).

[34] For a recent discussion, see Sawyer, *Sacred Languages*, 152–3.

[35] William W. Hallo, "Letters, Prayers and Letter-Prayers," in *Proceedings of the Seventh World Congress of Jewish Studies* (ed. Y. Gutman; Jerusalem: Perry Foundation, 1981), 17–27.

Lorton, "the *chery-hebet* or 'ritualist', whose title literally means 'the one who holds the ritual' (i.e., the papyrus on which the words of the ritual are written)."[36] Several tomb paintings, reliefs, and papyri illustrate this official as presiding over the ceremony, open scroll in hand.[37]

Jewish traditions also show developments in the ritual use of ritual texts. Ezra ritualized the public reading of the Torah (Nehemiah 8) by surrounding it with blessings and responses, obeisances, and a hierarchical arrangement of the assembled people. The Letter of Aristeas (second century B.C.E.) depicts King Ptolemy doing obeisance before Torah scrolls and, once the new Septuagint Greek translation has been completed, describes how the ceremony unveiling the translation concluded with public curses on anyone who might dare alter any part of that work (*Let. Aris.* 177).

In summary, texts were used in a variety of cultures to establish correct ritual performance and to legitimize the ritual practices of priests, kings, and temples. Thus the idea of enacting written instructions, that is, "doing it by the book," involved first of all doing rituals. There is also some evidence that texts began to be manipulated and read as part of the rituals themselves. Therefore as texts validated the accuracy and efficacy of rituals, rituals elevated the authority of certain texts to iconic status.

---

[36] David Lorton, "The Theology of the Cult Statues in Ancient Egypt," in *Born in Heaven, Made on Earth: The Making of the Cult Image in the Ancient Near East* (ed. Michael Dick; Winona Lake: Eisenbrauns, 1999), 149.

[37] The Papyrus of Ani (19th Dynasty, ca. 1295–1186 B.C.E., from Thebes; in the British Museum, EA 10470/6) shows a figure holding up an open scroll while the ceremony is performed. A New Kingdom tomb painting shows "artisans applying the finishing touches to two anthropoid sarcophagi" while "a man holds an open papyrus on which the words 'performing the Opening of the Mouth' are written" (Lorton, "Theology of Cult Statues," 158; a photo of the painting appears in Eberhard Otto, *Die Ägyptische Mundöffnungsritual* [Ägyptische Abhandlungen 3; Wiesbaden: Harrassowitz, 1960], vol. 2, fig. 13). Moses was depicted in a similar pose in the synagogue at Dura-Europa (3rd century C.E.). Perhaps the Pompeian mural in the Villa of the Mysteries of a boy reading (1st century C.E.) represents a similar situation in a Roman ritual.

The Authority of Torah

In the case of Judaism, the Torah's *ritual* authority seems to have preceded its authority in other matters. A chronological summary of a series of incidents involving books or references to books illustrates the widening scope of the Torah's authority.

According to 2 Kings, Josiah's reading of a "book of law" ca. 620 B.C.E. stimulated changes in cult furnishings, the monopolization of the most important rituals by the Jerusalem temple, and the revival of the celebration of Passover (2 Kings 22–23). However, despite the long-standing critical consensus that Josiah's law book was more or less the biblical book of Deuteronomy, 2 Kings offers no indication that Josiah acted on Deuteronomy's extensive civil and criminal legislation. In fact, the king's active enforcement of ritual mandates actually contradicts Deuteronomy's restrictive view of kingship.[38]

The book of Ezra reports that, ca. 535 B.C.E., the returning exiles built an altar in Jerusalem and celebrated *Sukkot* (the Feast of Tabernacles) "according to what is written in the Law of Moses, the man of God" (Ezra 3:2–5). In 520, they installed the priests and Levites according to the Torah (Ezra 6:18). Here again, Torah regulated the affairs of religious festivals and personnel only.

In the following century, however, Ezra reformed the Jerusalem community's marriage practices on the basis of a "book of the law of Moses" (Ezra 9:11–12 with specific reference to Deut 7:3). Was this the first attempt to mandate the book's legislation beyond temple and ritual matters? Was Ezra the innovator who turned a ritual book into a law book? Perhaps, but other episodes from the same period suggest uneven developments, at the very least. Nehemiah legislated against debt slavery without reference to Torah laws (Neh 5:1–13). The only laws mentioned explicitly in the historical review in Nehemiah 9 are the Sabbath commandment (9:14) and laws against idolatry and blasphemy (9:18, 26). The communal covenant of Nehemiah 10

---

[38] Knoppers, *Two Nations under God*, 2:164–9.

emphasized separation from neighboring peoples, no intermarriage, Sabbath and sabbatical years (including debt cancellation), tithes and offerings to the temple, a wood offering (not in the Torah), and so on. So only the issues of intermarriage and separation from foreigners seem to depart from the pattern of invoking the Torah's authority solely for ritual and temple matters. And ritual concerns probably motivated these as well. Note that the priests and Levites lead the lists of those who divorced their foreign wives (Ezra 10:18–23), that Nehemiah "drove away" a grandson and brother of high priests because he had married into the royal family of Samaria (Neh 13:28), and that the Book of Nehemiah concludes by emphasizing that Nehemiah purified the priests and Levites "of everything foreign" (13:29–30).[39] An explicit reference to Numbers grounds the exclusion of Ammonites and Moabites from the community (Neh 13:1–3), but Nehemiah must "purify" the temple room after expelling Tobiah the Ammonite from it (vv 9), which suggests again cultic concerns behind the policy of exclusion. After all, Leviticus describes the separation of holy and common, clean and unclean, as a chief task for ritual specialists, the priests (Lev 10:10). So the ritual purification of both temple and community focuses naturally on priests and seems to motivate Ezra's and Nehemiah's use of Torah as well. Once again, they used an old text to validate their *ritual* practices.

Within a few decades of these events, Persian authorities mandated Torah-orthodox Passover instructions for the Jewish community in Elephantine, Egypt. The letters from Elephantine suggest that at the end of the fifth century B.C.E., the Jerusalem hierarchy extended the

---

[39] References in Ezra and Nehemiah to the actions and roles of priests, and especially high priests, are nevertheless sparser than one would expect in a society presumably centered on its temple. On this, see Deborah W. Rooke, *Zadok's Heirs: The Role and Development of the High Priesthood in Ancient Israel* (Oxford: Oxford University Press, 2000), 152–74, who argued that the priests' authority was limited to the temple. She noted, however, that this literature depicts the Jerusalem priests, and especially the high priestly family, unfavorably because of their intermarriage with non-Jews (163).

Torah's ritual instructions, at least those regarding the date of Passover, to other Jewish cult centers outside Jerusalem. The Elephantine letters, however, show no awareness of an authoritative text, only of the Jerusalem priesthood's expertise in such matters. The Elephantine community also appealed to the Jerusalem priests and elders for support for their temple rebuilding project but received help only from Persian governors in Judea and Samaria. Perhaps the failure of the Jerusalem hierarchy to respond to this request reflects their desire to centralize Jewish worship in Jerusalem alone, something mandated by Deuteronomy.[40] The Persian authorities limited the Elephantine temple's offerings to nonanimal offerings, which perhaps also reflected Jerusalem's wish to monopolize animal sacrifice.[41] But even if written Torah was informing these decisions, its authority was not invoked in any of the extant correspondence.

The brother of Jerusalem's high priest was installed in a new Samaritan temple on Mt. Gerizim in the late fourth century, according to Josephus (*Ant.* 11.8).[42] The Samaritans also claimed the Torah as their scripture. Though Josephus does not link the two, I wonder if the priest and the book traveled to Mt. Gerizim together. Both would have served to authorize and validate the rituals of the Samaritan temple

[40] Rooke, *Zadok's Heirs*, 181–2. The Aaronide priests of the Second Temple period did not, however, show as much concern for centralizing cultic activity in Jerusalem as they did for monopolizing it for themselves wherever it occurred (see Chapter 7 of this book). There is no indication whether the Elephantine temple was served by Aaronide priests or not.

[41] The letters are translated by Bezalel Porten, ed., *The Elephantine Papyri in English* (Leiden: Brill, 1996), texts B13–14, B17, B19–21.

[42] The historicity of Josephus' account has been questioned on grounds of chronology and also because it looks as though he adapted a story in Neh 13:23 of intermarriage between the ruling family of Samaria and the high priestly family to serve as anti-Samaritan polemic (see Grabbe, *Judaism from Cyrus to Hadrian*, 174; Rooke, *Zadok's Heirs*, 222, n. 5). Samaritan traditions agree that they share a priestly lineage with Jews, but date the split in priestly lines much earlier, to premonarchic times when Eli established a sectarian (that is, Jewish) priesthood (see *The Samaritan Chronicle, or The Book of Joshua the Son of Nun* [tr. Oliver Turnball Crane; New York: John B. Alden, 1890], chap. 43; reprinted in Robert A. Anderson and Terry Giles, eds., *Tradition Kept: The Literature of the Samaritans* [Peabody, MA: Hendrickson, 2005]).

on the basis of Israel's ancient traditions. Subsequent controversies between Samaritans and Jews often centered on whose temple and priesthood accorded better with the Torah of Moses.[43] Nevertheless, Josephus made no mention of written Torah at the time of this temple's founding.

By the second century B.C.E., however, wider applications of the Torah's directives appear in much of the surviving literature. Thus the book of Tobit (ca. 200 B.C.E.) describes not only the tithe of the firstfruits but also a marriage contract being conducted "according to the law of Moses" (1:8; 7:12–13). 1 Maccabees (ca. 100 B.C.E.), like the book of Ezra, is careful to note compliance with Torah directives in the cleansing and restoration of the temple in 164 B.C.E. (1 Macc 4:47, 53). It maintains that the Maccabean revolt (167–164 B.C.E.) began over the question of compliance with Torah in making sacrifices (1 Macc 2:15–50). But similar compliance with Torah directives is noted in military matters as well (1 Macc 3:47). The principal legal (*halakhic*) concerns of the books of Maccabees revolve around sacrifices, altars, sabbath restrictions, circumcision, and food laws (*kashrut*), the latter clearly involving affairs far beyond the temple and its priests. The book of Judith (second century B.C.E.) is notable for highlighting Judith's observance of rules regarding fasting and purity (8:2–7; 9:1; 10:5; 12:2, 7–9, 19; 16:18). She seems to act in accord with Torah regulations, but unlike the story of Tobit, this narrative never refers to written laws. So the source of Judith's knowledge could have been oral teachings. The story of Susannah (ca. 100 B.C.E.), however, tells us explicitly that Susannah was trained in the law of Moses (v 3). When Daniel proves her accusers to be liars, the community executed them "according to the law of Moses" (v 62). This story thus explicitly applies written Torah to an issue of criminal law for the first time. It is also in the literature of this time that we first find references to the Torah scrolls themselves becoming the targets of attacks on Jewish ritual practices

---

[43] Josephus, *Ant.* 13.3; see van der Horst, "Anti-Samaritan Propaganda in Early Judaism," 31–2, 37–9.

(1 Macc 1:56–57). What is privileged by ritual may also be desecrated and destroyed as a symbolic means of undermining communal identity. So in the practices and literature of the second century B.C.E., we find clear signs that the authority of Torah was extended beyond the ritual realm to criminal and civil matters, and that Torah scrolls had become symbols of Jewish identity and practice.

Or perhaps the better way to put it is this: at that time the *ritual authority* of the Torah was extended beyond the temple to other aspects of daily life that, by falling under the Torah's precepts, were ritualized as well. The sectarian *halakhah* (legal interpretation) of the Qumran scrolls and related materials provide the best examples of this tendency.[44] The Qumran *Temple Scroll,* likely also a late second- or early first-century B.C.E. composition, literally extends the purity laws of the temple to the whole city of Jerusalem. Though the scroll deals with other concerns as well, especially the king, its principal interest remains in temple rituals, purity requirements, and the proper performance of festivals. The sectarian literature's interest in civil procedures seems limited to repeating the Torah's provisions with little amplification, except when it comes to regulating the internal life of the sectarian community itself, as in the *Community Rule* and the *Damascus Document.* These documents add many rules of behavior and disciplinary procedures to the biblical mandates. When we remember, however, that the sectarians conceived of their communities as reproducing the conditions of purity and holiness expected of the Jerusalem temple but not achieved there, these community rules appear once again to be extensions of the rules of the sanctuary. The temple's rules were applied to people insofar as they are (or should be) within the extended temple community.

---

[44] E.g., the *Temple Scroll* (11Q19), the *Rule of the Community* (1QS), and the *Halakhic Letter* (4QMMT) from Qumran; closely related are the *Damascus Document* and *Jubilees.* For translations of the Qumran material, see Florentino García Martínez, *The Dead Sea Scrolls Translated* (2nd ed.; Leiden: Brill; Grand Rapids: Eerdmans, 1996). For a brief survey of *halakhah* at Qumran, see Devorah Dimant, "Qumran Sectarian Literature," in *Jewish Writings of the Second Temple Period* (ed. Michael E. Stone; Philadelphia: Fortress, 1984), 489–502, 526–30.

Several recent studies have argued that concerns for ritual purity in late Second Temple Judaism were far more widespread than the example of the Qumran Essenes might suggest. Literary and archeological evidence suggests that bathing and hand-washing were not primarily focused on temple rituals but were common Jewish practices both in Judea and in the diaspora.[45] My argument that the Torah's authority originated in temple ritual and was only gradually extended beyond it does not dispute this possibility, any more than it challenges the widespread practice of criminal law in ancient Judaism. It simply points out that mere references to purity practices, as in the book of Judith, were not necessarily meant to invoke the written Torah; they may simply reflect traditional practice as taught by elders and priests. The invocation of written scripture to reinforce or to reform such practices outside the temple seems to have become common only in the Judaism of the second century B.C.E. and later.

Conclusion

This chapter can only sketch broad patterns of practice and outline developments in the ritual use of texts and the textual authorization of rituals in antiquity. Much more detailed research remains to be done on how texts were used to justify ritual practices and how rituals elevated the authority of texts in various cultures and time periods. This initial survey, however, suggests that, more than any other factor, it was the authority of the temple's ritual traditions that established the Pentateuch's prestige. That authority was grounded in the assertion that the priests were practicing the ancient ritual traditions for that local cult. The validity of that claim was defended by invoking a book that claimed to be much older than the disruptions in cult practice

---

[45] See the review and analysis by John C. Poirer, "Purity beyond the Temple in the Second Temple Era," *JBL* 122 (2003): 247–65.

caused by the destruction of the first temple and the Babylonian exile. As in other cultures of roughly the same time period, ritual and text supported each other: the prestige of the temple elevated the status of the book, which in turn guaranteed the legitimacy of the temple's rites.

Only when the ritual authority of the Torah was generally recognized did its other materials (civil and criminal laws, stories) gain special "scriptural" status. This development finds no clear parallel in other ancient cultures. Notwithstanding the profound cultural influence of texts like the Instruction of Kemit in Egypt, Gilgamesh in Mesopotamia, and Homer's Iliad in Greece, one searches ancient literatures in vain for assertions that they authorize particular beliefs or legitimate certain practices in the way that Torah is invoked in Judaism and other scriptures in later religious traditions. That observation does not dispute the fact that the Hebrew Bible did and does serve an enculturating educational role, as Carr has argued. It is, however, its ritual contents and function that have given it a distinctive authority characteristic of what we call "scriptures." That authority came about because the Torah's rhetorical structure combined lists of ritual instructions with criminal laws, narratives, and sanctions. It did so to persuade Jews to accept it as the Torah of the Jerusalem temple and community.[46] Once that was achieved, claims for its authority gradually increased in scope as various groups expanded the definition and geographic boundaries of the temple community.

Thus the origin of the religious authority of Western scriptures derived primarily from the use of old texts and books for validating rituals. The idea of scripture was grounded first and foremost in the ritual use of texts. The traditional dichotomy in Western, especially Christian, traditions between text and ritual disguises the fact that the authority of the scriptures originated in ritual concerns and continues to be maintained by ritual practices.

---

[46] For a full exposition of the rhetorical effect of the Torah's contents, see Watts, *Reading Law.*

Ironically, the Torah's particular emphasis on ritual offerings no longer applies in either Judaism or Christianity. Because of historical changes in both traditions, they no longer recommend the literal application of many of the ritual instructions. Therefore other aspects of Torah and Bible, such as the stories and the moral laws, came to be considered more central to the message of scripture. Hence the many attempts, ranging from ancient *halakhah* and allegory to modern literary analysis and structuralist anthropology, to interpret the Torah's ritual regulations in terms of ethics and theology.[47]

This development began almost as soon as the Torah's civil laws and narratives gained authoritative status, and long before the Romans' destruction of the Second Temple rendered much of the ritual instruction moot. Philo of Alexandria described the Sabbath observance in an Essene synagogue in the early first century C.E.: "Then one, indeed, takes up the books and reads them, and another of the men of the greatest experience comes forward and explains what is not very intelligible for a great many precepts are delivered in enigmatic modes of expression, and allegorically, as the old fashion was" (*Good Person*, 7:82).[48]

---

[47] This tendency is pervasive throughout the commentary literature from antiquity to the present (see Chapter 1). Contemporary examples include, among many others, Jacob Milgrom, who expounded at great length on "the ethical foundation of the dietary system" found in Leviticus (*Leviticus*, 1:704–42); Mary Douglas, who revised her famous comparative theory of impurity (*Purity and Danger*) to make an exception for priestly legislation in the Torah, which she describes as "philosophical doctrines in the forms of rules of behaviour" (*Leviticus as Literature*, 39); and Terence Fretheim, who argued that "law is a God-given means by which the creation can be made whole once again" (*The Pentateuch* [Nashville: Abingdon, 1996], 126). This strongly felt *need* within the religious and academic traditions to interpret the ritual regulations of scripture in theological and ethical ways does not seem to have been shared by the writers of the early chapters of Leviticus, as the rhetorical analysis of this book has shown. Carr also concluded from his study of the Hebrew Bible as an "educational-enculturational text" that there is "little evidence that the sorts of broader ideological structures focused on in biblical theology were of central concern to those who shaped and consolidated biblical literature" (*Writing*, 292). Cf. also Bergen, *Reading Ritual*, 53, 74.

[48] *The Works of Philo* (tr. C. D. Younge; Peabody, MA: Hendrickson, 1993), 689–70, as revised by Lawrence H. Schiffman, *Text and Traditions: A Source Reader for the*

Here the need to *do* the ritual correctly had already expanded into a need to *understand* the ritual text correctly and the ritual's meaning as interpreted through that text. Eventually, for many communities that treasure scriptures, understanding the text and its meaning was enough, and many of the rituals mandated *in* the text fell into disuse. Instead, rituals *of* the text arose that reinforced its iconic place at the center of worship.

Study of Second Temple and Rabbinic Judaism (Hoboken, NJ: Ktav, 1998), 283. The Qumran *Rule of the Community* (1QS 6.7–8) described it this way: "The Many shall be on watch together for a third of each night of the year in order to read the book, explain the regulation, and bless together" (translation by García Martínez, *Dead Sea Scrolls,* 9).

Bibliography

Achenbach, Reinhard. *Die Vollendung der Tora: Studien zur Redaktionsgeschichte des Numeribuches im Kontext von Hexateuch und Pentateuch.* BZABR 3. Wiesbaden: Harrassowitz, 2002. 130–40.

Alter, Robert. *The Five Books of Moses: A Translation with Commentary.* New York: Norton, 2004.

Anderson, Robert A. and Terry Giles, eds. *Tradition Kept: The Literature of the Samaritans.* Peabody, MA: Hendrickson, 2005.

Baker, David W. "Division Markers and the Structure of Leviticus 1–7." In *Studia Biblica 1978.* Ed. E. A. Livingstone. JSOTSup 11. Sheffield: JSOT, 1979. 193–94.

———. "Leviticus 1–7 and the Punic Tariffs: A Form Critical Comparison," *ZAW* 99 (1987): 193–94.

Barkley, Gary Wayne, ed. and tr. *Origen: Homilies on Leviticus 1–16.* Washington, DC: Catholic University Press of America, 1990.

Bataille, Georges. *Theory of Religion.* Tr. R. Hurley. New York: Zone, 1992 (French original, 1948).

Baumgarten, Albert I. "*Ḥaṭṭāʾt* Sacrifices." *RB* 103 (1996): 337–42.

Beal, Timothy K. and Tod Linafelt. "Sifting for Cinders: Strange Fire in Leviticus 10:1–5." *Semeia* 69/70 (1995): 19–32.

Begrich, J. "Die priesterliche Tora." In *Wesen und Werden des Alten Testaments.* Ed. P. Volz. BZAW 66. Berlin: A. Töpelmann, 1936. 63–88.

Bell, Catherine. *Ritual: Perspectives and Dimensions.* Oxford: Oxford University Press, 1997.

Bellah, Robert N. "Civil Religion in America." In *Beyond Belief: Essays on Religion in a Post-Traditional World.* New York: Harper & Row, 1970. 168–89.

Bergen, Wesley J. *Reading Ritual: Leviticus in Postmodern Culture.* JSOTSup 417. London: T&T Clark, 2005.

Bergquist, Birgitta. "Bronze Age Sacrificial Koine in the Eastern Mediterranean? A Study of Animal Sacrifice in the Ancient Near East." In *Ritual and Sacrifice in the Ancient Near East.* Ed. J. Quaegebeur. Leuven: Peeters, 1993. 11–43.

Berman, Louis A. *Akedah: The Binding of Isaac.* Boulder: Rowman & Littlefield, 1997.

Bertholet, Alfred. *Leviticus.* Kurzer Hand-Commentar zum Alten Testament. Tübingen: Mohr Siebeck, 1901.

Bibb, Bryan D. "Nadab and Abihu Attempt to Fill a Gap: Law and Narrative in Leviticus 10.1–7." *JSOT* 96 (2001): 83–99.

———. "This Is the Thing that the Lord Commanded You to Do: Ritual Words and Narrative Worlds in the Book of Leviticus." Ph.D. Dissertation, Princeton Theological Seminary, 2005.

Binkley, Roberta and Carol Lipson, eds. *Rhetoric before and beyond the Greeks.* Albany: SUNY Press, 2004.

Blenkinsopp, Joseph. *The Pentateuch: An Introduction to the First Five Books of the Bible.* New York: Doubleday, 1992.

———. *Sage, Priest, Prophet: Religious and Intellectual Leadership in Ancient Israel.* Louisville: Westminster John Knox, 1995.

Bloch, Maurice. *Prey into Hunter: The Politics of Religious Experience.* Cambridge: Cambridge University Press, 1992.

Boecker, Hans Jochen. *Law and the Administration of Justice in the Bible and the Ancient Near East.* Tr. Jeremy Moiser. Minneapolis: Augsburg, 1980.

Borger, R. "Gott Marduk und Gott-König Šulgi als Propheten." *Bibliotheca Orientalis* 28 (1971): 3–24.

Boyarin, Daniel. *Dying for God.* Stanford, CA: Stanford University Press, 1999.

Brichto, Herbert Chanan. "On Slaughter and Sacrifice, Blood and Atonement." *HUCA* 47 (1976): 19–55.

Brueggemann, Walter. *Theology of the Old Testament: Testimony, Dispute, Advocacy.* Minneapolis: Fortress, 1997.

Buc, Philippe. *The Dangers of Ritual: Between Early Medieval Texts and Social Scientific Theory.* Princeton: Princeton University Press, 2001.

Budd, Philip J. *Leviticus.* New Century Bible. Grand Rapids: Eerdmans, 1996.

Burke, Kenneth. A *Rhetoric of Motives.* Berkeley: University of California, 1950.

Burkert, Walter. *Homo Necans: The Anthropology of Ancient Greek Sacrificial Ritual and Myth.* Berkeley: University of California Press, 1983.

———. "The Problem of Ritual Killing." In *Violent Origins.* Ed. H. Hamerton-Kelly. Stanford: Stanford University Press, 1987. 149–88.

Caesar, C. Julius. *Caesar's Gallic War.* Tr. W. A. McDevitte and W. S. Bohn. New York: Harper & Brothers, 1869.

Çambel, H. *Corpus of Hieroglyphic Luwian Inscriptions.* 2 vols. Berlin: De Gruyter, 1999.

Carr, David M. *Writing on the Tablet of the Heart: Origins of Scripture and Literature.* Oxford: Oxford University Press, 2005.

Carter, Jeffrey, ed. *Understanding Religious Sacrifice: A Reader.* London: Continuum, 2003.

Caspi, Mishael Maswari. *Take Now Thy Son: The Motif of the Aqedah (Binding) in Literature.* North Richland Hills, TX: Bibal Press, 2001.

Cave, Roy C. and Herbert H. Coulson. *A Source Book for Medieval Economic History.* Milwaukee: Bruce, 1936; reprinted, New York: Biblo & Tannen, 1965.

Clines, David J. A. *Ezra, Nehemiah, Esther.* New Century Bible. Grand Rapids: Eerdmans, 1984.

Cothey, Antony. "Ethics and Holiness in the Theology of Leviticus." *JSOT* 30 (2005): 131–51.

Crane, Oliver Turnball, tr. *The Samaritan Chronicle, or The Book of Joshua the Son of Nun.* New York: John B. Alden, 1890.

Cross, Frank Moore, Jr. "A Reconstruction of the Judean Restoration." *JBL* 94 (1975): 4–18.

Dahm, Ulrike. *Opferkult und Priestertum in Alt-Israel: Ein kultur- und religionswissenschaftlicher Beitrag.* BZAW 327. Berlin: De Gruyter, 2003.

Damrosch, David. "Leviticus." In *The Literary Guide to the Bible.* Ed. Robert Alter and Frank Kermode. Cambridge, MA: Belknap/Harvard, 1987. 66–77.

———. *The Narrative Covenant: Transformations of Genre in the Growth of Biblical Literature.* San Francisco: Harper & Row, 1987.

Davis, Avroham, ed. *The Metsudah Chumash/Rashi.* Hoboken: Ktav, 1998.

Delaney, Carol. *Abraham on Trial: The Social Legacy of Biblical Myth.* Princeton: Princeton University Press, 1998.

Detienne, Marcel. "Culinary Practices and the Spirit of Sacrifice." In *The Cuisine of Sacrifice among the Greeks.* Ed. M. Detienne and J.-P. Vernant. Tr. P. Wissing. Chicago: University of Chicago, 1989 (French 1979). 1–20.

Díaz del Castillo, Bernal. *The Discovery and Conquest of Mexico.* Tr. A. P. Maudslay. New York: Farrar, Straus & Cudahy, 1956.

Dimant, Devorah. "Qumran Sectarian Literature." In *Jewish Writings of the Second Temple Period.* Ed. Michael E. Stone. Philadelphia: Fortress, 1984. 489–530.

Douglas, Mary. *In the Wilderness: The Doctrine of Defilement in the Book of Numbers.* JSOTSup 158. Sheffield: Sheffield Academic Press, 1993.

———. *Leviticus as Literature.* Oxford: Oxford University Press, 1999.

———. *Purity and Danger: An Analysis of Concepts of Pollution and Taboo.* New York: Praeger, 1966.

Driver, G. R. "Studies in the Vocabulary of the Old Testament, VI." *JTS* 34 (1933): 34–8.

Driver, Tom F. *The Magic of Ritual: Our Need for Liberating Rites that Transform Our Lives and Our Communities.* New York: Harper San Francisco, 1991.

Durkheim, Emile. *Elementary Forms of Religious Life.* Tr. J. W. Swain. New York: Free Press, 1965 (French original 1912).

Eberhart, Christian. *Studien zur Bedeutung der Opfer im Alten Testament. Die Signifikanz von Blut- und Verbrennungsriten im kultischen Rahmen.* WMANT 94. Neukirchen-Vluyn: Neukirchener Verlag, 2002.

Ehrenreich, Barbara. *Blood Rites: Origins and History of the Passions of War.* New York: Metropolitan, 1997.

Eliasen, Karen C. "Aaron's War Within: Story and Ritual in Leviticus 10." *Proceedings – Eastern Great Lakes and Midwest Biblical Societies* 20 (2000): 81–98.

———. "Getting a Feel for a Concept: A Ritual-Critical Reading of the Nadab and Abihu Incident in Lev 10," conference paper presented at the Eastern International Region meeting of the American Academy of Religion in Ithaca, NY, March 30–31, 2001.

Elliger, Karl. *Leviticus.* Handbuch zum Alten Testament 4. Tübingen: Mohr (Siebeck), 1966.

Evans-Pritchard, E. E. *Nuer Religion.* New York: Oxford University Press, 1974 (1956).

Fleming, Daniel E. "The Biblical Tradition of Anointing Priests." *JBL* 117 (1998): 401–14.

Foster, Benjamin. *Before the Muses: An Anthology of Akkadian Literature.* 3rd ed. Bethesda, MD: CDL, 2005.

Foster, John L. *Ancient Egyptian Literature: An Anthology.* Austin: University of Texas Press, 2001.

Frantzen, Allen J. *Bloody Good: Chivalry, Sacrifice, and the Great War.* Chicago: University of Chicago Press, 2004.

Frazer, James George. *The Golden Bough: A Study in Magic and Religion.* Abridged ed. New York: Macmillan, 1922, 1960.

Fretheim, Terence. *The Pentateuch.* Nashville: Abingdon, 1996.

Freud, Sigmund. "Obsessive Actions and Religious Practices," 1907; reprinted in *Readings in Ritual Studies.* Ed. Ronald L. Grimes. Upper Saddle River, NJ: Prentice Hall, 1996. 212–17.

———. *Totem and Taboo: Resemblances between the Psychic Lives of Savages and Neurotics.* Tr. A. A. Brill. New York: Vintage, 1918.

Gane, Roy E. *Cult and Character: Purification Offerings, Day of Atonement, and Theodicy.* Winona Lake: Eisenbrauns, 2005.

———. *Ritual Dynamic Structure.* Piscataway, NJ: Gorgias, 2004.

García Martínez, Florentino. *The Dead Sea Scrolls Translated.* 2nd ed. Leiden: Brill / Grand Rapids: Eerdmans, 1996.

Geertz, Clifford. *The Interpretation of Culture.* New York: Basic, 1973.

Gellman, Jerome I. *Abraham! Abraham! Kierkegaard and the Hasidim on the Binding of Isaac.* Aldershot: Ashgate, 2003.

Gellner, Ernest. "Concepts and Society." In *Sociological Theory and Philosophical Analysis.* Ed. Dorothy Emmet and Alasdair MacIntyre. New York: Macmillan 1970. 115–49.

Gerstenberger, Erhard S. *Leviticus: A Commentary.* Old Testament Library. Tr. D.W. Stott. Louisville: Westminster John Knox, 1996 (German 1993).

Giegerich, Wolfgang. "Killings: Psychology's Platonism and the Missing Link to Reality." *Spring* 54 (1993): 5–18.

———. "Once More the Reality/Irreality Issue: A Reply to Hillman's Reply." Online at http://www.rubedo.psc.br/reply.htm.

———. *Tötungen: Gewalt aus der Seele.* Frankfurt: Lang, 1994.

Gilders, William K. *Blood Ritual in the Hebrew Bible: Meaning and Power.* Baltimore: Johns Hopkins University Press, 2004.

———. "*Ḥaṭṭāʾt* as 'Sin Offering': A Reconsideration," conference paper presented at the International Society of Biblical Literature meeting, Cambridge, UK, July, 2003.

Girard, René. "Generative Scapegoating." In *Violent Origins*. Ed. R. G. Hamerton-Kelly. Stanford: Stanford University Press, 1987. 73–8.

———. *Violence and the Sacred*. Baltimore: Johns Hopkins University Press, 1977 (French original, 1972).

Gordon, Richard. "Religion in the Roman Empire: The Civic Compromise and Its Limits." In *Pagan Priests: Religion and Power in the Ancient World*. Ed. Mary Beard and John North. Ithaca: Cornell University Press, 1990. 235–55.

Gorman, Frank H., Jr. *The Ideology of Ritual: Space, Time and Status in the Priestly Theology*. JSOTSup 91. Sheffield: JSOT Press, 1990.

———. *Leviticus: Divine Presence and Community*. Grand Rapids: Eerdmans, 1997.

Gottwald, Norman K. *The Hebrew Bible: A Socio-Literary Introduction*. Philadelphia: Fortress, 1985.

Grabbe, Lester L. "Josephus and the Reconstruction of the Judean Restoration." *JBL* 106 (1987): 231–46.

———. *Judaism from Cyrus to Hadrian, Vol. 1: The Persian and Greek Periods*. Minneapolis: Fortress, 1992.

———. *Leviticus*. Old Testament Guides. Sheffield: Sheffield Academic Press, 1993.

———. *Priests, Prophets, Diviners, Sages: A Socio-Historical Study of Religious Specialists in Ancient Israel*. Valley Forge, PA: Trinity Press International, 1995.

Gradwohl, R. "Das 'fremde Feuer' von Nadab und Abihu." *ZAW* 75 (1963): 288–96.

Graham, William A. *Beyond the Written Word: Oral Aspects of Scripture in the History of Religion*. Cambridge: Cambridge University Press, 1987.

Gray, George Buchanan. *Sacrifice in the Old Testament: Its Theory and Practice*. New York: Ktav, 1971 (1st ed., 1925).

Green, William Scott. "Romancing the Tome: Rabbinic Hermeneutics and the Theory of Literature." *Semeia* 40 (1987): 147–68.

Greenstein, Edward L. "Deconstruction and Biblical Narrative." *Prooftexts* 9 (1989): 43–71.

Grimes, Ronald. *Beginnings in Ritual Studies*. Rev. ed. Studies in Comparative Religion. Columbia: University of South Carolina Press, 1995.

———. *Ritual Criticism: Case Studies in Its Practice, Essays on Its Theory*. Columbia: University of South Carolina Press, 1990.

Hallo, William W. "Letters, Prayers and Letter-Prayers." In *Proceedings of the Seventh World Congress of Jewish Studies*. Ed. Y. Gutman. Jerusalem: Perry Foundation, 1981.

Hartley, John E. *Leviticus*. WBC 4. Dallas: Word, 1992.

Hayes, John H. "Atonement in the Book of Leviticus." *Interpretation* 52 (1998): 5–15.

Heald, Suzette, Lester L. Grabbe, Don Handelman, Alan F. Segal, and Ronald S. Hendel. "Book Review Forum on Mary Douglas's *Leviticus as Literature*." *Journal of Ritual Studies* 18/2 (2004), 152–85.

Heesterman, J. C. *The Broken World of Sacrifice: An Essay in Ancient Indian Ritual*. Chicago: University of Chicago Press, 1993.

Heyman, George P. *Martyrdom and Sacrifice: Roman and Christian Representations of Power*. Minneapolis: Fortress, 2007.

Hillman, James. "Once More into the Fray: A Response to Wolfgang Giegerich's 'Killings.'" *Spring* 56 (1994): 1–18.

Hobbs, T. R. *2 Kings*. WBC 13. Waco: Word, 1985.

Horst, Pieter W. van der. "Anti-Samaritan Propaganda in Early Judaism." In *Persuasion and Dissuasion in Early Christianity, Ancient Judaism, and Hellenism*. Ed. Pieter W. van der Horst et al. Leuven: Peeters, 2003. 25–44.

Houston, Walter J. "Tragedy in the Courts of the Lord: A Socio-Literary Reading of the Death of Nadab and Abihu." *JSOT* 90 (2000): 31–9.

Hubert, Henri and Marcel Mauss. *Sacrifice: Its Nature and Function*. Chicago: University of Chicago Press, 1964 (French original, 1898).

Janowski, Bernd. *Sühne als Heilsgeschehen: Studien zur Sühnetheologie der Priesterschrift und zur Wurzel KPR im Alten Orient und im Alten Testament*. WMANT 55. Neukirchen-Vluyn: Neukirchener Verlag, 1982.

Janzen, David. *The Social Meanings of Sacrifice in the Hebrew Bible: A Study of Four Writings*. BZAW 344. Berlin: De Gruyter, 2004.

Jay, Nancy. *Throughout Your Generations Forever: Sacrifice, Religion, and Paternity*. Chicago: University of Chicago Press, 1992.

Jones, G. H. *1 and 2 Kings*. New Century Bible. Grand Rapids: Eerdmans, 1984.

Josephus, Flavius. *The Antiquities of the Jews*. In *The Works of Flavius Josephus*. Tr. W. Whiston. Philadelphia: Winston, n.d.

Kaufmann, Yehezkel. *Toledot ha'Emunah haYisre'elit*. 4 vols. 2nd ed. Jerusalem: Mosad Bialik, 1952.

Kessler, Edward. *Bound by the Bible: Jews, Christians and the Sacrifice of Isaac*. Cambridge: Cambridge University Press, 2004.

Kirschner, Robert. "The Rabbinic and Philonic Exegesis of the Nadab and Abihu Incident." *JQR* 73 (1983): 375–93.

Kiuchi, Nobuyoshi. *The Purification Offering in the Priestly Literature: Its Meaning and Function.* Sheffield: JSOT Press, 1987.

Klawans, Jonathan. *Purity, Sacrifice, and the Temple: Symbolism and Supersessionism in the Study of Ancient Judaism.* Oxford: Oxford University Press, 2006.

———. "Ritual Purity, Moral Purity, and Sacrifice in Jacob Milgrom's Leviticus." *Religious Studies Review* 29/1 (2003): 19–28.

Kleinig, John W. *The Lord's Song: The Basis, Function and Significance of Choral Music in Chronicles.* JSOTSup 156. Sheffield: Sheffield Academic Press, 1993.

Klingbeil, Gerald A. *A Comparative Study of the Ritual of Ordination as Found in Leviticus 8 and Emar 369.* Lewiston: Edwin Mellon, 1998.

———. "Ritual Time in Leviticus 8 with Special Reference to the Seven Day Period in the Old Testament." *ZAW* 109 (1997): 500–13.

———. " 'Who did what when and why?' The Dynamics of Ritual Participants in Leviticus 8 and Emar 369." In *Inicios, Paradigmas y Fundamentos: Estudios teológicos y exegéticos en el Pentateuco.* Ed. G. A. Klingbeil. San Martín, Argentina: Universidada Adventista del Plata, 2004. 105–34.

Knierim, Rolf P. *The Task of Old Testament Theology: Method and Cases.* Grand Rapids: Eerdmans, 1995.

———. *Text and Concept in Leviticus 1:1–9: A Case in Exegetical Method.* Forschungen zum Alten Testament 2. Tübingen: Mohr [Siebeck], 1992.

Knohl, Israel. *The Sanctuary of Silence: The Priestly Torah and the Holiness School.* Minneapolis: Fortress, 1995.

Knoppers, Gary N. *Two Nations under God: The Deuteronomistic History of Solomon and the Dual Monarchies. Volume 2: The Rise of Jeroboam, the Fall of Israel and the Reign of Josiah.* Harvard Semitic Monographs 53. Atlanta: Scholars Press, 1994.

———. "Hierodules, Priests, or Janitors? The Levites in Chronicles and the History of the Israelite Priesthood." *JBL* 118 (1999), 49–72.

———. "The Relationship of the Priestly Genealogies to the History of the High Priesthood in Jerusalem." In *Judah and the Judeans in the Neo-Babylonian Period.* Ed. Oded Lipschits and Joseph Blenkinsopp. Winona Lake, IN: Eisenbrauns, 2003. 109–33.

Koch, Klaus. "Alttestamentliche und altorientalische Rituale." In *Die Hebräische Bibel und ihre zweifache Nachgeschichte: Festschrif für Rolf*

Rendtorff. Ed. E. Blum et al. Neukirchen-Vluyn: Neukirchener Verlag, 1990. 75–85

———. "Ezra and Meremoth: Remarks on the History of the High Priesthood." In *"Sha'arei Talmon": Studies in the Bible, Qumran, and the Ancient Near East Presented to Shemaryahu Talmon.* Ed. Michael Fishbane and Emanuel Tov. Winona Lake, IN: Eisenbrauns, 1992. 105–10.

———. *Die Priesterschrift von Exodus 25 bis Leviticus 16: eine überlieferungsgeschichtliche und literarkritische Untersuchung.* FRLANT 53. Göttingen: Vandenhoeck & Ruprecht, 1959.

———. "*ḥṭ.*" *TDOT* 4:318.

Kornfeld, Walter. *Levitikus.* Die Neue Echter Bibel. Würzberg: Echter, 1983.

Krakauer, Jon. *Under the Banner of Heaven: A Story of Violent Faith.* New York: Anchor, 2003.

Kraus, F. R. "Ein zentrales Problem des altmesopotamischen Rechts: Was is der Codex Hammu-Rabi?" *Genava* 8 (1960): 283–96.

Kugel, James L. *Traditions of the Bible: A Guide to the Bible As It Was at the Start of the Common Era.* Cambridge, MA: Harvard University Press, 1998.

———. "Levi's Elevation to the Priesthood in Second Temple Writings," *Harvard Theological Review* 86 (1993): 1–63.

Lamb, W. R. M., ed. and tr. *Lysias.* London: Heinemann; New York: G. P. Putnam's Sons, 1930.

Lambert, W. G. "Donations of Food and Drink to the Gods in Ancient Mesopotamia." In *Ritual and Sacrifice in the Ancient Near East.* Ed. J. Quaegebeur. Leuven: Peeters, 1993. 191–201.

Lang, Bernhard. "*Kipper.*" *TDOT* 7:288–303.

Laughlin, John C. "The 'Strange Fire' of Nadab and Abihu." *JBL* 95 (1976): 559–65.

Lemardelé, Christophe. "Le sacrifice de purification: un sacrifice ambigu?" *VT* 52 (2002): 284–9.

Levenson, Jon D. *The Death and Resurrection of the Beloved Son: The Transformation of Child Sacrifice in Judaism and Christianity.* New Haven: Yale University Press, 1993.

Levine, Baruch A. "The Descriptive Tabernacle Texts of the Pentateuch." *JAOS* 85 (1965): 307–18.

———. "The Descriptive Ritual Texts from Ugarit: Some Formal and Functional Features of the *Genre.*" In *The Word of the Lord Shall Go Forth: Essay in Honor of David Noel Freedman.* Ed. C. L. Meyers and M. O'Conner. Winona Lake: Eisenbrauns, 1983. 467–75.

————. *In the Presence of the Lord: A Study of Cult and Some Cultic Terms in Ancient Israel.* Studies in Judaism in Late Antiquity 5. Leiden: Brill, 1974.

————. *Leviticus.* JPS Torah Commentary. Philadelphia: Jewish Publication Society, 1989.

————. *Numbers 1–20, Numbers 21–36.* Anchor Bible 4. 2 vols. Garden City: Doubleday, 1993, 2000.

————. "Silence, Sound and the Phenomenology of Mourning in Biblical Israel." *JANES* 22 (1993): 89–106.

————. "Ugaritic Descriptive Rituals." *JCS* 17 (1963): 105–11.

Levine, Baruch A. and William W. Hallo. "Offerings to the Temple Gates at Ur." *HUCA* 38 (1967): 17–58.

Levine, Baruch A. and Jean-Michel de Terragon. "The King Proclaims the Day: Ugaritic Rites for the Vintage (KTU 1.41//1.87)." *RB* 100 (1993): 76–115.

Levinson, Bernard M., ed. *Theory and Method in Biblical and Cuneiform Law: Revision, Interpolation and Development.* JSOTSup 181. Sheffield: Sheffield Academic Press, 1994.

————. "The First Constitution: Rethinking the Origins of Rule of Law and Separation of Powers in Light of Deuteronomy." *Cardozo Law Review* 27 (2006): 1853–88.

Lichtheim, Miriam. *Ancient Egyptian Literature.* 3 vols. Berkeley: University of California, 1973–80.

Lienhard, Joseph T. *Exodus, Leviticus, Numbers, Deuteronomy.* Ancient Christian Commentary on Scripture, Old Testament 3. Downers Grove, IL: InterVarsity, 2001.

Lincoln, Bruce. "Sacrificial Ideology and Indo-European Society." In *Death, War and Sacrifice: Studies in Ideology and Practice.* Chicago: University of Chicago Press, 1991. 167–75.

Lipiński, E. "Rites et sacrifices dans la tradition Phénico-Punique." In *Ritual and Sacrifice in the Ancient Near East.* Ed. J. Quaegebeur. Leuven: Peeters, 1993. 257–81.

Livy. *History of Rome.* Ed. Ernest Rhys. Tr. Canon Roberts. Everyman's Library. New York: E. P. Dutton, 1912.

Longman, Tremper, III. *Fictional Akkadian Autobiography: A Generic and Comparative Study.* Winona Lake, IN: Eisenbrauns, 1991.

Lorton, David. "The Theology of the Cult Statues in Ancient Egypt." In *Born in Heaven, Made on Earth: The Making of the Cult Image in the Ancient Near East.* Ed. Michael Dick. Winona Lake: Eisenbrauns, 1999. 123–210.

Marvin, Carolyn and David Ingle. *Blood Sacrifice and the Nation: Totem Rituals and the American Flag.* Cambridge: Cambridge University Press, 1999.

Marx, Alfred. "Sacrifice pour les péchés ou rites de levee de sanction." *ZAW* 100 (1988): 183–98.

———. *Les systèmes sacrificiels de l'Ancien Testament: Formes et functions du culte sacrificial à Yhwh.* VTSup 105. Leiden: Brill, 2005.

———. "The Theology of Sacrifice According to Leviticus 1–7." In *The Book of Leviticus: Composition and Reception.* Ed. R. Rendtorff and R. A. Kugler. VTSup 93. Leiden: Brill, 2003. 103–20.

McCarthy, Dennis J. *Treaty and Covenant: A Study in Form in the Ancient Oriental Documents and in the Old Testament.* 2nd rev. ed. Analecta Biblica 21. Rome: Pontifical Biblical Institute, 1981.

McKay, J. W. *Religion in Judah under the Assyrians.* Naperville, IL: Allensen, 1973.

Metzger, David. "Pentateuchal Rhetoric and the Voice of the Aaronides." In *Rhetoric Before and Beyond the Greeks.* Ed. Carol Lipson and Roberta Binkley. Albany: SUNY Press, 2004.

Milgrom, Jacob. "The Changing Concept of Holiness in the Pentateuchal Codes with Emphasis on Leviticus 19." In *Reading Leviticus: A Conversation with Mary Douglas.* Ed. J. F. A. Sawyer. JSOTSup 227. Sheffield: Sheffield Academic Press, 1996. 65–75.

———. *Cult and Conscience: The Asham and the Priestly Doctrine of Repentence.* Leiden: Brill, 1976.

———. *Leviticus 1–16, Leviticus 17–22, Leviticus 23–27.* Anchor Bible 3. 3 vols. New York: Doubleday, 1991, 2000, 2001.

———. *Numbers Bmdbr.* JPS. Torah Commentary. Philadelphia: Jewish Publication Society, 1990.

———. "Prolegomenon to Lev 17:11." *JBL* 90 (1971): 149–156; reprinted in idem, *Studies in Cultic Theology and Terminology.* SJLA 36; Leiden: Brill, 1983. 96–103.

———. "Rationale for Cultic Law: The Case of Impurity." *Semeia* 45 (1989): 103–10.

———. "Systemic Differences in the Priestly Corpus: A Response to Jonathan Klawans." *RB* 112 (2005): 321–29.

Mizruchi, Susan L. "The Place of Ritual in Our Time." *American Literary History* 12/3 (2000): 467–92.

———. *The Science of Sacrifice: American Literature and Modern Social Theory,* Princeton, NJ: Princeton University Press, 1998.

Modéus, Martin. *Sacrifice and Symbol: Biblical* Šelāmîm *in a Ritual Perspective*. CB:OT 52. Stockholm: Almqvist & Wiksell, 2005.

Moor, Johannes C. de. *An Anthology of Religious Texts from Ugarit*. Nisaba 16. Leiden: Brill, 1987.

Murnane, William J. *Texts from the Amarna Period in Egypt*. WAW 5. Atlanta: Scholars Press, 1995.

Najman, Hindy. *Seconding Sinai: The Development of Mosaic Discourse in Second Temple Judaism. Journal for the Study of Judaism* Supplement 77. Leiden: Brill, 2003.

Nelson, Richard D. *Raising Up a Faithful Priest: Community and Priesthood in Biblical Theology*. Louisville: Westminster John Knox, 1993.

Niditch, Susan. *Oral World and Written Word: Ancient Israelite Literature*. Louisville: Westminster John Knox, 1996.

Nihan, Christophe. "The Death of Nadab and Abihu and the Priestly Legislation on Perfume Offering: Leviticus 10 in the Context of the Final Editing of Leviticus," conference paper, Biblical Law Section of the Society of Biblical Literature Annual Meeting, 2003; online at http://www.law2.byu.edu/Biblical_Law/annual_meeting.htm.

Nissinen, Marti. *Prophets and Prophecy in the Ancient Near East*. WAW 12. Atlanta: SBL, 2003.

Noort, Ed and Eibert Tigchelaar, eds. *The Sacrifice of Isaac: The Aqedah (Genesis 22) and Its Interpretations*. Leiden: Brill, 2002.

North, John A. "Sacrifice and Ritual: Rome." In *Civilizations of the Ancient Mediterranean: Greece and Rome*. Ed. M. Grant and R. Kitzinger. New York: Scribner's, 1988. 981–6.

Noth, Martin. *Leviticus: A Commentary*. Old Testament Library. Philadelphia: Westminster, 1965 (German, 1962).

Olyan, Saul M. *Rites and Rank: Hierarchy in Biblical Representations of Cult*. Princeton: Princeton University Press, 2000.

Otto, Eberhard. *Die Ägyptische Mundöffnungsritual*. Ägyptische Abhandlungen 3. Wiesbaden: Harrassowitz, 1960.

Overholt, Thomas W. *Channels of Prophecy: The Social Dynamics of Prophetic Activity*. Minneapolis: Fortress, 1989.

Paran, Meir. *Forms of the Priestly Style in the Pentateuch: Patterns, Linguistic Usages, Syntactic Structures* (Hebrew). Jerusalem: Magnes, 1989.

Pardee, Dennis. *Ritual and Cult at Ugarit*. WAW 10. Atlanta: SBL, 2002.

Patrick, Dale and Allen Scult. *Rhetoric and Biblical Interpretation*. JSOTSup 82. Sheffield: Almond, 1990.

Péter-Contesse, René. "Le Sacerdoce." In *The Book of Leviticus: Composition and Reception*. Ed. Rolf Rendtorff and Robert Kugler. VTSup 93. Leiden: Brill, 2003. 189–206.

Poirer, John C. "Purity beyond the Temple in the Second Temple Era." *JBL* 122 (2003): 247–65.

Porten, Bezalel. *The Elephantine Papyri in English*. Leiden: Brill, 1996.

Qimron, E. and J. Strugnell. *Qumran Cave 4. V. Miqsat Ma'ase ha-Torah*. Discoveries in the Judean Desert 10. Oxford: Clarendon, 1994.

Quaegebeur, Jan. "L'autel-à-feu et l'abattoir en Égypte tardive." In *Ritual and Sacrifice in the Ancient Near East*. Ed. J. Quaegebeur. Leuven: Peeters, 1993. 329–53.

Rad, Gerhard von. *Deuterononium-Studien*. Rev. ed. Göttingen: Vandenhoeck & Ruprecht, 1948. Translated by D. Stalker as *Studies in Deuteronomy*. Studies in Biblical Theology 9. London: SCM, 1953.

Rainey, Anson F. "The Order of Sacrifices in Old Testament Ritual Texts." *Bib* 51 (1970): 485–98.

Rappaport, Roy. *Ritual and Religion in the Making of Humanity*. Cambridge: Cambridge University Press, 1999.

Redford, Donald B. "The So-Called 'Codification' of Egyptian Law under Darius I." In *Persia and Torah: The Theory of Imperial Authorization of the Pentateuch*. Ed. James W. Watts. SBL Symposium Series 17. Atlanta: Society of Biblical Literature, 2001.

Rendtorff, Rolf. "Another Prolegomenon to Leviticus 17:11." *Pomegranates and Golden Bells: Studies . . . in Honor of Jacob Milgrom*. Ed. David P. Wright, David Noel Freedman, and Avi Hurvitz. Winona Lake, IN: Eisenbrauns, 1995. 23–8.

———. *Die Gesetze in der Priesterschrift: eine gattungsgeschichtliche Untersuchung*. FRLANT 44. Göttingen: Vandenhoeck & Ruprecht, 1954.

———. *Leviticus*. Biblischer Kommentar: Altes Testament 3/1. Neukirchen-Vluyn: Neukirchener Verlag, 1985.

Rooke, Deborah W. *Zadok's Heirs: The Role and Development of the High Priesthood in Ancient Israel*. Oxford: Oxford University Press, 2000.

Sawyer, John F. A. *Sacred Languages and Sacred Texts: Religion in the First Christian Centuries*. London: Routledge, 1999.

Schenker, Adrian. "Interprétations récente et dimension spécifiques du sacrifice ḥaṭṭā't." *Bib* 75 (1994): 59–70.

———. "Once Again, the Expiatory Sacrifices." *JBL* 116 (1997): 697–99.

———. *Studien zu Opfer und Kult im Alten Testament*. Tübingen: Mohr Siebeck, 1992.

———. "Der Unterschied zwischen Sündopfer *ḥṭʾt* und Schuldopfer *ʾšm* im Licht von Lev 5, 17–19 und 5, 10–6." In *Pentateuchal and Deuteronomistic Studies.* Ed. C. Brekelmans and J. Lust. BETL 94. Leuven: Peeters, 1990. 115–123. Reprinted in *Recht und Kult im Alten Testament: Achtzehn Studien.* OBO 172. Freiburg: Universitätsverlag / Göttingen: Vandenhoeck & Ruprecht, 2000. 104–12.

Schiffman, Lawrence H. *Text and Traditions: A Source Reader for the Study of Second Temple and Rabbinic Judaism.* Hoboken, NJ: Ktav, 1998.

Schniedewind, William M. *How the Bible Became a Book.* Cambridge: Cambridge University Press, 2004.

Schwartz, Baruch J. "The Bearing of Sin in the Priestly Literature." *Pomegranates and Golden Bells: Studies . . . in Honor of Jacob Milgrom.* Ed. David P. Wright, David Noel Freedman, and Avi Hurvitz. Winona Lake, IN: Eisenbrauns, 1995. 3–21.

———. "Prohibitions Concerning the 'Eating' of Blood in Leviticus 17." In *Priesthood and Cult in Ancient Israel.* Ed. Gary A. Anderson and Saul M. Olyan. JSOTSup 125. Sheffield: Sheffield Academic Press, 1991. 34–66.

———. "Selected Chapters of the Holiness Code – A Literary Study of Leviticus 17–19" (Hebrew). Ph.D. Dissertation, Hebrew University of Jerusalem, 1987.

Segal, Peretz. "The Divine Verdict of Leviticus 10:3." *VT* 39 (1989): 91–5.

Singer, Itamar. *Hittite Prayers.* Writings from the Ancient World 11. Atlanta: SBL, 2002.

Sklar, Jay. *Sin, Impurity, Sacrifice, Atonement: The Priestly Conceptions.* Hebrew Bible Monographs 2. Sheffield: Sheffield Phoenix Press, 2005.

Smith, Jonathan Z. "The Domestication of Sacrifice." In *Violent Origins.* Ed. R. G. Hamerton-Kelly. Stanford: Stanford University Press, 1987. 191–235.

———. *Map Is Not Territory: Studies in the History of Religion.* Leiden: Brill, 1978.

———. *To Take Place: Toward Theory in Ritual.* Chicago: University of Chicago Press, 1987.

———. "Trading Places." In *Ancient Magic and Ritual Power.* Ed. M. Meyer and P. Mirecki. Leiden: E. J. Brill, 1995. 13–28.

Smith, Mark S. *The Pilgrimage Pattern in Exodus.* JSOTSup 239. Sheffield: Sheffield Academic Press, 1997.

Smith, William Robertson. *Lectures on the Religion of the Semites.* 2nd ed. London: Black, 1894 (1st ed. 1889).

Snaith, N. H. *Leviticus and Numbers.* New Century Bible. London: Nelson, 1967.

Sommer, Benjamin D. "Expulsion as Initiation: Displacement, Divine Presence, and Divine Exile in the Torah." In *Beginning/Again: Toward a Hermeneutics of Jewish Texts.* Ed. Aryeh Cohen and Shaul Magid. New York and London: Seven Bridges, 2001. 23–48.

Spiegel, Shalom. *The Last Trial: On the Legends and Lore of the Command to Abraham to Offer Isaac as a Sacrifice: The Akedah 1899–1984.* Tr. Judah Goldin. New York: Schocken, 1967, 1993.

Staal, Fritz. "The Meaninglessness of Ritual." *Numen* 26/1 (1979): 2–22.

Staubli, T. *Die Bücher Levitikus, Numeri.* NSKAT 3. Stuttgart: Kohlhammer, 1996.

Stott, Katherine. "Finding the Lost Book of the Law: Re-reading the Story of the 'Book of the Law' (Deuteronomy–2 Kings) in Light of Classical Literature." *JSOT* 30 (2005): 145–69.

Stowers, Stanley K. "On the Comparison of Blood in Greek and Israelite Ritual." In *Hesed ve-Emet: Studies in Honor of Ernest S. Frerichs.* Ed. Jodi Magness and Seymour Gitin. Brown Judaic Studies 320. Atlanta: Scholars Press, 1998. 179–94.

Strenski, Ivan. "Between Theory and Specialty: Sacrifice in the 90s." *Religious Studies Review* 22/1 (1996): 10–20.

———. *Contesting Sacrifice: Religion, Nationalism, and Social Thought in France.* Chicago: University of Chicago Press, 2002.

Swartz, Michael D. "The Semiotics of the Priestly Vestments in Ancient Judaism." In *Sacrifice in Religious Experience.* Ed. Albert I. Baumgarten. Numen 93. Leiden: Brill, 2002. 57–80.

Sweeney, Marvin K. *King Josiah of Judah: The Lost Messiah of Israel.* Oxford: Oxford University Press, 2001.

Thompson, Dorothy J. "The High Priests of Memphis under Ptolemaic Rule." In *Pagan Priests: Religion and Power in the Ancient World.* Ed. Mary Beard and John North. Ithaca: Cornell University Press, 1990. 95–116.

Thureau-Dangin, F. *Rituels accadiens.* Paris: E. Leroux, 1921.

Turner, Victor. *The Forest of Symbols: Aspects of Ndembu Ritual.* Ithaca: Cornell University Press, 1967.

———. *The Ritual Process: Structure and Anti-Structure.* Ithaca: Cornell University Press, 1969.

Tylor, Edward B. *Primitive Culture.* New York: Brentano's Books, 1871.

Utzschneider, Helmut. *Das Heiligtum und das Gesetz: Studien zur Bedeutung der Sinaitischen Heiligtumstexte (Ex 25–40; Lev 8–9).* OBO 77. Freiburg: Universitätsverlag / Göttingen: Vandenhoeck & Ruprecht, 1988.

————. "Vergebung im Ritual: Zur Deutung des *ḥaṭṭāt* Rituals (Sündopfer) in Lev 4,1–5,13." In *Abschied von der Schuld? Zur Anthropologie und Theologie von Schuldbekenntnis, Opfer und Versöhnung.* Ed. Richard Riess et al. Stuttgart: Kohlhammer, 1996. 96–119.

Van Gennep, Arnold. *The Rites of Passage.* Tr. M. B. Vizedom and G. L. Caffee. Chicago: University of Chicago Press, 1960.

Vanderkam, James C. *An Introduction to Early Judaism.* Grand Rapids: Eerdmans, 2001.

————. *From Joshua to Caiaphas: High Priests after the Exile.* Minneapolis: Augsburg Fortress, 2004.

————. "Jewish High Priests of the Persian Period: Is the List Complete?" In *Priesthood and Cult in Ancient Israel.* Ed. Gary A. Anderson and Saul M. Olyan. JSOTSup 125. Sheffield: Sheffield Academic Press, 1991. 67–91.

Vaux, Roland de. *Ancient Israel.* Tr. John McHugh. New York: McGraw-Hill, 1961.

Walfish, Barry D. "An Introduction to Medieval Jewish Biblical Interpretation." In *With Reverence for the Word: Medieval Scriptural Exegesis in Judaism, Christianity, and Islam.* Ed. J. D. McAuliffe, B. D. Walfish, and J. W. Goering. Oxford: Oxford University Press, 2003. 3–12.

Watts, James W. "Biblical Psalms outside the Psalter." In *The Book of Psalms: Composition and Reception.* Ed. Peter W. Flint and Patrick D. Miller. VTSup 99. Leiden: Brill, 2004. 288–309.

————. " '*Olah*: The Rhetoric of Burnt Offerings." *VT* 66 (2006): 125–37.

———— (ed.). *Persia and Torah: The Theory of Imperial Authorization of the Pentateuch.* Atlanta: SBL, 2001.

————. *Psalm and Story: Inset Hymns in Hebrew Narrative.* JSOTSup 139. Sheffield: JSOT Press, 1992.

————. "Psalmody in Prophecy: Habakkuk 3 in Context." In *Forming Prophetic Literature: Essays on Isaiah and the Twelve in Honor of John D. W. Watts.* Ed. James W. Watts and Paul R. House. JSOTSup 235. Sheffield: Sheffield Academic Press, 1996. 209–23.

————. *Reading Law: The Rhetorical Shaping of the Pentateuch.* The Biblical Seminar 59. Sheffield: Sheffield Academic Press, 1999.

————. "The Rhetoric of Ritual Instruction in Leviticus 1–7." In *The Book of Leviticus: Composition and Reception.* Ed. Rolf Rendtorff and Robert A. Kugler. VTSup 93. Leiden: Brill, 2003. 79–100.

————. "Ritual Legitimacy and Scriptural Authority." *JBL* 124 (2005): 401–17.

―――. "Story-List-Sanction: A Cross-Cultural Strategy of Ancient Persuasion." In *Rhetoric before and beyond the Greeks.* Ed. Roberta Binkley and Carol Lipson. Albany: SUNY Press, 2004. 197–212.

―――. " 'This Song': Conspicuous Poetry in Hebrew Prose." In *Verse in Ancient Near Eastern Prose.* Ed. Johannes C. de Moor and Wilfred G. E. Watson. AOAT 42. Neukirchen-Vluyn: Neukirchener Verlag, 1993. 345–58.

Weinfeld, Moshe. "Social and Cultic Institutions in the Priestly Source against Their Ancient Near Eastern Background." In the *Proceedings of the Eighth World Congress of Jewish Studies.* Jerusalem: Magnes, 1983. 95–129.

Weitzman, Steven. *Surviving Sacrilege: Cultural Persistence in Jewish Antiquity.* Cambridge, MA: Harvard University Press, 2005.

Wellhausen, Julius. *Prolegomena to the History of Israel.* Gloucester, MA: Peter Smith, 1973 (German 1st ed., 1878).

―――. "Israel," *Encyclopaedia Britannica,* 9th ed.; reprinted in *Prolegomena,* 429–548.

Wenham, Gordon J. *The Book Leviticus.* New International Commentary on the Old Testament. Grand Rapids: Eerdmans, 1979.

Widengren, Geo. "The Persian Period." In *Israelite and Judaean History.* Ed. John H. Hayes and J. M. Miller. OTL. Philadelphia: Westminster, 1977. 489–539.

Williamson, Hugh G. M. *1 and 2 Chronicles.* New Century Bible. Grand Rapids: Eerdmans, 1982.

―――. *Ezra, Nehemiah.* WBC 16. Waco: Word, 1985.

―――. "The Historical Value of Josephus' Jewish Antiquities." *JTS* 28 (1977): 49–67.

Wilson, Robert R. *Prophecy and Society in Ancient Israel.* Philadelphia: Fortress, 1980.

Wyatt, N. *Religious Texts from Ugarit: The Words of Ilimilku and His Colleagues.* Biblical Seminar 53. Sheffield: Sheffield Academic Press, 1998.

Yoo, Yohan. "A Theory of Purity from the Perspective of Comparative Religions." Ph.D. Dissertation, Syracuse University, 2005.

Younge, C. D., ed. and tr. *The Works of Philo.* Peabody, MA: Hendrickson, 1993.

Index of Biblical Citations

Index of Other Ancient Literature

See also "ritual texts" in Subject Index.

Index of Authors

Achenbach, Reinhard, 146
Alter, Robert, 82n10, 219
Anderson, Robert A., 211n42, 219

Baker, David W., 55, 219
Barkley, Gary Wayne, 18, 152n24, 219
Bataille, Georges, 177, 177n14, 219
Baumgarten, Albert I., 81, 81n5, 219
Beal, Timothy K., 100, 101n14, 127,
    127n61, 219
Begrich, J., 39n4, 219
Bell, Catherine, 3n6, 6n16, 220
Bellah, Robert N., 187n34, 220
Bergen, Wesley J., 14, 14n39, 15,
    15n41, 28n81, 29, 29n83, 30n86,
    73n22, 95, 95n33, 138n14, 184n28,
    216n47, 220
Bergquist, Birgitta, 74n24, 75n28,
    75n29, 220
Berman, Louis A., 186n31, 220
Bertholet, Alfred, 98n1, 124n54, 220
Bibb, Bryan D., 10n24, 101, 101n16,
    107n27, 112n37, 129n63, 220

Binkley, Roberta, 35n94, 220
Blenkinsopp, Joseph, 58n58, 220
Bloch, Maurice, 178, 178n17, 179,
    186n33, 220
Boecker, Hans Jochen, 195n5, 220
Borger, R., xii, 51n37, 51n38, 220
Boyarin, Daniel, 77n35, 186n32, 220
Brichto, Herbert Chanan, 131,
    131n4, 131n5, 220
Brueggemann, Walter, 167, 220
Buc, Philippe, 1, 1n1, 1n2, 2, 32, 33,
    33n91, 122, 122n52, 154, 155n26,
    193, 193n1, 199n15, 221
Budd, Philip J., 108n30, 221
Burke, Kenneth, 35n93, 101n17, 221
Burkert, Walter, 9, 9n22, 176,
    176n10, 178, 180, 180n21, 186n33,
    221

Çambel, H., 49n32, 221
Carr, David M., 38n2, 103n19,
    168n47, 197, 197n12, 198n13,
    198n14, 215, 216n47, 221

244

Index of Subjects